Exploring Sex Differences

Exploring Sex Differences

edited by

BARBARA LLOYD

*School of Social Sciences, University of Sussex,
Brighton, England*

JOHN ARCHER

*Psychology Division, Preston Polytechnic,
Preston, England*

1976

Academic Press
London · New York · San Francisco
A Subsidiary of Harcourt Brace Jovanovich, Publishers

ACADEMIC PRESS INC. (LONDON) LTD.
24/28 Oval Road,
London NW1

United States Edition published by
ACADEMIC PRESS INC.
111 Fifth Avenue
New York, New York 10003

Library of Congress Catalog Card Number 76-10488
ISBN: 0-12-453550-X

Printed by
Whitstable Litho,
Straker Brothers Ltd.

CONTRIBUTORS

JOHN ARCHER, *Division of Psychology, Preston Polytechnic, Preston, Lancashire, England.*

MICHAEL R. CUNNINGHAM, *Department of Family Social Science and Psychology, University of Minnesota, Minneapolis, Minnesota, U.S.A.*

BARBARA B. LLOYD, *School of Social Sciences, University of Sussex, Falmer, Brighton BN1 9QN, Sussex, England.*

DOROTHY McBRIDE KIPNIS, *10 Windsor Avenue, Melrose Park, Philadelphia, Pennsylvania, 191267, U.S.A.*

DIANE McGUINNESS, *Department of Psychology, Hatfield Polytechnic, Hertfordshire, England.*

PETER MAYO, *School of Cultural and Community Studies, University of Sussex, Falmer, Brighton BN1 9QN, England.*

PETER R. MESSENT, *Animal Studies Department, Pedigree Pet Foods Ltd., Melton Mowbray, England.*

LESLEY ROGERS, *Department of Physiology, Monash University, Clayton, Victoria, Australia.*

PAUL ROSENBLATT, *Department of Family Social Science and Psychology, University of Minnesota, Minneapolis, Minnesota, U.S.A.*

MARILYN STRATHERN, *Department of Anthropology, University, P.O. Box 4820, University of Papua New Guinea, Papua, New Guinea.*

DOROTHY Z. ULLIAN, *Department of Psychology, Wheelock College, Boston, Massachusetts, U.S.A.*

PREFACE

Following the challenge to traditional sex roles by the
Women's Movement, sex differences have recently received re-
newed attention as an academic subject of study. This topi-
cal interest has provoked demands for courses on the psychology of women and on sex differences and has been a catalyst
for the publication of a variety of books from a range of
disciplines. In our own book psychologists, biologists and
an anthropologist examine the question of sex differences in
the terms of their own specialities. We have asked our contributors to write about problems of particular interest to
them. Thus some chapters contain straightforward summaries
of research while others are more personal and speculative.
　　Academic research on sex differences cannot be value-
free and must reflect to some degree the debate about sex
roles current in the larger society. The problems which investigators choose to study, the methods by which they approach them and the manner in which results are reported,
both to the scientific community and the public, reflect not
only personal values and commitments but also general social
values. These issues are considered at greater length in
the first chapter.
　　Using a cognitive-developmental model, Dorothy Ullian
looks at six stages in the child's growing understanding of
sex roles in American society, in terms both of their descriptive and prescriptive elements. Her review of both psychoanalytic and social learning approaches to the acquisition
of male and female sex roles prefaces the presentation of her
own research.
　　Ranging more widely and drawing examples from her studies of the *Hagan* of New Guinea and from Women's Liberation
writings, Marilyn Strathern, a social anthropologist, discusses the use of gender constructs as symbols reflecting a society's values and cultural preoccupations. Gender is seen not
simply as an obvious elaboration of sex differences but in
terms of its contribution to and as a product of its perception and use in male-female relations.

Paul Rosenblatt and Michael Cunningham, social psychologists, review and comment on the available cross-cultural evidence on the division of labour by sex and discuss reproductive and temperamental differences which might form a basis for frequently occurring forms of labour-division. They conclude that the most important sex difference is the woman's reduced mobility as a consequence of her role in childbearing and child care; man's greater aggressiveness may also be significant. They conclude however, that there is sufficient evidence of plasticity to allow for considerable changes to occur in sex roles in our society.

In the next chapter, the theme of work is examined again but in terms of the educational prerequisites for and status accorded to various occupations in modern Western societies. Among Dorothy Kipnis' thought-provoking observations is her highlighting of the changes in the pattern of sex differences in intelligence as the participation of men and women in further education has altered.

The development of differences in intellectual performance is examined by Diane McGuinness, an experimental psychologist. She describes how early sensory and perceptual differences interact with environmental events, such as parental responses and educational influences, to produce a range of sex-typical cognitive abilities in adulthood.

In two chapters specifically concerned with the relation of sex hormones and behaviour, Peter Messent and Lesley Rogers examine some of the dimensions which have already been discussed in earlier chapters, e.g. differences in attention in relation to performance on spatial-visual tasks and sensory threshold changes during the menstrual cycle. In a detailed review of psychopathological behaviour, Peter Mayo examines both biological evidence and the consequences of sex role differentiation in terms of relative stress, in an attempt to explain the documented sex differences in mental health.

The temptation to use biological evidence and speculation in constructing simple explanations of the sex differences observed in our culture in the incidence of mental illness and on psychological tests is great. We are particularly sensitive to the risks involved. The final chapter takes up this theme in detail and a variety of theories purporting to link biological variables with human sex differences in behaviour are critically examined.

Overall our book contains a variety of approaches and

viewpoints but is unified by an effort to consider both biological and social factors in explaining sex differences.
As editors we have attempted to guide our authors into an
interactionist position when using these factors to account
for behavioural differences between males and females. Thus
we would like to thank the contributors both for their tolerance of our ideological commitment and for the general speed
and willingness with which they have prepared their chapters
for our volume.

     Thanks are also due to Peter Lloyd, Richard Andrew and
Lynda Birke for their helpful comments on parts of the manu-
script, to Yvette Ashby, Adrienne Hirshfeld and Ann Moscatelli
for typing some chapters.

Barbara Lloyd

John Archer

CONTENTS

xi

1. SOCIAL RESPONSIBILITY AND RESEARCH ON SEX DIFFERENCES

Barbara B. Lloyd

In opening the discussion of sex differences, I shall consider political, scientific, methodological and conceptual
problems surrounding the investigation and application of
knowledge in this field. Conventional ideology in our society holds that the scientist, guided by his conscience, is
free to study those problems which he finds interesting, to
employ the methods he believes most adequate and to report
his results in the terms which he considers most illuminating.
That this freedom can be constrained is seen when considering the changes in attitude which have taken place in the
last few decades, both in the scientific community and the
general public, towards the study of sexuality. Today the
names of Freud, Havelock Ellis, Kinsey, Masters and Johnson,
rather than stirring controversy, are an establishment roll-
call in sex research. Many of our unquestioned assumptions,
such as the effect of cultural factors in determining standards of acceptable sexual behaviour, are hypotheses which
have survived the successful battles of these pioneers.
     Alfred Kinsey only began to study human sexuality after
he had established a solid professional reputation with twenty years of research on the anatomy and physiology of gall
wasps. Despite his achievements in entomology, some university colleagues refused to speak to him when he began studying human sexual behaviour, attempts were made to curtail
his research funds and his family suffered social ostracism.
But progress towards modifying social attitudes about the
scientific study of human sexuality was made by Kinsey. His
major works, *Sexual behaviour in the human male* (1948) and
human female (1953) provoked general discussion and became
best sellers. Although as a young physician, William Masters
was counselled to follow Kinsey's example and only begin the
study of the sexual response in middle age when he had esta-

blished himself as an authority in an orthodox field, his
research, undertaken with Virginia Johnson, has met with less
hostility. Nevertheless, Masters maintains a clinical practice which supports his investigations of the sexual response
as funds are still not readily available for the study of
human sexuality.

Moving from the human sexual response into the area of
sex differences, the impact of the wider society on the object of study quickly becomes apparent. Social constraints
will be considered both as they affect the definition of sex
differences and the data which are reported. The rhetoric
of the discussion will be examined in terms of the explanatory concepts used to account for sex differences. As an
example, explanations stressing biological determinants will
be compared with an interactionist model. (See Chapter 10
for further consideration of biological theories.)

DEFINING SEX DIFFERENCES

The term scientist was employed loosely in the opening
paragraph and only a moment's reflection is necessary to realize that the problem of defining a sex difference is not
the same when faced by a geneticist, an embryologist, a psychologist or a sociologist. The geneticist, examining the
evidence for 46 chromosomes in the normal human being has
little difficulty in identifying the 22 pairs which are the
same in males and females, the autosomes, and then in distin-
guishing the xx pair and relating it to the development of
the anatomically normal female or the xy pair to the normal
male. Admittedly there are occasional developmental mishaps
and infants are born whose genital anatomy is either ambiguous or belies their genetic identification, but the certainty
with which these anomalies can be recognized testifies to
the advances which have been made. A tissue sample from the
lining of the newborn's mouth allows the geneticist to determine whether the individual's cells carry two x chromosomes
or only one and the embryologist's understanding of the role
of androgens allows him to account for the masculinisation
of a genetic female or the reverse (Money and Ehrhardt, 1972).
The picture becomes more complex when behaviour is the
object of study. Definitional problems abound in the social
sciences although hopes for a resolution have been raised by
the introduction of methods from the study of animal behaviour. Ethologists claim that they can investigate sex differ-

ences by observing "the occurrence of small, easy to describe items of behaviour" (Blurton-Jones and Konner, 1973, p. 692). It is too early to judge the validity of these claims but in past research on sex differences two types of definitional problem can be identified. One variety follows from the use of the same term with different implications in different disciplines, while the other is the more general consequence of defining concepts empirically.

The strategy of seeking differences in the scores of males and females on specific behaviours such as aggression or verbal fluency, an extension of research on individual differences, has been identified by Hochschild (1973) as typifying the psychological approach to the study of sex roles. The term sex role is also employed by anthropologists, e.g. when examining the division of labour in a society (see Chapter 4 by Rosenblatt and Cunningham) and by sociologists concerned with explaining the impact of socialization on role-taking. While it is possible to suggest aspects of sex role investigations which are the distinctive interest of different social sciences, i.e. the examination of behaviour, or the structure of relationships, Angrist (1969) has argued that the term sex role is used with much ambiguity. Psychologists, anthropologists and sociologists conceptualize sex roles distinctly but there is considerable overlap and no general consensus within a single discipline of the theoretical implications.

Psychologists traditionally expect greater clarity from their experimentally oriented colleagues that from those involved in other social sciences. It is thus surprising, as well as instructive, to note the definitional slippage and loss of clarity which has occurred when the concept of emotionality was borrowed from personality theory and applied to a constellation of rat behaviour including movement in an open field and rate of defecation (Archer, 1973). The conceptual confusion has been increased by efforts to apply findings from research on emotionality in rats to explain human sex differences in affect (Gray, 1971; Archer, 1971).

Psychologists, emulating the methods of the natural sciences, have sought to avoid definitional issues by adopting a resolutely empirical approach. In choosing this stance it has been relatively easy to step unconsciously from describing "what is" to prescribing "what ought to be". (See Chapter 2 by Ullian for a consideration of prescriptive aspects of sex role definition.) Ingleby (1974) has spelt out the

consequences in the field of child psychology. He has argued
that instead of pursuing a value-free scientific study, psychologists have produced a theory of child development which
reflects contemporary power relationships and is a defence
of the status quo. He contends that the device which allows
psychologists to ignore the social and political forces
which affect the raising of children is the abstract conceptualization of cultural factors in terms of socialization.
Once they are encapsulated within scientific jargon, their
precise content can be ignored. In a positive vein Ingleby
has suggested methods for psychologists and others working
in the "people professions" to use to bring about change.

The impact of society on psychological research in sex
differences *per se* has been examined by Bem (1972). She has
rejected the conventional definitions employed in the study
of masculinity and femininity and argued that these characteristics are not opposite ends of a single continuum but
rather that individuals should be assessed in terms both of
their masculine-assertive and instrumental dispositions, and
their feminine-expressive and yielding natures. The idea of
these dual aspects of human personality is not new but most
research on sexual identity has been dominated by an "either
or" viewpoint. Jung (1954) used the terms animus and anima
to describe the male and female in everyone; Bakan (1966) has
more recently theorized about agency and communion which he
views as masculine and feminine but embodied to some extent
in all human beings, while Block (1973) has used Bakan's perspective in studying the development of sex role identification.

Bem has constructed scales employing her two-dimensional
conceptualization of masculinity and femininity and used them
to identify individuals who are traditional in their endorsement of items so there is a large difference in their masculine and feminine scores as well as people whose positions
on both variables are similar (Bem, 1974). In terms of conventional values the latter group could be labelled "undifferentiated" and possibly be considered deviant but Bem pre-
fers to describe them as "androgynous". She has shown that
"androgynous" people, those whose masculine and feminine
scores are similar, are also more flexible in behaviour
across situations, being able to act nurturantly or instru-
mentally depending on the problem confronting them (Bem,
1975).

In considering why psychologists have overlooked "andro-

gynous" people Bem has highlighted the influence of American
sex role values and also noted the limitations of a trait
theory approach in explanations of personality. As an additional example of the impact of social norms in explanations of gender identity, she cited a study in which 336
families were interviewed but one-third discarded because
neither parent could be identified as dominant (Hetherington,
1965). While Bem's own research and theorizing question
accepted ideology, conventional values have a considerable
impact on most psychological theories in this area. The
pervasiveness of the acceptance of "what is" as "what ought
to be" can be further documented by the observation that
while psychologists may dispute the process whereby the
child develops his appropriate masculine or feminine gender
identity, i.e. whether it is best explained as social learning, identification with the same sex parent, or as a complex cognitive-developmental process, none of the contending
theorists challenge the prescribed outcome - that individuals
should develop clearly differentiated sex role identities
(see Chapter 2).

The impact of societal norms in defining sex differences
and the acceptance of these norms by professionals can be
documented in other areas. One such report, already considered a classic and reprinted in books of readings, is that
of Broverman and her colleagues (1970; Bardwick, 1972) in
which they investigated clinicians' definitions of mental
health. Doctors and social workers were required to use a
122 item scale to describe either a healthy, mature, socially
competent male, female or adult person. Earlier research
had shown that a third of the items were polarized and applied in a consistently stereotyped manner to men or women,
but of these 38 items only 11 were applied positively to
women. Spelt out more concretely, the results indicated
that healthy women who were appropriately typed and thus
characterized by the feminine pole on the male items and
vice versa were more submissive, less independent, less adventurous, more easily influenced, less aggressive and competitive, more excitable, emotional and sensitive and so
forth. It is hardly surprising that the concept of the
healthy adult and the healthy male were very similar while
that of the healthy female differed from both of them. Clinicians were thus shown to be using a dual standard of mental health which paralleled the socially sanctioned view
of male-female differentiation. Here we have an example

which goes beyond academic interest alone as it is reasonable
to presume that these therapists would be trying to ensure
that their patients' progress and adjustment were in line
with their ideas of sex-appropriate healthy behaviour.

I have examined here a few of the conceptual problems
encountered in studying sex differences; in the next section
I look at some methodological issues. Although theory and
method cannot be separated when undertaking research on males
and females, this division may alert the reader to problems
which are normally a professional concern. It is important
to consider not only biases in the results which scientists
report but also the difficulties encountered in producing
noteworthy findings.

A major contribution to the psychological study of differences is the extensive review undertaken by Maccoby and
Jacklin (1974). Their exhaustive survey of the literature
and scholarly integration of its findings has, however, documented significant sex differences only in aggression and in
verbal, mathematical and spatial skills.

METHODOLOGICAL ISSUES

In seeking to document the hypothesis that scientific
research on sex differences is consciously or more often unconsciously shaped by conventional social values I quoted a
number of published studies. Here I shall consider the
norms of publication as a further source of bias. The issues, which range from the survival of spurious facts to the
impact of using a probability model for testing psychological hypotheses, can be broadly described as methodological
but there is overlap between these problems and the conceptual questions surrounding the definition of sex differences.

The possibility that "scientific facts" about sex differences may be revealed as comfortable fictions is demonstrated in a paper by Reynolds (1966) reporting his failure to
find empirical data to support the familiar statement that
women are better at discriminating colours than men. The only evidence he could locate, an experimental study published
in the 1930's, described colour preferences in infants
(Staples, 1932). A telling datum is the reply Reynolds received from Lindesmith whom he queried about the source he
had used to verify the statement when it appeared in his
textbook (Lindesmith and Strauss, 1956). Lindesmith suggested that the fact was self-evident and required no evidence.

The perpetuation of half truths through reliance on review
articles and other secondary sources occurs in other areas
of psychology. Recently Loftus (1974) has re-examined an
original research report and found that subjects tracking
one message when two were being delivered through head-
phones, one to each ear, did not invariably report their own
names when they were transmitted on the irrelevant channel,
as had been suggested in a number of textbooks. Breakthroughs
were actually reported 30 or 33 per cent of the time depending upon the method of presentation. An important difference in these examples is that in the field of sex differences gender stereotypes provide intuitive justification for
creating generalizations from little or no evidence, whereas
in other research areas this source of bias is less apparent.
        The maintenance of scientific fictions concerning sex
differences is worrying, but equally disturbing are the factors which may lead to the failure to report them, either
because there has been no systematic attempt to evaluate
them or because no statistically significant differences
were found. Maccoby and Jacklin (1974) have dealt with
these sources of bias in their survey by seeking additional
data from the original investigators and by undertaking further statistical analyses where the data permitted.
        Problems surrounding the failure to report sex differen-
ces can be formulated in a number of ways (cf. Maccoby and
Jacklin, 1974, especially pp. 4-6). Empirical research has
shown that authors may not only fail to report the sex of
the experimenter who carried out the study but also that of
the individuals who were investigated (Harris, 1971). An
analysis of recent volumes of four major psychology journals
produced statistically significant results showing that female researchers were more likely than males to report having undertaken analysis for sex differences but it is noteworthy that even among female investigators sex differences
were ignored in the majority of papers (Harris, 1972).
        One outcome of the failure to report sex differences is
the tendency of psychologists to treat their experimental
subjects as one undifferentiated mass or, if results which
include females are unclear, to ignore these and construct
theories congruent with findings from males alone. As a result much psychological theory has a masculine bias; one
female practitioner has suggested that psychological theory
might be quite different if it were formulated by women
about women (Carlson, 1972). In the controversial realm of

achievement reviewers of research on females have concluded:

> First, like much psychological theory, achievement
> motivation theory was developed to explain the be-
> haviour of males. Then attempts were made to use
> that theory for females. Not surprisingly, it does
> not work well for females. (Stein and Bailey, 1973,
> p. 362.)

An analysis of articles published in a major journal lends
further support for this conclusion. Dan and Beekman (1972)
found that in 92 per cent of studies based solely on male
subjects no mention was made of their sex in the discussion
or conclusions. There were 13 articles in which females
were the only subjects and only 62 per cent of these general-
ized their results without specifying the sex of the individuals upon whom the data had been collected. Concretely
this means that 49 studies based upon male results and 8 reports of female behaviour failed to take account of sex in
their theoretical discussions. The conceptual importance of
these practices lies in the development of a range of psychological theories more suited to males and such that female
performance is likely to appear unpredictable or deviant.

The developing consciousness of female psychologists
may lend impetus to the demand that researchers sample both
sexes and report any sex differences that they find; but a
host of statistical issues lie behind the general failure of
researchers to publish such analyses consistently. The criteria of scientific rigour dictate that psychologists test
their hypotheses empirically, and, to evaluate these results,
statistical procedures based upon probability theory are employed. Thus, to show that females speak more quickly than
males, measures of individual speaking speeds would be tested against the hypothesis that there is no difference in the
average speaking speed of men and women. The null hypothesis states that the average speaking speed of men and women
is the same. Conventionally, psychologists are only willing
to reject the null hypothesis if their statistical tests
indicate that a difference as large as the one obtained
could only be expected 5 times in 100 sets or less frequently. In rejecting the null hypothesis the researcher asserts
that the difference he has found would not be frequently encountered by chance; such positive results are publishable.
Failure to reject the null hypothesis cannot be taken as evidence that the population means are the same as it only says

that the obtained difference is not rare. Since the investigator who fails to reject the null hypothesis is unable to
assert the converse, that he has shown definitively there is
no difference, these results are generally not published.
Greenwald (1975) has considered the consequences of adopting
this strategy and using both a mathematical model to simu-
late the publication process and analyses of individual
cases has shown that, in the area where the null hypothesis is
indeed true, the result is few publications. Greenwald was
concerned to demonstrate the detrimental effects of this
conventional approach to social psychology but his conclusions are also of critical importance for the psychological
study of sex differences.

The consequence of employing the traditional null hypothesis strategy in the field of sex differences is that we
have little evidence of behaviours on which no differences
in the performance of men and women have been found. (See
Chapter 10 by Archer for a further discussion.) Moreover,
from the assortment of differences which have been reported
we are often unable to determine how many comparisons have
been made and whether the significant differences which
were reported could be only a few from a large array in
which case some significant results would be expected by
chance. In research on cyclical changes in females both of
these problems are important and were raised by Messent (see
Chapter 8) when considering alternatives to physiological
explanations of premenstrual symptoms. Detailed examination
of the problems of inference raised by significance testing
and multiple comparisons along with the further question of
adequate controls led Parlee to conclude that "as a scientific hypothesis the existence of a premenstrual syndrome has
little other than face validity" (1973, p. 463). While
these issues have been recognized and considered in the limited area of premenstrual behaviour it is reasonable to assume that they affect much of the research and subsequent
theorizing about the nature of male-female differences in
a wide range of behaviours. As noted earlier, Maccoby and
Jacklin found only limited empirical evidence of developmental sex differences but they suggest that the picture is incomplete since investigators oversample newborns, nursery
school age and college students and use different variables
at the various ages.

Granted that our knowledge of both the similarities and
significant differences in the performances of men and women

is limited, one further caution is necessary. Even when a
statistically significant result is reported it generally
reflects a small difference in the average levels of behaviour in the two sexes. Even on those dimensions such as physical aggression and spatial perception where differences
have been repeatedly reported there is much overlap in the
distributions and it is generally impossible to predict an
individual's performance on the basis of knowing only his
sex.

EXPLANATIONS OF SEX DIFFERENCES

In the sections which follow I shall consider the debate on sex differences from two perspectives. First I shall
describe an approach which I identify as biological determinism. Next I consider an interactionist explanation which
I believe to be not only more complex but also more satisfactory.

Biological Determinism

Behaviourism has been under strong attack for over a
decade and during this period psychologists have rediscovered
biology. Although the heated nature-nurture debates of the
past have been replaced by a general recognition that neither
of these sources are sufficient alone to explain development,
controversy still flares about the explanation of sex differences. Identification of the major protagonists and their
positions may help to clarify the issues which divide them.
Two female psychologists, Judith Bardwick in the United
States and Corinne Hutt in England are major proponents of
the viewpoint which I have labelled biological determinism.
In the introduction to her book on sex differences Hutt
states:

Having met, repeatedly, with rejections of any suggestion, however covert, that some human sex differences may be of biological origin, it seemed important to set the "sexual differentiation" story in
perspective. ...In much developmental and social
psychological writing too little cognizance is taken
of the structure and function of the brain, much
less of the constraints set by the nature of its
organization. I make no apology, therefore, for

stating the case for the biological bases of psychological sex differences. (1972, p. 17.)

In a similar vein Bardwick begins the second chapter of her
book on the psychology of women by asserting:

I have nonetheless taken the apparently eccentric
position that the body makes direct contributions to
the psyche of the individual. I am going to have to
make conceptual leaps from the data but I shall try
to demonstrate that differences in the behavioural
responses of males and females exist even before
parents differentiate the sexes in their handling
of infants; the differences in personality characteristics begin to develop *before birth* and they
are responded to differentially by the parents.
(1971, p. 21.)

In *Contemporary Psychology*, the journal devoted exclusively to reviews, Hutt and Bardwick came under attack for
their admittedly biological bias. The similarity in the two
reviews ends there as Money's (1973) comments on the Hutt
book were brief but vitriolic while Maccoby (1972) admired
Bardwick's courage and understanding yet was sceptical about
her biological emphasis and willingness to leap from congeni-
tal differences in internal biochemical climates to sex differences in behaviour. If you enjoy heated controversy
these reviews may provide a diversion but it is unlikely that
arguments will alter the beliefs of those fully committed to
biologically based explanation.
    The question for us is what are the basic assumptions
which separate the authors from their reviewers? Both Hutt
and Bardwick believe that it is currently possible to theo-
rize in a meaningful way about the direct influence of biological variables on behaviour. In order to show that there
are behavioural differences which are scarcely mediated by
experience Bardwick has listed a range of responses, e.g.
gross motor activity and pain sensitivity, on which newborn
males and females have been reported to differ significantly.
Although Maccoby admitted that she intuitively agreed that
there probably are inherent response differences, she demonstrated, by re-analysing the studies Bardwick cited, that the
data presented do not show such consistent and clear differences between the sexes. Maccoby is arguing for the influence of experience on behaviour and thus having shown the

difficulty in demonstrating sex differences in newborns assumes that she had challenged the predominantly biological
explanation offered by Bardwick. Further consideration of
the problems of establishing reliable measures of neonatal
sex differences is contained in Chapter 6 in which McGuinness
has suggested that the immaturity of the infant nervous system may prevent our measuring sensory thresholds precisely
enough to yield consistent differences and that the greater
physical maturity of females who are the same gestational
age at birth as males may make comparison difficult.

The main issue is not one of fact. In an analysis of
the old nature versus nurture problem Lehrman (1970) has
made this point, arguing that the issue could not be resolved
empirically. He suggested looking instead at the problems
which different workers choose to make central to their research and to try and understand how the scientific concepts
and the language of their argument were influenced by the
original choice. Viewed in this perspective the analyses of
both Hutt and Bardwick can be considered attempts to set
right a balance of biological and experiential factors which
had in the past swung too heavily to the nurture side by
taking advantage of the considerable strides which have been
made in the biological sciences. It is hardly surprising
that experiments such as those of Harris (1970) or Levine
(1966) which show the permanent impairment of oestrous cy-
cling or of typical female sexual behaviour as the result of
a hormonal implant when the female rat is only four days old,
should argue for the potency of biological variables.

An Interactionist Model

Whether a sex difference has a biological or experiental
origin, cannot be settled empirically, but in the discussion
which follows I argue that adherence to a primarily biological perspective distorts our understanding by lessening attention to environmental variables. The brains of mammals
may be differentially organized either prenatally or just after birth to produce cyclical or acyclical hormonal release
but this observation leaves a large gap in any complex, full
or subtle explanation of the many reputed sex differences in
adult behaviour. As Hinde has observed:

> ... if we hold the aim of ontogenetic studies to be
> the unravelling of the pattern of changes occurring

in time, data as to the source of behaviour differences are only a first step. It is necessary to ask
further how the genetic or environmental factors in
question produce the difference in behaviour. Nevertheless the examination of successive differences
produced by successive types of experimental interference is the only way of breaking open the onto-
genetic interaction. (1968, p. 12.)

   Focus on biological factors reduces the likelihood that
environmental variables will be thoroughly explored. Typical of this one sided emphasis is the discussion of sex differences in motivation by Hutt (1972, pp. 110-119). Her
overview of the development of aggression included, along
with a consideration of the brain and circulating hormones,
examination of environmental factors and an example from her
own research which she has suggested shows an interaction of
predisposition and opportunity in the aggressive behaviour
of pre-school boys and girls. Nonetheless, she finally concluded, "... thus we may have here a common neurochemical
basis for aggression, drive and attention." (p. 119). It
would seem just as likely that we also have a common set of
norms or expectation about the behaviour of boys and girls
but given Hutt's general conclusion it is likely that social
variables will not be investigated.
   Commitment to an interactionist model prevents an exclusive focusing on either biological or social factors. This
effect is clear in a study of the development of synchrony
in the menstrual cycle of students at an American Liberal
Arts College reported by McClintock (1971) who collected reports of the onset and duration of menstruation over a six
month period. Synchrony in animal populations has been explained in terms of the number of daylight hours, or of
special behaviour-activating odours, pheromones. Observations of synchrony in human females have been made but explanations are incomplete. Perhaps a biological explanation
is to be expected since most research on the menstrual cycle,
when it shows correlations with other behaviours, is interpreted causally to imply hormonal changes. McClintock assessed the developing similarity in dates of onset in pairs
of room-mates and of close friends, i.e. girls who spent
considerable time together, and showed an effect in comparison with random pairings. These results ruled out common
diet and daily routine as causal factors and further analyses

based upon divisions of the total sample into larger groups
based upon time spent together and living units determined
geographically, found the synchronization effect only in
friendship groups. McClintock's conclusion that the increasing similarity in dates of onset depends on "some interpersonal physiological process" may lack precision but it is
probably a more suggestive explanation than is usually encountered in the literature on the menstrual cycle. Ideally,
it will lead to further research to elucidate the nature of
the interpersonal effect.

John Archer and I have discussed at some length elsewhere the nature of an interactionist explanation (Archer
and Lloyd, 1974) so I shall only summarize our argument here.
Central to an interactionist explanation and that which distinguishes it from an additive one is the concept of feedback. Thus a research strategy based upon an interactionist
model would involve study not only of the effects of hormone
levels on behaviour but similarly the effects of behaviour
on levels of circulating hormones. The process is two way,
a affects b but b also affects a. I have cited McClintock's
study at length since it focuses upon the modification of
hormonal function as the result of social behaviour, while
most research has sought to show how fluctuations in hormone
level influence behaviour (see Chapter 8 by Messent). An
interactive approach might lead to further study seeking to
show the effects of menstrual synchrony and associated changes on other behaviours. Ideally further study would reveal
the effect of menstrual synchrony and the associated hormonal
changes on behaviour. At this stage it is speculation to
suggest that one result of synchrony might be to ensure continued interaction as girls with similar cycles might, as
the result of similar levels of circulating hormones, experience similar mood variation. Quickly this becomes a chicken
and egg problem - in essence an interactionist explanation.
Possibly it is a desire for clarity which attracts many theorists to simpler forms of explanation. Those who reject biological determinism might with equal comfort adopt a social
learning view and thus neglect biological variables.

In considering the application of an interactionist explanation thus far I have only looked at short term changes.
After all, McClintock found that modifications in the direction of greater synchrony levelled off after four months;
but what of long term development which continues throughout
an individual's lifetime? Theories which seek to account

for such changes are bound to be complex. The preliminary
explanation which Sherman (1967) has suggested to account
for the superior spatial ability of males but linguistic
facility of females involves a combination of the generally
slower male development coupled with later talking but greater masculature interacting with parental response to these
characteristics (see Chapters 6 and 10). Sherman has argued
that concentration upon any one dimension can provide little
understanding of the origin of sex differences in cognitive
skills. The combination of variables and a time perspective
is necessary for an adequate explanation of the complex development we seek to describe.

SCIENTIFIC FINDINGS AND SOCIETY

I have already tried to show that social norms and values affect the outcome of research on sex differences as a
consequence of the adoption of an empirical method in the
social sciences. In describing sex roles as he finds them,
the scientist may inadvertently lend support to the status
quo. Here I shall consider more fully the complementary effect - the impact of research findings on the wider society.
In Chapter 3 Marilyn Strathern discusses the general
problem of the uses to which a society puts its cultural
stereotypes of maleness and femaleness, i.e. its gender concepts, as well as their employment in scientific theories.
I shall explore the uses to which knowledge of sex differences and explanations of their origins can be put. The discussions overlap insofar as the dichotomy between nature and
culture or biological and social variables is important to
both arguments.
Crook (1970) has observed that explanations of animal
behaviour by ethologists such as Lorenz in terms of fixed
action patterns and sign stimuli or American behaviourists
imbued with the plasticity of human nature, reflected the
spirit of their times, being congruent with the racism of
the Third Reich or the (then still credible) American ideal
of an ethnically diverse, open society. But the analysis
can be taken further. In Germany only research which could
give ideological support to National Socialist programmes was
tolerated and those social scientists whose views were incompatible with a nativistic explanation of human variation
were forced to leave. The growth of the social sciences, in
both England and America, reflected the exodus from Austria

as well as Germany, during the 1930's. Greater diversity
within the scientific community has been tolerated both in
England and America. Although there has long been considerable support for a nativist view of individual differences
in intelligence (see Kipnis, Chapter 5 and Kamin, 1974) a
one-sided environmentalist approach held great sway in
America until this decade (Richards, 1974). The availability
of competing views in a pluralistic society makes it tempting
to consider why particular scientific theories enjoy a vogue
at a particular time.

Currently biological explanations of sex differences
are popular; so it is relevant to ask why this should be and
to consider the possible impact on society of the results of
scientific studies sympathetic to this view (cf. Rose and
Rose, 1973 for a discussion of the politics of biological
explanations). Crook has suggested that one substitute for
the ethical code lost when orthodox religious beliefs were
abandoned has been found in simple theories of biological
determinism. As an example he has suggested that ideas
about "territoriality" can be employed to provide moral legitimacy for withdrawal into racial enclaves. Writing at a
different level, Strathern proposes that attributes which
have their origins in nature may appear more personal and immutable while those of cultural origin are artificial, arbi-
tary and changeable since they are man made. Especially
when viewed from the perspective of Women's Liberation, cultural objects and indeed society are particularly suspect.
As a psychologist I think that the illusion of normlessness
and lack of boundaries which popular discussions of the "per-
missive society" create also furnish impetus to a search for
universal, immutable verities, which biologically based explanations appear to supply.

In exploring the impact of "biological facts" of sex
differences on society I am not covertly espousing a one-
sided explanation. As I argued in the previous section, I
believe that only through an analysis of the interaction of
biological and social variables can we begin to approach an
adequate understanding of the few reliable differences in
the intellectual and temperamental behaviour of men and
women which have been reported. Equally, we need to consider both the impact of society on science and the reaction
of society to scientific findings.

There is a surprising degree of consensus on a set of
sex differences which those disposed to a biological determi-

nist view list as established fact (Bardwick, 1971; Garai
and Scheinfeld, 1968; Hutt, 1972). These include greater
size and musculature of the male but the faster physical development and greater biological resistance both to infection
and genetic defect in females. Males are always described as
more active, impulsive, aggressive and object oriented while
females are oriented to people, consistent and reactive.
Males excel in verbal comprehension and reasoning, mathematics, spatial perception and abstract thinking but female
performance in terms of verbal fluency, spelling, manual dexterity, clerical skills and rote memory is notably better.
As might be expected, males are more competitive and achievement oriented while females are nurturant and dependent.
Since these authors are in agreement on the facts it is worth
examining their recommendation to the larger society on the
basis of this evidence, though it should also be noted that
the most recent and comprehensive summary in this area
(Maccoby and Jacklin, 1974) only finds evidence to support
some of these conclusions.

Hutt is perhaps the most extreme both in asserting the
biological origin of sex differences and in disclaiming responsibility as a scientist for the consequences. She stated: "That sex differences do exist is an incontrovertible
biological fact. Whether such differences should result in
differential treatment of males and females is a social decision" (p. 133). Her suggestions ultimately favour the
status quo, a conclusion she reached and supported by considering reports of return to traditional sex roles in kib-
butzim, observations that occupations outside the home in
Eastern Europe resulted in married women having two jobs and
little leisure, and English studies suggesting that traditional roles in England were still acceptable though some
women gained satisfaction through a career as well as in
marriage.

Both Bardwick and Garai and Scheinfeld used the same
"facts" but were also interested in directing change.
Bardwick, whose approach is female-oriented, concentrated on
using the facts to facilitate the adjustment of women to
their traditional roles in maternity and child care but also
suggested that rigid sex role differentiation not only deprived women who sought career achievement but also stifled
men from expressing the feminine-nurturant, people-oriented
sides of their nature. Thus while she accepted the "biological facts" she argued for tolerance.

The most detailed proposals were produced by Garai and
Scheinfeld who were also cautious in pointing out that on
most questions additional findings would be necessary before
a definitive answer could be given. They sought, nonetheless,
to give practical advice to deal with the slower development
of boys, the failure of women in science subjects, the need
to create a more masculine atmosphere in primary schools and
the less successful problem-solving of females. They suggested the possibility of single-sex education in certain subjects
and at certain ages, the desirability of offering "brain-
storming" and other creativity exercises to girls, ideally
by male teachers, and the prospect that subjects such as en-
gineering which fail to attract women, might in future be
taught by specially talented female teachers and in a feminine manner.

Although the various prescriptions start with the same
set of facts the practical suggestions are diverse. In one
sense they reinforce Hutt's contention that the use to which
such information is put depends on the wider society. Each
of the authors I have considered made their suggestions in
terms of personal values rather than scientific rules. But
recognition of the scientist's responsibility in this sphere
still leaves questions to be answered. One of the important
issues is the use to which scientific reports may be put.

Writing in the context of ethological research, Crook
(1970) has argued that in presenting scientific theories and
results to the lay public there is often oversimplication
and distortion. Evidence of this phenomenon is not difficult to find. Even quality newspapers such as *The Guardian*
succumb from time to time. Mary Stott, writing on "women's
studies" extolled Elaine Morgan as the one female ethologist
who has challenged accepted evolutionary doctrines with a
theory both "beautifully simple and remarkably convincing".
Although Mary Stott recognized that the aquatic theory was
originally advanced by Hardy she mistakenly implied that
Elaine Morgan was a professional ethologist. Her comment
that Morgan's theory is simple and convincing must be regarded in the light of her error. Scientists are authorities
whose views receive special attention. Thus while I have
some reservations about the ability of logical argument to
alter opinion, I do believe that material presented as scientific evidence is used to buttress opinion and to lend
credence to views already held. In this regard simple theories are most appealing.

Bardwick, Hutt and others who acknowledge the interactive nature of social and biological variables yet nonetheless stress the latter in order to right what they see as an
imbalance, fail to appreciate the danger of their approach.
Although professional colleagues might be presumed to understand, once beyond this charmed circle misinterpretation is
very likely. Hutt (1972, p. 118) for example noted that
testosterone increased attention and her account implied
that the studies were carried out on men. She did, however,
furnish two references so that the cautious reader could discover for himself that the subject of these studies were
male chicks. By the time the finding is reported in *The
Female Woman* (Stassinopoulos, 1973) retrieval of this important qualification becomes much less likely as the reference
only appears at the end of the book and in the text the subjects have become "men with high androgen levels - identified by their excretion of certain chemicals, their thickset
physique with large chests and biceps, their large amounts
of pubic hair..." (1973, p. 33). Thus I believe that the
responsible scientist must give as complete and unambiguous
account as possible. In the chapters which follow efforts
have been made to fulfil this dictum. Authors have explored
their specialist topics fully and have furnished generous
references.

REFERENCES

Angrist, S.S. (1969). The study of sex roles. *Journal of
Social Issues,* 25, 215-232.

Archer, J. (1971). Sex differences in emotional behaviour:
a reply to Gray and Buffery. *Acta Psychologica,* 35, 415-
429.

Archer, J. (1973). J. Tests for emotionality in rats and
mice: a review. *Animal Behaviour,* 21, 205-235.

Archer, J. and Lloyd, B.B. (1974). Sex roles: biological
and social interactions. *New Scientist,* 21 November, 582-
584.

Bakan, D. (1966). "The Duality of Human Existence". Rand
McNally, Chicago.

Bardwick, J.M. (1971). "Psychology of Women: A Study of
Bio-Cultural Conflicts". Harper and Row, New York.

Bardwick, J.M. (1972). (ed.) "Readings in the Psychology of Women". Harper and Row, New York.

Bem, S.L. (1972). Psychology looks at sex roles: Where have all the androgynous people gone? Paper presented at University of California, Los Angeles Symposium on Women.

Bem, S.L. (1974). The measurement of psychological androgyny. *Journal of Consulting and Clinical Psychology*, 42, 155-162.

Bem, S.L. Sex-role adaptability: one consequence of psychological androgyny. *Journal of Personality and Social Psychology*. In press.

Block, J.H. (1973). Conceptions of sex roles: some cross-cultural and longitudinal perspectives. *American Psychologist*, 28, 512-526.

Blurton-Jones, N.G. and Konner, M.J. (1973). Sex differences in the behaviour of London and Bushman children. *In* "Comparative Ecology and Behaviour of Primates", (R.P. Michael and J.H. Crook, eds.) Academic Press, London and New York.

Broverman, I.K., Broverman, D.M., Clarkson, F.E., Rosenkrantz, P.S. and Vogel, S.R. (1970). Sex roles stereotypes and clinical judgments of mental health. *Journal of Clinical and Consulting Psychology*, 34, 1-7. Reprinted in Bardwick, J.M. (ed.) "Readings in the Psychology of Women".

Carlson, R. (1972). Understanding women: Implications for personality theory and research. *Journal of Social Issues*, 28, 17-32.

Crook, J.H. (1970). *Introduction to* "Social Behaviour in Birds and Mammals: Essays on the Social Ethology of Animals and Men". Academic Press, London and New York.

Dan, A.J. and Beekman, S. (1972). Male versus female representation in psychological research. *American Psychologist*, 27, 1078.

Garai, J.E. and Scheinfeld, A. (1968). Sex differences in mental and behavioural traits. *Genetic Psychology Monographs*, 77, 169-299.

Gray, J.A. (1971). "The Psychology of Fear and Stress". Chapter 6. World University Library, London.

Greenwald, A.G. (1975). Consequences of prejudice against the null hypothesis. *Psychological Bulletin*, 82, 1-20.

Harris, G.W. (1970). Hormonal differentiation of the developing nervous system with regard to patterns of endocrine function. *Philosophical transactions of the Royal Society of London*, 259, 165-177.

Harris, S.L. (1971). Influence of subject and experimenter sex in psychological research. *Journal of Consulting and Clinical Psychology*, 37, 291-294.

Harris, S.L. (1972). Who studies sex differences? *American Psychologist*, 27, 1077-1078.

Hetherington, E.M. (1965). A developmental study of the effects of sex of dominant parent on sex-role preference, identification and imitation in children. *Journal of Personality and Social Psychology*, 2, 188-194.

Hinde, R.A. (1968). Dichotomies in the study of development. *In* "Genetic and Environmental Influences on Behaviour". (J.M. Thody and A.S. Parkes, eds.) Oliver and Boyd, Edinburgh.

Hochschild, A.R. (1973). A review of sex role research. *American Journal of Sociology*, 78, 1011-1029.

Hutt, C. (1972). "Males and Females". Penguin Books, Harmondsworth.

Ingleby, D. (1974). The psychology of child psychology. *In* "The Integration of a Child into a Social World". (M.P.M. Richards, ed.) Cambridge University Press, London.

Jung, C.C. (1954). "Psychological Types" *from* "The Collected Works of C.C. Jung". Vol. 7. Routledge and Kegan Paul, London.

Kamin, L.J. (1974). "The Science and Politics of I.Q.". Lawrence Erlbaum Associates, Hillsdale, New Jersey.

Kinsey, A.C., Pomeroy, W.B., Martin, C.E. and Gebhard, P.H. (1948). "Sexual Behaviour in the Human Male". Saunders, Philadelphia.

Kinsey, A.C., Pomeroy, W.B., Martin, C.E. and Gebhard, P.H. (1953). "Sexual Behaviour in the Human Female". Saunders, Philadelphia.

Lehrman, D.S. (1970). Semantic and conceptual issues in the nature-nurture problem. *In* "Development and Evolution of Behaviour". (L.R. Aronson, E. Tobach, D.S. Lehrman and J.S. Rosenblatt, eds.) Freeman, San Francisco.

Levine, S. (1966). Sex differences in the brain. *Scientific American*, 214, 84-90.

Lindesmith, A.R. and Strauss, A.L. (1956). "Social Psychology" Dryden Press, Hinsdale, Illinois.

Loftus, E.F. (1974). On reading the fine print. *Quarterly Journal of Experimental Psychology*, 27, 324.

McClintock, M.K. (1971). Menstrual synchrony and suppression. *Nature*, 229, 244-245.

Maccoby, E.E. (1972). The meaning of being female. (Review of J.M. Bardwick's "Psychology of Women: A Study of Bio-Cultural Conflicts") *Contemporary Psychology*, 17, 369-372.

Maccoby, E.M. and Jacklin, C.N. (1974). "The Psychology of Sex Differences". Stanford University Press, Stanford.

Money, J. (1973). Biology = ♂/♀ Destiny: a woman's view. (Review of C. Hutt's "Males and Females") *Contemporary Psychology*, 18, 603-604.

Money, J. and Ehrhardt, A.A. (1972). "Man Woman: Boy Girl". John Hopkins University Press, Baltimore and London.

Parlee, M.B. (1973). The premenstrual syndrome. *Psychological Bulletin*, 80, 454-465.

Reynolds, L.T. (1966). A note on the perpetuation of a "scientific fiction". *Sociometry*, 29, 85-88.

Richards, M.P.M. (1974). "The Integration of a Child into a Social World". Cambridge University Press, London.

Rose, E.P.R. and Rose, H. (1973). "Do not adjust your mind, there is a fault in reality" - Idealogy in neurobiology. *Cognition*, 4, 479-501.

Sherman, J.A. (1967). Problem of sex differences in space perception and aspects of intellectual functioning. *Psychological Review*, 74, 290-299.

Staples, R. (1932). The responses of infants to color. *Journal of Experimental Psychology*, 15, 119-141.

Stassinopoulos, A. (1973). "The Female Woman". Davis-Poynter, London.

Stein, A.H. and Bailey, M.M. (1973). The socialization of achievement orientation in females. *Psychological Bulletin,* 80, 345-366.

2. THE DEVELOPMENT OF CONCEPTIONS OF MASCULINITY AND FEMININITY

Dorothy Z. Ullian

Most of the research on sex-role development may be divided
into two divergent, often antithetical views about the nature
and source of sex differences. The first approach, which is
based on a Freudian model of sex-role development is characterized by its emphasis on anatomical differences as the primary basis for differences in the male and female personality.
The second approach, which includes more recent formulations
of analytic theory as well as the work of social learning
theorists, proposes that sex differences are due primarily to
social environmental conditions which shape and influence the
male and female personality. In contrast to Freud's stress
on biology, this approach focuses on society as the prime determinant of masculinity and femininity.

The purpose of this paper is to examine these two theoretical positions in a critical light, and to propose a new
model for the examination and interpretation of sex differences. The model to be presented does not view the development
of male and female personalities as a function of biology,
nor as a function of social conditioning. Rather, it suggests that both biological and societal factors may be differentially important at various levels of development. It
is postulated that with increasing age, there are shifts in
the kinds of interpretations the individual gives to biological and social differences between males and females. It
is the nature of these interpretations, rather than of the
biological and social differences *per se*, which shed light
on the psychological aspects of masculinity and femininity.

Two main issues are addressed by psychoanalytic and
learning theories of sex-role development. First, they propose a theory about the nature of masculinity and femininity,
and second, they consider the process by which such traits
are acquired. The following section will include an outline

of the two major theories, a summary of the relevant empirical studies, and a critical analysis of these two perspectives. The final section will present an alternative model
of sex-role development, and review some preliminary empirical findings which illustrate and support such an approach.

PSYCHOANALYTIC AND SOCIAL LEARNING THEORIES OF DEVELOPMENT

Psychoanalytic Theory

Regardless of the form in which it is presented, psychoanalytic theory makes the critical assumption that a predetermined relationship exists between the nature of genital
differences and the psychological characteristics of males
and females. Freud assumed that there are sex-typed differences in aggressiveness, dependency, jealousy, and passivity,
differences which represent an inevitable emotional response
to unconscious fears and impulses about genital differences.
Thus, men were accorded a greater sense of justice than women because of the preponderance of penis envy in the lives
of females; female narcissism was viewed as a compensation
for the sexual inferiority of women. Modesty was seen as
originating from a desire to hide the deficiency of female
genitals, and the prevalence of women in the craft of weaving
was traced to the unconscious motive of attaching hairs so
as to veil the inadequate genitals. According to Freud, direct penis envy or some compensatory defence mechanism is
the constant determining factor in the development of the
female personality. Freud maintained that this relationship
between biology and psychological identity persists throughout development. Writing originally in 1933 on this subject,
Freud observed:

> ...she clings for a long time to get something like
> it (penis), and believes in the possibility for an
> extraordinary number of years; and even at a time
> when her knowledge of reality has long since led her
> to abandon the fulfillment of this desire as being
> quite unattainable, analysis proves that it still
> persists in the unconscious, and retains a consider-
> able charge of energy. (pp. 160-161.)

Thus, whether explaining the female's greater sense of modesty or the male's superior sense of morality, a direct correspondence is assumed to exist between biological and psy-

chological differences.

According to Freudian theory, the major differences between males and females evolve during the oedipal stage of development, when sexual rivalries between the child and its parents force the child to identify with the same-sex parent. It is the process of identification which ensures the acquisition of appropriate male and female traits. Thus, Freud's conception of the development of sex-role identity is dominated by the proposition of a unitary mechanism which establishes masculine and feminine identity in the first years of life, and persists unchanged throughout development.

An alternative psychoanalytic formulation of masculinity and femininity has been introduced by Erikson (1950). In an effort to go beyond the Freudian emphasis on penis envy, Erikson postulates that the nature of both the male and female sexual organs lead to distinctly different ways of orienting in the world, and that these orientations correspond to differences in the male and female personality. Thus, the external, intrusive nature of the male sex organ is presumed to correspond to an active, pragmatic orientation which is known as "outer space". According to Erikson, this basic masculine orientation is responsible for the progress as well as the potential destruction of Western technological society. The female body, with its internal, expectant reproductive system is assumed to correspond to the gentle, peaceful and static orientation known as "inner space". This basic orientation is thought to predispose the female to commit herself to the love of a man and to the care of both their offspring.

In short, Erikson's central thesis is that the male and female sexual topography corresponds to basic personality schemata which become the defining attributes of masculinity and femininity. Erikson makes less clear the process by which physical differences are translated into personality schemata. In some instançes, the connection between "inner" or "outer" space and masculinity-femininity appears to be symbolic or metaphorical, while at other points, Erikson appears to be arguing in functional evolutionary terms.

Thus, insofar as they are attempting to highlight the sexual aspects of personality functioning, both Erikson and Freud postulate a predetermined relationship between the nature of male and female biology and later psychological functioning.

Social Learning Theory

If psychoanalytic theory may be said to assume a relationship between anatomical differences and psychological
functioning, social learning theory may be said to assume a
correspondence between external events and internal psychological functioning. The social learning position asserts
that few, if any, sex differences in personality exist that
are not a function of learning. Masculinity and femininity
reflect norms and values which are internalized by children
through direct cultural transmission.
    Proponents of this model may be classified according to
two different perspectives: positions which reflect both a
theoretical and ideological distinction. The first group
views development in terms of increasing conformity to
social norms and standards, and considers conformity to male
and female stereotypes as the standard of normal sex-role
development (Kagan, 1964; Mussen, 1969). The studies derived
from this approach focus on the ages at which children's beliefs conform to socially accepted standards of masculinity
and femininity and attempt to isolate the background variables
which are related to sex-typing (Greenstein, 1966; Hetheringtor
1965). The data indicate that children are aware of the toys
and activities culturally appropriate to their gender by four
or five years of age (Brown, 1958). In addition, from pre-
school age onwards, children label the mother as more nurturant and nicer, while the father is viewed as more competent,
powerful, punitive, and fear-arousing (Kagan and Lemkin, 1960;
Emmerich *et al.* 1971). According to this perspective, these
attributes are acquired through observation (Mussen, 1969),
modelling (Bandura, 1968), identification (Sears, 1970), and
imitation (Bandura, Ross and Ross, 1963).
    The second group of studies is characterized by its re-
jection of conformity to sex-role stereotypes as the end
point of development. Although these theorists agree that
masculine and feminine traits develop as a result of environmental conditions, they reject a) the notion of conformity
to cultural stereotypes as the standard of adequacy or nor-
mality in development, b) the inequities of the social, political, and economic institutions which shape concepts of masculinity and femininity, and c) the prejudicial and unwar-
rented emphasis on the anatomical or biological differences

between the sexes.

According to this view, psychoanalytic concepts such
as penis envy, narcissism, castration anxiety, etc. are considered to be either psychologically false or, insofar as
they exist, to be more adequately explained by the social
and economic inequities of a particular society. Seidenberg,
(1973) for example, reformulates the issue of "castration"
in women from a societal point of view. Instead of attribu-
ting the castration complex to the sexual rivalry between
women for the father's love, he focuses instead on the negative consequences of a male dominated social system:

> ...therefore the daughter's fantasy of being "cut off"
> is not an irrational fantasy - but a social reality.
> She is in fact "cut off" from the world which we have
> always defined as being most meaningful and relevant.
> The castration complex is no myth, as psychoanalysis
> would have it. (p. 311.)

In addition to these recent attempts to revise psychoanalytic concepts from a more environmentalist perspective
(Mitchell, 1974; Miller, 1973; Strouse, 1974), empirical
studies have been conducted to document the role of prejudicial environment on the development of male and female stereotypes. In a series of studies designed to investigate the
nature of sex-role stereotyping, the data indicate that individuals of both sexes rated males as competent, independent,
powerful, and aggressive, while females were viewed as with-
drawn, conceited, nurturant, and dependent (Rosenkrantz *et
al*. 1968). The researchers found moreover, that an independent group of psychiatrists tended to rate "male" attributes
as consistent with their model of a "normal healthy adult"
while female traits bore no such relationship to professional
concepts of mental health (Broverman *et al*. 1970). The
investigators cite these findings as important evidence of
the devaluation of female attributes in society.

In contrast to the traditional model which defines
sex-role identity in terms of the degree of conformity to
masculine and feminine stereotypes, recent models have been
proposed which view optimal development in terms of greater
"androgyny" (Bem, 1974) or an increased integration of
"agency" and "communion" (Block, 1973). These concepts
refer to the tendency for individuals to display sex-role
flexibility across situations without regard for sterotyping
behaviours as more appropriate for one sex or another.*

This tendency is assumed to represent a psychologically
healthier, as well as a developmentally more advanced orientation to sex-role identity.

Thus, despite the theoretical and ideological dispari-
ties within the social learning framework, the significant
feature of the social learning model is its exclusive focus
on the environment as the determining aspect of masculinity
and femininity.

Both the psychoanalytic and the social learning models
raise a series of theoretical and methodological issues.
First, each of these approaches postulates a single factor
which is presumed to play an important role at all stages of
development. From the psychoanalytic perspective, the biological factor is a critical determinant of sex-role identity
from early childhood through adulthood; while for social
learning theorists, the nature of the social system, with its
differential roles, norms and expectations is seen as the
salient factor at all ages. The question may be raised
whether either of these factors operate as independently and
uniformly as each theory suggests, or whether each assumes
a differential importance at particular levels of development.

Second, much of the theorizing about the development of
sex-role identity is based on empirical data which indicate
conformity to socially accepted stereotypes by 4 to 5 years
of age. The findings are based primarily on the use of
forced-choice questionnaires on which masculinity and femininity are viewed as a continuous dimension composed of a
series of dichotomous traits. Age-related shifts are measured in terms of increases in the amount of responses which
differentiate males and females along a particular dimension.

* Both Bem and Block's constructs are operationally defined
by the degree to which an individual's self-assessments on
forced-choice questionnaires include an equal endorsement of
both masculine and feminine traits. Both the measures, however, fail to specify whether the self-ratings of "androgynous" or "agentic and communal" individuals necessarily reflect the individual's judgments about the desirability of
expressing cross-sex traits. From this methodological perspective, one must assume psychological equivalence among
all "androgynous" individuals, regardless of whether their
self-ratings simultaneously reflect an acceptance or rejection of such traits.

It is important to note that forced-choice questionnaires permit only a quantitative assessment of the degree of conformity to socially expected norms and values. Such a methodology prevents the observation or examination of potential qualitative changes in thinking about sex-roles, and reveals little about the meaning or importance of non-conforming responses.

A DEVELOPMENTAL MODEL OF SEX-ROLE CONCEPTS

An alternative to the psychoanalytic and social learning theories outlined above is the view that masculinity and femininity are concepts which develop in accordance with the changing nature of the child's thinking about the biological, social, and psychological differences between males and females. In other words, masculine and feminine identities are not merely a function of biological propensities; nor are they solely the result of particular societal conditions. Rather, they represent developmentally changing ways of viewing and interpreting differences between the sexes. This approach is based on the assumption that masculine and feminine identities are not stable, invariant phenomena which persist unchanged throughout development. Rather, it assumes that conceptions of masculinity and femininity undergo significant changes as a result of cognitive and social development.

From this perspective, I undertook a study (Ullian, 1976) to explore these hypotheses. In particular, the following three hypotheses were examined:

1. There are age-related changes in the mode of conceptualizing male and female differences. In contrast to the conformity model described previously, this hypothesis suggests that significant developmental shifts occur in the qualitative nature of judgments made about males and females, rather than in the degree to which they approximate adult stereotypes.

2. Two classes of sex-role judgments can be distinguished: the descriptive and the prescriptive. While the former refers to judgments and beliefs about the nature of male and female differences, the latter refers to judgments about the need or desirability to conform to masculine and feminine stereotypes. Thus, in addition to the descriptive aspect of sex-typing, one may distinguish a related sequence of prescriptive judgments which define the individual's views of permissable behaviour for males and females.

3. Sex-role development proceeds beyond the level of
conformity to socially accepted stereotypes. At the final
level, an attempt is made to adopt standards of masculinity
and femininity which are consistent with the moral requirements of equality and human freedom. This form of thinking
about male and female roles may be viewed within a developmental sequence, rather than as exceptional instances of
"liberated" or "androgynous" individuals.

The approach adopted here derives from a model of development which views the organism as developing through stages
of interaction with the physical and social environment
(Piaget and Inhelder, 1969; Werner, 1961). Each stage of
development involves a qualitatively different organization
of experience that is a progressive transformation of the
previous stage. This model has previously been adopted in
the area of sex-role development to explain the development
of concepts of masculinity and femininity from three to eight
years of age (Kohlberg, 1966).

Our study examined sex-role development from childhood
to adolescence. Seventy males and females ranging in age
from 6 to 18 were individually interviewed in an open-ended
clinical fashion. The interview was designed to allow examination of beliefs about men and women along four general
dimensions: competence, power, nurturance, and activity
level.* The items included both direct questions on these
dimensions (Who do you think is more intelligent - men or
women? Why?), as well as a series of questions about males
and females within the social context of work, family, and
interpersonal relationships (Who should be the boss in the
family? Why?). Each subject was questioned extensively
about the basis on which sex-role judgments were made, as
well as on the need or desirability to conform to masculine
and feminine stereotypes (Do you think it is important for
a man to act masculine and a woman to act feminine? Why?).
For purposes of the present analysis, the data of male and

* *Although all subjects were interviewed about each of the
four dimensions, the content and style of the questions were
adapted to suit the vocabulary and experiences of different
age groups. On the dimension of power, for example, the
younger children were asked "Who should be the boss in the
family?" while older individuals were asked "Who do you
think should ultimately be responsible for the important
decisions in the family?"*

female subjects were combined.

An analysis of the interview responses indicates support for each of the three hypotheses. First, the data support the notion of developmental levels in the individual's conceptualization of masculinity and femininity. Seven age groups of male and female subjects were studied, and six distinct levels emerged from this analysis. Each level consists of a particular way of describing sex differences (descriptive) and a mode of judging what is appropriate behaviour for males and females (prescriptive). Table I presents a summary of the developmental sequence, which proceeds from sex-typed judgments based on a) biological factors to b) societal factors to c) psychological factors.*

The descriptive and the prescriptive aspects of each level may be characterized by the following themes:

Level I (6 years)

Descriptive: Subjects at this level view differences between males and females primarily as a result of biological and physical propensities. The salient features on which sex-role judgments are based include size, strength, length of hair, and voice characteristics. While the child also recognizes differences in social and occupational roles, these are assumed to derive from innate physical differences, and are therefore viewed as fixed and unchangeable. For example, while the capacity for work is seen as responsible for the male's greater power and competence, it is equated with obvious differences in size and strength. Thus, when a child was asked whether a woman could ever make as much money as a man, one child responded categorically:

> "No. Because the man knows how to make more money because a man could do work better than a lady sometimes." (*Why is that?*) "A lady doesn't know so much about working in an insurance agency." (*How*

---

* *For purposes of the present analysis, "psychological" is used to refer to the individual's concern with issues of personal identity and interpersonal relationships in conceptualizing masculinity and femininity. This orientation is in marked contrast to the societal orientation, in which masculine and feminine traits are viewed in terms of their relationship to the external social system (norms, duties, expectations, etc.).*

TABLE I

Summary of Six Levels of Sex-Role Conceptualization

Biological Orientation

Level I: Masculine and feminine traits are based primarily
on external bodily differences, such as size, strength,
length of hair, etc. While social and psychological differences are also recognized, they are assumed to derive from
external physical differences. Conformity to sex differences
is viewed as necessary in order to maintain and express gender differences.

Level II: There is an awareness that masculine and feminine
traits may exist independently from biological and physical
features. Emphasis is placed on the ability of the individual to act according to choice, since he or she is no longer limited by physical or biological constraints.

Societal Orientation

Level III: Masculine and feminine traits are seen as inherent in the requirements of a system of social roles and are
viewed as fixed and unchangeable. Conformity to masculine
and feminine standards is based on the need to satisfy external demands of the social system.

Level IV: There is an awareness that the system of social
roles is arbitrary and variable, and may function independently of sex of individual. Stress is put on the individual's freedom to act according to individual self-interest.

Psychological Orientation

Level V: Masculine and feminine traits are based on the
adoption of an appropriate psychological identity by males
and females. Deviation is viewed as "sick" or "abnormal"
and conformity to external standards is seen as required
for maintenance of marriage and the family.

Level VI: There is an awareness that masculinity and femininity may exist independent from conformity to traditional
standards, roles and behaviours. Principles of equality and
freedom are proposed as standards for behaviour, and are used
to define an ideal model of personal and interpersonal functioning.

come she couldn't learn as much as the father?) "Because a father can get more money, the father can do
more things than the lady because as I was saying, a
lady has delicate skin, a man has tougher skin."

The six-year-old's confusion between biological and social
reality is further illustrated by the following comment.
Asked why she believes men to be stronger, the child replied:

"Because they were born to be stronger. They were
born to be stronger than girls because they do more
work than girls."

It can be seen, then, that sex differences in competence,
power, nurturance and activity level are viewed as an inevitable consequence of the biological nature of males and females.
    Prescriptive: In accordance with the six-year-old
child's emphasis on physical, observable differences between
males and females, sex-role conformity is based on the need
to maintain and express external differences. Deviation
from existing observable differences is viewed as a violation
of the laws of physical reality, as well as a threat to one's
gender identity. While sex-role conformity is required to
ensure the maintenance of gender identity, little concern is
expressed about parental and peer expectations. For example,
when a child was asked her opinion of a girl with very short
hair, she responded:

"She would kind of look like a boy." (*Would that be
right or wrong?*) "Wrong, because it doesn't look
nice if a boy has long hair and a girl has short
hair." (*Why?*) "Because if there was a girl and a
boy together, and say the girl has short hair like
the boy, some people would say 'I like these two
boys', but one is really a girl."

Here we see that deviations from any of the usual external
signs of one's sex (clothing, hair style) are perceived as
a possible change in one's real or perceived basic gender
identity. As a result, others will think the person to be
of the opposite sex and consequently will see that person as
funny, bizarre, or distorted.

Level II (8 years)

    Descriptive: Responses at this level reflect a rejection of the previous mode of viewing masculinity and femininity in terms of their biological or physical correlates. There is an increasing recognition that gender identity exists independently from one's external bodily characteristics (such as hair style, ornamentation, clothing). The eight-year-old child indicates an awareness of a subjective "self" which intervenes between one's physical attributes, and the behaviours and activities labelled as masculine or feminine. In addition, children at this level show an emerging awareness that particular aspects of masculinity and femininity are a function of training, habit, and social conditions.

While the content of the Level II child's ideas about males and females do not necessarily differ from those at Level I, those differences which were previously seen as inate or physically determined are no longer viewed as inevitable and unchangeable. On the issue of competence, for example, a child was asked:

> (*Who do you think should make the important decisions around the house?*) "My father does things like that. I don't know how to put this, but he is stronger and I think he knows what is going to happen if you do that." (*Do you think he knows better than your mother?*) "If he has to fix something and my mother says he should do it one way and he says this is the way, he knows that that was the way he was supposed to do it." (*How come he knew and your mother didn't?*) "Because my father is trained to know how to do more." (*Do you think fathers are better at knowing things than women?*) "It depends on the kind of man."

This example illustrates two important shifts in thinking from Level I to Level II. First, in spite of a continuing belief in male superiority, the child has begun to distinguish the physical from the psychological. Competence is no longer tied to concrete differences in size and strength, but is now related to one's level of training or education. Once the child is able to differentiate masculine and feminine attributes from their biological correlates, the child is free to consider the possibility of men and women as equal along each of the four dimensions. For example, when a student was asked who would make a better President, she answered:

> "It depends on what kind of man and what kind of

woman it is, and if she is smarter than the man,
then I think she should be."

Thus, particular roles and duties are no longer seen as inherent in the individual's sexual gender; rather, the child
is aware that sex-role identity is partly a function of experience and environment, which allows for possible variation
in the range of roles and behaviour that an individual of
either sex may engage in.

   Prescriptive: In contrast to the Level I child, the
Level II child's prescriptive judgments are based on the recognition that gender identity remains constant, in spite of
variations in physical and bodily characteristics. Since
masculine and feminine traits are now viewed as an expression
of individual choice, rather than as a result of biological
properties, children at this level express a commitment that
each individual can and should choose from a wide range of
male and female behaviours, roles and activities. For example, an eight-year-old girl was posed with the question:

   (*Some people say girls should act like girls and
   boys like boys?*) "I don't think it's true. Because like the girls are the same as the boys.
   And the boys are the same as the girls. If you
   take her and put her in his clothes, they are the
   same, and some boys want to act pretty and some
   want to wear neckties and pants and they don't
   like tuxedos, they are doing their own thing."

   This individualistic tendency in which personal choice
takes precedence over external standards of appropriate behaviour is further evidenced by a child's reflection on her
mother's attempts to encourage her femininity:

   (*What would you think of a woman with big muscles?*)
   "I don't think it is nice. Well, it is alright.
   Some people say it is not feminine. I think it is
   alright. What is the matter with having big muscles?
   I am always lifting things for my mother and father
   and my mother always says 'you should not do that'.
   Well, there is nothing the matter with it. I am not
   trying to be fresh with her, but I don't think there
   is anything the matter with it."

In summary, the Level II child recognizes that a sense of
self does, in fact, intervene between one's sexual gender

and the traits or behaviours associated with it. Thus, the child actively rejects the conception of biology dictating sex-role identity, and focuses on the subjective personality which governs human behaviour.

Level III (10 years)

   Descriptive: Children at this level show an increasing awareness of a social system which distinguishes between males and females in terms of social roles. Within this context, sex differences are now related not only to past experience or training, but also to one's future role in the social and economic system. Based on the differentiation of sexes by roles, the child automatically attributes the required abilities and qualities to members of each sex to fulfil those roles. A ten-year-old child was asked, for example, to judge which sex is more intelligent:

> "Men are smarter because they have to do a lot of things like thinking. They have to work at their jobs. They have to think a lot and they have to work and they have to figure things out."

At this point in development, the child ceases to rely on what is physically possible for males and females, and focuses instead on what is socially required as the basis for his judgments. In short, the child attempts to accommodate his conception of masculinity and femininity to the constraints of future social roles, which are viewed as inevitable and unchangeable. For example, when a ten-year-old child was asked about a boy playing with dolls, he responded:

> "No, I don't think he should be dainty, he should take care of the home and things." (*Why?*) "Because he has a big responsibility to look for a job and he has the ability to be responsible."

Unlike the older students, the Level III child accepts the demands of the conventional social system as logically correct and consistent. The child believes that a proper match exists between one's acquired traits and abilities, and one's future role in the familial, occupational, and social system.
   Prescriptive: In contrast to the Level II child's view that all behaviour should be tolerated because it is biologically possible, the prescriptions of children at Level III show an increasing tendency to align behaviour with socially

accepted standards and expectations. Unlike their younger counterparts, these children are concerned with peer and parental responses to non-conforming behaviour. When a child was asked if a boy should ever be dainty, for example, he responded:

> "I don't think anybody would like it if he did because the lady sort of does the dainty part and wears earrings and necklaces and fancy dresses and stuff, but the man has different kinds of jewelry." (*Would it be wrong if the man wore jewelry?*) "Well, women wouldn't just go wearing men's things. You could, it would be right, but everyone would say, 'look at him', and he would not get a job if he wanted to and nobody would accept him; they would think he was a weird guy."

Thus, while children at this level view conventional male and female behaviour as only one of several possibilities, social norms and conventions are relied upon to provide guidance and direction in determining sex-appropriate behaviour.

Level IV (12 years)

   Descriptive: In contrast to the ten-year-old children, the twelve-year-olds are aware that masculine and feminine attributes are largely a function of social and historical forces: as a result they are no longer viewed as inevitable and immutable. Thus, males and females are assumed to be essentially equal in terms of potential, while particular social and cultural circumstances influence the realization of that potential. A twelve-year-old student illustrates this point:

> (*Can you say who is nicer - a man or a woman?*) "No." (*Why?*) "Because it depends on the personality of the person, not whether he is a woman or man." (*Who is smarter?*) "Same thing as the other question, you can't tell, it is a matter of your brain, it is not whether you are a woman or a man. It's whether you are smart."

This level is of interest in that it marks the point at which children recognize that masculine and feminine traits are no longer a function of biological or social necessity, but originate instead in the somewhat arbitrary nature of social and historical forces.

    Prescriptive: Based on an "egalitarian" notion of masculinity and femininity, the prescriptive judgments at this level stress that behaviour should be governed by individual needs and preferences. While the twelve-year-old children are aware of socially acceptable standards and norms, they are no longer viewed as fixed or uniform, and deviation from them is permissable. Therefore, when a student was asked what he would think of a woman doing a man's job, for example, he replied:

> "Well, if she could handle it, it's okay. If a girl just wants to prove a point, then she really shouldn't do it. But if she can do a heavy working job, then she should be able to do it." (*What would you think of a strong, tough girl?*) "She might be a tomboy, but I wouldn't think anything different, as long as she was a girl." (*What do you think of boys who act girlish?*) "There is nothing wrong with them, it is just that a lot of people tease them and everything."

Both Level II and Level IV children reject conformity to male and female stereotypes. However, it is important to distinguish the bases on which their judgments are made. At Level II prescriptive judgments are based on the recognition that males and females are physically or biologically capable of engaging in cross-sex activities and therefore ought to pursue those activities, whereas at Level IV the prescriptive judgments are based on the recognition that masculine and feminine attributes are merely a function of social convention, which is seen as arbitrary and variable. Thus, while the Level II child's judgments reflect a rejection of his previous notion of biological determinism, the Level IV child's judgments similarly represent his rejection of the notion of social determinism.

Level V (14-16 years)

    Descriptive: At this level, sex-linked attributes such as competence, power, etc., are no longer determined by sexual gender or by social necessity. Sex differences are now viewed as the result of social standards which are externally imposed and which may in fact be discrepant from the true nature of men and women. For example, when a student was asked about the differences in male and female power, she remarked:

> "They are more protective of women than the other
> way around." (*Why is that?*) "Because society ex-
> pects women to pretend they can't protect them-
> selves and let the men do it. In fact, they are
> just as able as men to do it, but they're not sup-
> posed to."

Nevertheless, adolescents tend to define internal psychological differences between male and females which are
independent of, or prior to, the social sex-roles they play.
A student remarks:

> "They (girls) have a lot of views on things, they
> are more – I think they have more emotions than
> men do and they show it more than men do."

All the usual psychological sex-role stereotypes are present;
women are more sympathetic, more dependent, more emotional,
less sexually driven. Although these differences are viewed
as a function of habit or cultural conditioning, they are
assumed to be a salient aspect of male and female identity.

Prescriptive: In spite of the adolescent's recognition
that sex-role stereotypes do not necessarily reflect the true
nature of male and female differences, their prescriptive
judgments indicate a strong insistence that members of either
sex conform to social and cultural norms. While these students endorse the right of each individual to act freely and
independently, stereotypes tend to dictate what is "right"
in a socio-moral sense, and conformity is used as a basis for
moral evaluations of the self and others. A fourteen-year-
old student, a self-confessed feminist, was asked what she
would think of a man who dressed in midi coats and heeled
shoes:

> "I wouldn't go near him, ugh!" (*Why not?*) "They have
> some psychological problem." (*Why?*) "They must have
> something wrong with them, maybe they were brought up
> that way, because they shouldn't act feminine, that
> is our identity, that is our position, not theirs.
> They should be masculine." (*Why?*) "Because that is
> the way it is always – men are masculine and women
> are feminine. If they were feminine, it would really
> be strange."

The prescriptive judgments of the adolescents differ

from those of the younger children in several ways. They
are not based on the need to conform to physical reality,
nor are they viewed as necessary for the maintenance of
social roles, duties and obligations. Rather, they spring
from a concern with maintaining one's personal identity and
respecting one's true sexual nature. At this point in development, personal identity is equated with the degree of conformity to socially accepted standards of male and female
behaviour. "Being oneself" is defined by following the dic-
tates of conventional society, and deviation from these standards is judged as abnormal or unauthentic.

In addition to the adolescent's concern with personal
identity, conformity to stereotypes is directly related to
anticipated success in heterosexual relationships. Despite
the adolescent's awareness of non-traditional alternatives,
deviation from traditional roles and duties is viewed as a
threat to the survival of both marriage and family. When a
student was asked, for example, if it is important to maintain roles, she responded:

> "Yah, I think the marriage would be shattered there,
> if I was smarter than he." (*What comes to mind?*)
> "You would be thinking more than he and you would
> think he was a dumbbell and you would overpower him
> and it was supposed to be him being the leader and
> you would become the leader after a while and you
> would probably go to work - and I can't imagine the
> family."

Despite the individual's awareness of the basic inequality
of traditional male and female roles, conformity to these
stereotypes is still strongly urged both for the maintenance
of one's identity or self-esteem, and for the success or con-
tinuance of heterosexual relationships.

Level VI (18 years)

Descriptive: Although these students acknowledge stereotyped differences between males and females, they do not believe that such differences are basic to their personal identity, nor are they necessary for optimal heterosexual relationships. Rather, they are seen as the product of conventional expectations and norms internalized by children.
These social stereotypes are viewed as a product of an unjust,
prejudicial, male-dominated society. A male student pointed

out, for example:

> "Women get put into a role; by the nature of them
> being born men and women they're put into social
> positions and their social actions are laid out
> for them and they are expected to do certain things
> and not to do other things. Men are expected to be
> aggressive and dominant, and the characteristics
> associated with masculinity."

Attempting to go beyond customary sex-role stereotypes, the
college student tries to construct a set of attributes which
have validity for males and females, as well as those which
might enhance the smooth functioning of heterosexual relationships. Asked to define the ideal woman, a student responded:

> "Personally, the ideal woman to me can be beautiful,
> and soft, but the ideal man may also be soft in the
> same way, because he is soft-spoken, not domineering
> over anyone, but still with ambition so he can get
> things done."

Despite the college student's rejection of conventional
norms as the basis of masculinity and femininity, and despite his attempts to formulate a principle of equality which
governs heterosexual relationships, his/her *personal* preferences of masculinity and femininity closely resemble traditional stereotypes of male superiority. While males are encouraged to be childrearers, teachers and nurses, women are
encouraged to become lawyers, doctors, and scientists, and
male-female relationships are expected to be equitable and
fair, each student would personally prefer a relationship
in which the male is slightly more competent than the female.
When a student remarks, "I say stereotypes should be abolished,
but I can't help what has been put into me during the years",
he expresses the dilemma of this developmental level: that
of reconciling abstract moral principles of equality and individual freedom with personal values and choices in one's
private experience. This leads the student to dissociate
himself from his judgments, labelling himself as "moronic",
"biased", or "male chauvinist". Unlike the fourteen-year-
old students who view conformity to male and female stereotypes as morally and socially required, the college students
view conformity or non-conformity as a personal choice. In
short, college students recognize that their personal judg-

ments about masculinity and femininity are undoubtedly influenced by their own particular experiences in a traditional
environment. However, they simultaneously view their own experience as only one of many possible alternatives and thus
refuse to judge any form of masculine or feminine behaviour
as inherently right or wrong.

The analysis so far has delineated a series of levels
which indicate a sequential concern with biological, societal, and psychological factors in determining judgments about
masculinity and femininity. At the earliest levels, (Levels
I and II), the children's responses to the issues of masculinity and femininity were based on the physical or biological differences between the sexes. At the middle levels,
(Levels III and IV), judgments about sex-roles were organized
around conceptions of societal roles and obligations. At the
final level, (Levels V and VI), masculinity and femininity
were defined according to the psychological requirements of
individual and interpersonal functioning. In summary, the
analyses presented here lend support to the three main hypotheses. First, they indicate that masculinity and femininity
are not unitary concepts which are acquired in a linear way
through development. If that were the case, the responses
at Levels I through VI would be expected to reflect increasing acceptance of sex-role conventions. In fact, the results
suggest a pattern of alternating acceptance and rejection of
sex-role norms. Furthermore, the nature of changes in sex-
role concepts may be characterized by their sequential focus
on a) biological, b) societal and c) psychological factors
as the determinants of masculinity and femininity.

Second, the study indicates that sex-role development
must be viewed in terms of two separate issues; the descriptive as well as the prescriptive. The results indicate that
despite the child's growing awareness of the arbitrary or
socially-determined nature of male and female differences,
there are significant developmental shifts in the way that
information is used to make judgments about the need or desirability to conform to stereotypes of masculinity and femininity. In the absence of such a distinction, studies on
sex-role stereotyping continue to reveal a relatively uni-
form degree of stereotyping from childhood to adulthood.

Finally, the study reveals that the end point of sex-
role development proceeds beyond the mere acceptance of conventional notions of masculinity and femininity. At Level
VI, an attempt is made to construct a set of ideal standards

which have universal validity, and which are consistent with
principles of equality and human freedom. While past studies
have categorized individuals in dichotomous terms (normal
versus deviant, or androgynous versus stereotyped), the developmental perspective proposed here offers a logical basis
for such non-stereotyped views, rather than merely a charac-
terological typology based on responses to a forced-choice
questionnaire.

While the results outlined above are based on preliminary observation, further analysis of the data will yield a
more complex description of the critical distinctions made
at various levels of development. Nevertheless, the developmental perspective provides an alternative framework from
which to understand the development of sex-role identity.
The results presented here offer no solution to the nature-
nurture question, but they do suggest that the salience of
biological versus social factors depends mainly on the interpretation given to them by the individual at various levels
of development. Finally, this approach establishes a model
from which existing sex differences may be interpreted and
understood. By examining the individual's changing beliefs
about masculinity and femininity, one may begin to identify
the source of sex differences which have heretofore been observed, but insufficiently explained.

REFERENCES

Bandura, A. (1968). Social learning theory of identificatory
    processes. *In* "Handbook of Socialization Theory and Re-
    search". (D. Goslin, ed.) Rand McNally and Co., Chicago.

Bandura, A., Ross, D. and Ross, S. (1963). A test of the
    status envy, social power and secondary reinforcement
    theories of identificatory learning. *Journal of Abnormal
    and Social Psychology,* 67, 527-534.

Bem, S.L. (1974). The measurement of psychological androgyny.
    Journal of Consulting and Clinical Psychology, 42, 155-
    162.

Block, J. (1973). Conceptions of sex-role: some cross-
    cultural and longitudinal perspectives. *American Psycho-
    logist,* 6, 512-526.

Brown, D.G. (1958). Sex-role development in a changing cul-
    ture. *Psychological Bulletin,* 55, 232-242.

Broverman, I., Broverman, D., Clarkson, F., Rosenkrantz, P. and Vogel, S. (1970). Sex-role stereotypes and clinical judgments of mental health. *Journal of Consulting and Clinical Psychology*, 34, 1-7.

Emmerich, W., Goldman, S. and Shore, R. (1971). Differentiation and development of social norms. *Journal of Personality and Social Psychology*, 18, 323-353.

Erikson, E. (1950). "Childhood and Society". W.W. Norton and Co. Inc., New York.

Fauls, L.B. and Smith, W.D. (1956). Sex-role learning of five year olds. *Journal of Genetic Psychology*, 89, 105-117.

Freud, S. (1957). "New Introductory Lectures on Psychoanalysis". The Hogarth Press Ltd., London. First published 1933.

Greenstein, J. (1962). Father characteristics and sex-typing. *Journal of Personality and Social Psychology*, 3, 271-277.

Hartley, R., Hardesty, F. and Gorfein, D. (1962). Children's perception and expression of sex-preferences. *Child Development*, 33, 221-227.

Hetherington, M. (1965). A developmental study of the effects of sex of the dominant parent on sex-role preference, identification, and imitation in children. *Journal of Personality and Social Psychology*, 2, 188-194.

Kagan, J. and Lemkin, J. (1960). The child's differential perception of parental attitudes. *Journal of Abnormal and Social Psychology*, 61, 440-477.

Kagan, J. (1964). Acquisition and significance of sex-typing and sex-role identity. *In* "Review of Child Development Research". (M. Hoffman and L. Hoffman, eds.) Vol. 1. Russell Sage, New York.

Kohlberg, L. (1966). A cognitive-developmental analysis of children's sex-role concepts and attitudes. *In* "The Development of Sex Differences". (E. Maccoby, ed.) Stanford University Press, California.

Miller, J. (1933). "Psychoanalysis and Women". Penguin Books Ltd., Middlesex, England.

Mitchell, J. (1974). "Psychoanalysis and Femininism". Random

House, New York.

Mussen, P. (1969). Early sex-role development. *In* "Handbook of Socialization Theory and Research". (D. Goslin, ed.) Rand McNally, Chicago.

Piaget, J. and Inhelder, B. (1969). "The Psychology of the Child". Basic Books, New York.

Rosenkrantz, P., Bee, H., Vogel, S., Broverman, I. and Broverman, D. (1968). Sex-role stereotypes and self-concepts in college students. *Journal of Consulting and Clinical Psychology*, 32, 287-295.

Sears, R. (1970). Relation of early socialization experiences to self-concept and gender role in middle childhood. *Child Development*, 2, 267-289.

Sears, R., Rau, L. and Alpert, R. (1965). "Identification and Child Rearing". Stanford University Press, California.

Seidenberg, R. (1973). Is anatomy destiny? *In* "Psychoanalysis and Women". (Jean Baker Miller, ed.) Penguin Books Ltd., Middlesex, England.

Strouse, J. (1974). (ed.) "Women and Analysis: Dialogues on Psychoanalytic Views of Femininity". Grossman Publishers, New York.

Ullian, D. (1976). "A Developmental Study of Conceptions of Masculinity and Femininity". Doctoral Dissertation, Harvard University.

Werner, H. (1961). "Comparative Psychology of Mental Development". Science Editions Inc., New York.

3. AN ANTHROPOLOGICAL PERSPECTIVE

Marilyn Strathern

Studies of sex differences, both popular and scientific, commonly explore the connection between cultural stereotypes about males and females (gender) and the physiological basis for discrimination (sex). Is man by nature more aggressive than woman? Does woman's mental development really take a different course? These are the kinds of questions we find interesting. This chapter is about the stereotypes themselves, or rather, about the activity of stereotype-making. Like any other behaviour it must be understood within its cultural context. In many cultures notions about differences and similarities between the sexes (gender constructs) are put to use, not just to order actual relations between men and women, but as a kind of language for talking about other things as well - for example, the respective prestige of certain occupations, or the correct relationship between a human being and his deity. Such a usage of gender draws upon sex differences as a source of symbolism. This means that a set of items or characteristics, those regarded as indicative of maleness or femaleness, stands for or is a kind of shorthand for talking about another set. For example, if a job is described as "woman's work" the speaker's hearers at once understand that it belongs to a class of activities which receive a particular rating. This classification not only links women to certain kinds of work but also suggests a relationship between this job and others, based partly on the relationship of women to men.

When sex differences are used in this way, the resultant stereotypes are likely to be related not simply to what men and women are like biologically or in their social life, but also to cultural preoccupations which may well be at a remove from men's and women's affairs. One might find the men in our example very interested in prestige and occupation hierarchies, so that the ascription of jobs as "male" or

"female" becomes a highly emotional matter. In order to insult or denigrate, they are able to dismiss others as doing
women's work. The relationship between men and women is
thus used to rank men among themselves. Again, consider one
form which our (Western) preoccupation with the boundary between nature and culture takes: a contrast between what are
innate, biological factors in the make-up of human beings and
what are of social origin has been a stimulus for scientific
investigation, as well as for ideologies such as that of the
women's liberation movements. We should at least be aware of
the possibility of feedback here - that in arriving at a
clearer understanding of the cultural and biological elements
in the make-up of the sexes we are also using sex differences
to illuminate and talk about, in short to symbolize, the relationship we see between nature and culture.

GENDER

Anthropologists are interested in the ways societies
utilize or ignore differences and similarities in men and
women to produce the gender categories "male" and "female".
Most cultures seem to place considerable emphasis on this
categorization, though, as we shall see, gender may be more
the product of the thinking of one sex than of the other.
The sex differences which gender ideas rest upon are
both gross anatomical characteristics and variations in quality of behaviour or mentality. The way the latter are perceived is largely a matter of social classification and evaluation. Frequently, however, all the differences and similarities so ascribed will be taken together and appear to be
based on biology. In most societies gender thus has the appearance of being a straightforward representation of natural
sex characteristics. The process may go something like this.
Culture emphasizes perceived differences in the muscular performance of the sexes. These become linked to contrasts between outside and inside work. The stereotype is that in
any outside situation requiring muscular exertion men will
perform better than women. Gender typing then allocates
roles to males which have some connection with this, so that
for example, lawn-mowing appears a more appropriate male contribution to the household than floor-washing. Lawn-mowing
has the characteristic of being visible but sporadic; floor-
washing invisible and routine. These characteristics themselves create further value links between aspects of male

and female qualities (men's routine work is done elsewhere). This process invests gender constructs with a concreteness and a naturalness which can be drawn upon as a source of symbolism. Thus: men are (physically) strong and that is why they are (socially) powerful. Power (as a cultural notion) is here a gender attribute. Power as an analytical notion, which involves an investigation on the observer's part into just what influence persons have in a society, may be another matter altogether. *Hagen* * culture proclaims that males are "powerful", though they can be threatened on occasion by weak females. An outsider would comment that the very fact that men fear women suggests a rather more equal distribution of interpersonal influence than the stereotype allows, and that males and females are both "powerful" in some respects. This example is of course a common one. In many societies males are represented as more powerful than females, whatever the actual degree of power discrimination there is between the sexes. So too we find some very common gender attributes such as the belief that women are capricious. This is easy to understand. If men visualize males as the natural possessors of power and prestige, single-minded devotion to their interests becomes devotion to a proper cause. Feminine single-mindedness directed towards female interests is evaluated as antisocial. An outsider will argue that the attribute of caprice is a direct function of perceived power relations; whereas an insider will say that men have to hold power because women by their nature are irresponsible. We should add that while attention to gender is universal, in many societies a major preoccupation, there are a handful of cultures[†] which do not seem to utilize it

* *A people in the Papua New Guinea Highlands with whom I have worked. To give some concreteness and continuity to my examples, I cite various illustrations from Hagen.*

† *I raise this as a point which needs further investigation. Three cultures which come to mind are those of the Mbuti pygmies of the Congo, who place little emphasis on gender (Turnbull, 1965); Hadza in Tanzania, who emphasise few social categorizations apart from gender (Woodburn, 1964); and Kaulong of Melanesia (New Britain), who use sex and sexuality to define social identities but produce a model that does not look much like gender at all (Goodale, 1973a and b — I am grateful for permission to refer to these as yet unpublished papers).*

to any great extent. This should alert us to the question
of what its uses might be.

Its support of power relations is a function of gender
which has been seized upon by modern feminists in their
"discovery" of mythology. Males are seen as a class with
interests to protect. They will thus tend to perpetuate
stereotypes about the relative powers and dangers of the opposite sex when it is to their advantage. The actual qualities which the power relations appear to rest on (e.g. women
are weak, capricious, emotional/men are strong, single-
minded, logical) are likely, as we have seen, to be as much
the rationale as the cause of this state of affairs. D'Andrad
(1967, p. 202) suggests that "some of the present biological *
sex differences ... may be due to selective factors operating as a result of cultural universals in the division of
labour". I would substitute "gender-typing" here, the division between the sexes being one sphere in which it appears,
for it itself is an arrangement based not on an *ad hoc* ap-
portionment but on a perception of appropriateness; and this
predicates the existence of gender. The idea of role must
involve some prior selective device which defines who is or
is not fit to play the part.

Gender is a set of ideas. It is at work in the way society classifies roles and sets up stereotypes. Each sex is
allocated certain roles (for example wage-earner/housekeeper),
and often congruent with this are ideas about how men and
women behave, think and feel, e.g. men are adventurous, have
enquiring minds, are proud of achievement/women prefer to
stay at home, accept conditions, and are sensitive to social
relationships. These are examples of stereotypes. Which
particular kinds of behaviour or types of personality are
held to characterize which sex vary somewhat from culture to
culture. Such sets of ideas amount to the way the sexes are
perceived; they are not in the first place rules or norms,
though they may have a normative effect. It is quite possible, even within one culture, for stereotypes to be inconsis-
tent. Thus *Hagen* women are characterized (by both sexes,
women here adopting a male viewpoint) as at the same time

---

* *Whatever their biological status there may be characteris-*
tics which are "cultural" insofar as they are the product of
social living, but "natural" insofar as they are constraints
in the make-up of a modern individual which he can do little
about.

soft-brained and hard-headed. The link between these con-
tradictory assertions is that women do not really have men's
interests at heart, whether because they shilly-shally or because they are obstinate. Stereotypes encourage the actors
to relate an individual's behaviour to the category to which
he or she belongs. They define how people in particular situations are expected to feel and react. This is carried to
the point where each sex is felt to have personality traits
which make certain tasks especially appropriate for it.

The achievement of gender stereotypes, then, is to make
it appear perfectly "natural" that men should be better suited to some and women to other roles. There is almost certain
to be feedback at work. Given the sexual definition of an
activity, "natural" data may be produced in support. This is
clear in one *Hagen* example. Among male stereotypes about
women's personalities and behaviour is the supposition that
women find it hard to be single-minded, which is why they
are basically untrustworthy. Since they are untrustworthy
they cannot share in the important decision-making processes
by which clans conduct their affairs. Their domain is the
household, with its relatively circumscribed tasks. One
rationale for this allocation of spheres lies in biological
facts as they are perceived. Some *Hageners* say that the female's mind is differently organized from the male's (it has
more compartments) and that this is an innate endowment.

Culturally demarcated differences between the sexes are
frequently defined in relation to one another, so that maleness and femaleness is each identified by reference to its
opposite. The sexes form a bounded pair of mutually exclusive terms (male = not female, and female = not male). The
structure of this contrast tends to be carried over into the
association of ideas attached to them, so that the constellation of attributes given to one sex is frequently related
to the attributes of the other. Thus males and females may
be contrasted in terms of strength and weakness – qualities
which, like the definition of male and female, are relative
to each other. Another *Hagen* view is that men are fitted
for the public life, and women for home life, there being a
polar, though not mutually exclusive, opposition between
public and domestic spheres of action. Because the sex contrast is bounded (unlike, say, that between mothers and
fathers: one cannot define a mother only as a non-father)
and appears to refer to phenomena (males and females) which
are qualitatively and naturally different, the effect is to

classify differences in degree behaviour and such like as
though they were qualitative ones also.

In the sets of characteristics recognized as differences between the sexes, we can usually discover two kinds of
relationship. The first is between opposed concepts (e₀g.
strength/weakness). The second is an internal linking -
which may or may not be explicit - between all the characteristics held to be typical of one sex, as when it is said
that because men are strong they are more suited to the public life₀

To the extent that the several items applied to the
sexes may be in some logical relationship to one another,
further characteristics are generated. The "sex-linking" of
attributes, like any classification device, may creatively
determine the direction of new linkages₀ Does this make
gender constructs adaptable to new ecological situations?
Take mobility, which Rosenblatt and Cunningham (Chapter 4)
identify as a common male trait₀ Whatever its origin, the
cultural ascription of such a quality to a set of "sex-linked"
roles will embed it in a matrix which may include various
spheres of activity - such as working outside the home, com-
mercial travelling, and outdoor sports. In wartime, women
may be brought into public life, but a new boundary between
the sexes is created in echo of the old one, so that it is
felt to be quite appropriate that women should run the country at home while men go off to fight abroad₀ The boundaries
shift, but the concept (who in the society is typically mo-
bile) remains as a clear discrimination of gender. Thus the
prior relationship between various characteristics (mobility,
working outside, whatever is defined as "outside") can influence how new characteristics (wartime roles) are to be defined.

Finally, ideas are played out in "real life", and there
is another kind of relationship to which an anthropologist
would draw attention: the behaviour of men and women towards
one another. Perceived differences in behaviour and temperament between the sexes which particular societies magnify or
minimize will both contribute to and be a product of actual
male-female relations₀ For instance, because men cherish
their attribute of strength, they may feel threatened by
women from time to time. Or, since public speaking is appropriate for males they may exclude females from open forums.

It is not enough, then, to say that gender classes are
obvious developments on sex differences₀ Many systems give

public prominence to men and put constraints on women's mobility, but there is infinite variation in the ideologies and
logic by which such ideas are elaborated. Gender constructs
are empty moulds into which all kinds of notions and values
are poured. What the moulds provide is the outline structure of contrast and relationship.
But whose constructs are we talking about?

DO WOMEN HAVE WORLD-VIEWS?

In recent years there has been a spate of studies addressed to the topic of male-female relations, and among the
questions which have been raised by anthropologists is whether women construe their social world in the same way as
men. Because of their position women are likely to have a
different vantage point, if not different interests, from
men's; or even rather different "models" of social reality.
Their model might resemble the viewpoint of a particular sub-
culture or minority group; or it might represent a kind of
alternative world-view. These questions turn directly on
two facets of social life: power relations between the sexes
and ideologies about their natures.

It was probably predictable, given the direction of popular ideas and their representation in women's liberation
literature, that an anthropologist should demonstrate how
most ethnographies are written from an androcentric (i.e.
male) point of view. This is true not only because many anthropologists have been men but because, if we are to believe
Edwin Ardener (1972), the discipline has a male bias. He
alleged that anthropologists are encouraged to discover those
structures in which males (both the researcher and those of
the society under study) are likely to have vested interests,
as, for example, bounded groups. An ethnographer is taught
to interpret roles in terms of jural norms and social identities; he looks for ideologies of particular kinds. Should
the "society" have named groups (tribes, clans and such) analysis is likely to be more straightforward than for those
field-workers who cannot find such groupings. If indeed
such elements do amount to an androcentric approach, this is
inherent in the discipline and is not related to the sex of
the field-worker.
Ardener suggests that whereas men tend to give a bounded
model of their society which will include both themselves and
women, the models women provide may not be "acceptable at

first sight to men or ethnographers ... They lack the meta-
language for its discussion ... (And) will not necessarily
provide a model for society as a unit that will contain both
men and themselves." (1972, pp. 138-139.)

He is concerned with the way men and women see themselves in relation to "society" and "nature". This also has
implications for notions about gender. Male models of society tend to encompass a definition of women (a theory of gender) but perhaps the reverse is not necessarily true.

Ardener's view is most starkly put in relation to social
theories about the nature of group structures. Proponents of
network or transactional theory might not come to this conclusion. Van Baal, in stressing the power advantages which
women's agreement to act as so-called "objects" in marriage
transactions brings them, states:

> (A society's) code of rules and mores is not the
> simple product of male discretion but the outcome
> of an incessant tug-of-war between the sexes.
> ... The supposition that a society's rules of con-
> duct are exclusively or predominantly male made is
> preposterous. The fact that the codification of
> the rules and the supervision of their observance
> very often are male prerogatives should not lead
> us to make the mistake of the cock perched on the
> hedge crowing because the hen laid an egg.
> (1970, pp. 299-300.)

Yet this does not really affect the argument about models.
It is presumably the cockerel's imaginative vision of the
respective roles of the sexes which leads him to sit in such
a prominent position.

Social anthropologists frequently refer to themselves
as observers. Is their androcentric emphasis a visual illusion or a mirror of reality? There is some evidence from
other disciplines* which suggests that men tend to be the
map-makers, and that "societies" as we know them are more
likely to be male rather than female constructs. Certainly
one would expect power-holders (males) to be more interested
than their counterparts in those classifications and defini-

---

* *Some of this is surveyed in Callan (1970) and Maccoby
(1967) cf. Tiger's (1969) analogy of male bonding as the
spinal column of a community, from which it derives its
structures and social coherence.*

tions which invest power in social categories. A gynocentric
(i.e. female) perspective on the part of the observer is not
necessarily going to help. Some societies may indeed yield
female as well as male models of the world, but in others
women may simply live in the shadow, or shelter, of men's
structures.

The procedural implications are intriguing. If "society" (or "culture") is to remain the focus of study for social anthropologists, then it is a matter of investigation
whether men and women both have the kind of social life which
the anthropologists can analyse. But if "people" are the focus, how can the discipline in its present form encompass
what may in some cases be behaviour which does not at all
look like "social" activity, or ideas which are not concerned
with classifications or with world-views? Ardener addresses
himself to the discovery of female models which are in effect
counterparts of male ones. The question is at least to be
raised whether such counterparts always exist.

Writers on male-female relations have stressed the frequently found ambiguity of women's place as "social persons"
in comparison with men. They are "persons" in that they become invested with roles which give them status in the society. But many societies also attribute to women a status
which is less complete than men's, so that women may be seen
as not so amenable to cultural control, as "closer to nature",
and so on. Essentially the same viewpoint is also found in
studies of the "position of women", which relate them to the
matrix of male social structures. Analyses of women as ambiguous beings, peripheral and asocial, are probably only one
step removed from male-created models in which women appear
as outside the mean, both powerful and powerless, both dependent and antisocial. Goodale (1973a) has suggested that almost everywhere females seem to be defined in less precise
terms than males. Dornbusch's observation (quoting Hartley,
1964) that there is "greater latitude for deviation granted
to females by the society", (1967, p. 211) would fit many
societies. This might suggest some feminine input into the
model, if it is also agreed that females are less interested
in the process of definition itself. For implicit in some
of the questioning of our assumptions is the notion that possibly women's cognitive functions differ from men's, and that
women would not make, if left to their own devices, the kinds
of boundary-drawing definitions which preoccupy the other sex.
This is the logical conclusion or *reductio ad absurdam*, de-

pending on one's stance, of the search for female models.

SYMBOLS

Social anthropology can perhaps make a distinctive contribution to the study of sex differences in the idea that
concepts are created to some purpose, that sex differences
as they appear in gender are used and manipulated. Gender
is a language in whose terms relations between the sexes are
considered. An allocation of spheres of activity, of super-
natural powers, of qualities such as nurturance and thrift,
all serve to regulate interaction between men and women.
But the contrasts and comparisons between male and female
behaviour can be further used themselves as a symbol for
other categories and values. One might define gender as the
application of various attributes to the sexes; or turn this
round and say that what also happens is the structuring of
certain attributes by the device of "sex-linkage". If the
middle-class characterize lower classes as emotional, cunning,
unfit to rule, their concatenation of qualities makes an implicit equation between lower class men and women. These
qualities are seen to be naturally connected as they appear
in the female sex, and applicable as a block to low status
men also. Millet (1971, pp. 228-232) gives a devasting
example of this process. When matrimony between husband and
wife signifies the unity of Christ and Church, and the husband is said to be the head of his wife as Christ is the
head of the Church, the doctrine draws upon the analogy of
relations between the sexes. The symbol of the authoritative
husband over the respectful wife, which is a metaphor for
the subordination of the Church to Christ, is derived from
the kind of interaction prescribed between spouses in society.
Gender is a convenient label to hang discriminations
upon because of its connotations of "naturalness" and inevitability. In Hagen the high evaluation which men put on
ceremonial exchange is demonstrated in exchange tallies worn
round their necks. Types of exchange activity are differentiated depending on whether shells or pigs are the chief val-
uable. Men wear tallies only for shell exchanges, and they
alone dance in celebration of these. Women are accorded
ceremonial roles when pigs are also involved; then they too
might dance with the men. One could say this represents the
sexes' participation in obtaining these valuables. Shells
can only be gained through transactions with other men,

whereas pigs are reared and it is the job of women to tend
them. Women's part is thus celebrated at pig - but not at
shell - exchanges, which is how *Hageners* put it. In fact
the real economics of the situation are less clear cut. A
man who obtains shells from a partner may keep them in his
wife's house for her to "look after", and the partner is
likely to be someone with whom he has connections through a
woman - his wife or sister. While it is quite true that
women's tasks include the tending of pigs, on an exchange
occasion as many animals will be raised through transactions
as come from the household. These discriminations are a
classification device; women are conceptually associated
with pigs. Linking types of valuables with the sexes probably has as much relevance for the structuring of exchanges
as for male-female roles in the society. Indeed, it provides a way of thinking about social activities, which makes
an explicit and evaluative contrast between work associated
with production (gardening, stock raising) and participation
in social transactions (ceremonial exchange, politics).

Let us sum up the aspects of gender-construction which
we have been considering. First, how the sexes are perceived
provides a mirror in which society can see itself. Thus the
Hagen example: men are associated with transactions, women
with production; politics and ceremonial exchange are socially more significant than gardening and house-keeping. These
associations do not just define maleness and femaleness;
they also define a relationship between politics and horti-
culture.

Secondly, once gender stereotypes have been formed they
can be used to symbolize things outside the male-female relationship. Apart from the feedback described above is the
metaphorical application of male-female stereotypes to other
domains. The practice of calling an enemy a woman rests on
gender constructs of the kind "females are weak/inferior".
Hagen people make a radical destinction between male and female in terms of potential achievement in public life. While
this excludes actual women from prominence on public occasions, it also bulwarks status differentiation between men.
Unsuccessful men are classified as "like women". They are
only like women in certain respects, but the definition of
the sexes in terms of public prominence and insignificance
is an important element in gender discrimination, and on
this score it is appropriate to refer to a rubbish man's activities as feminine. (In some respects women can transcend

their physiological sex and become "like men".)   In making
achievement appear to be "sex-linked", a big man can claim
the naturalness of his endowments; and because success rests
on mental rather than physiological qualities can also claim
his personal skill in making the best use of these. Contrasts between the potentials of males and females thus stand
for contrasts between the potentials for success or failure
among men themselves.

A third aspect remains for consideration. Anthropologists have long pointed to the relationship between cultural
classifications of the natural environment or of elements in
the physical body and the formation of divisions and categories within society itself. Thus natural classes may provide symbols for thinking about social classes, as concern
with bodily orifices and the containment of the flesh indicates concern with social boundaries. To the natural world
and the human body as sources of symbols we should add sex
differences. The most significant thing about gender constructs "based" on these is the implication of relationship.

Social relationships depend on classification and communication. Recognition of the class of person one is interacting with (a child, a chief) signals the appropriate
language. Processes of differentiation and communication
are probably basic to the ability to categorize, which in
turn is probably basic to the ability to form relationships
as we know them.* Relationship is inherent in the very construction of gender. Males and females are delineated as
social categories: gender sets up boundaries between the
sexes and also provides rules for communication between them.

Male-female relations thus provide powerful symbols,
for they express oppositeness and contrast while at the same
time including the possibility of complementarity or union.
Gender constructs put sex differences in relationship to one
another. In the evolution of society it is even possible
that gender ideas played a part in the conceptualization of
social relations. This conclusion receives some support
from Kohlberg's demonstration that at least for the individual the process of forming a gender identity is "a part of
the general process of conceptual growth" (1967, p. 98).
In other words, gender differentiation might well be linked

---

* Some modern experiments in communal living are attempts to
conduct relationships without categorization (though an en-
thropologist might say this was a contradiction in terms).

to the capacity to perceive relationships as such.

What I have described here in cognitive terms, Rosemary Firth (1970) applies to social behaviour. She points to one of the functions of gender concepts as being to regulate

> that complementary state which originates in biologi-
> cal distinction. And ... which forces the sexes to
> a social dependency which is even more important than
> their biological interdependence. (1970, p. 87)

When artificial lines are drawn around the activity of each sex, their physical differences become exaggerated by symbolic ones, and the high-lighting of difference increases the perceived need for dependency. Thus, she writes, the cultural regulation of human sexual behaviour

> is orientated towards mutual dependency; (which) is
> not only genetic and economic but, above all, social
> and symbolic. It involves a whole set of ideas about
> relationships, which are reinforced by the forms of
> art, ritual and religion which constitute specific
> human cultures. (1970, p. 91)

Yet if this formulation is set against those of some liberation writers it becomes clear that the language of analysis incorporates certain cultural biases. Firth implies that dependency is a good thing or at least essential for social life. Those concerned on the other hand to politicise gender see in every relationship an enactment of tyranny, and if that is what social life entails, would reject society.

THE ROLE OF GENDER IN LIBERATION IDEOLOGY

A central question which preoccupies certain radical feminists is how far a "woman" or "man" can be treated both as a member of a particular sex *and* as a person in her or his own right, the implication being that this is impossible. There is a widespread assumption that to consider someone as a member of a category or class, such as "female" or "male" is to denigrate their human status. Kate Millett, for example, argues that "humanity" must be freed from "the tyranny of sexual-social category" (1970, p. 363). This relates to the popular opposition between institutionalized ("social") relations and interaction with others on a purely affective basis.

In one form or another these oppositions refer to a

central dichotomy in Western thought: the "relationship" between "society" and the "individual".*   In the arguments over
the powers and freedom of the sexes in relation to one another
is mirrored the dilemma between the state with its control
over everyone's lives and the preservation of the individual's
liberties (an "individual" is typified as "a human being").
The issues of power relations between the sexes deals with
real inequalities between men and women; but much of its impetus is arguably derived from wider intellectual concerns.
Hence the popular polarization between social constraints
(state control, institutionalized relationships, social interaction, any kind of interpersonal influence) and individual
autonomy (human rights, spontaneous relationships, emotional
interaction, and the validity of personal feeling and experience).
      These concerns in turn are related, Douglas (1970) would
argue, to certain styles in our social life.   Indeed, Douglas'
analysis of cosmologies concerned with the inner life, where
there is no conception of offence but only of failure, where
the self is valued for its own sake although people suspect
others disregard their claims to be treated as persons, and
where spontaneous feeling is highly regarded, foreshadows
many of the preoccupations of writers associated with women's
liberation.   Germaine Greer states: "The surest guide to
the correctness of the path that women take is *joy in the
struggle*.   Revolution is the festival of the oppressed" (1970,
p. 330, original italics); and Mary Douglas (1970, p. 154):
"Protest against symbols is only against rituals of differentiation.   Rituals of enthusiasm are honoured."   Douglas sees
the apparent anti-ritualism of today as the adoption of one

* *Mitchell suggests that the new "politics of experience",
"the promotion of 'feelings' to the ranks of political action" (1971, p. 38) is a radical putting to the test of pie-
ties in capitalist ideology.   "(Women) are ... among the
first to gain from the radical 'capture' of emotionality from
capitalist ideology for political protest movements" (1971,
p. 38).   This takes the standpoint of women as a prior interest group ("class").   One could with equal cogency stand the
proposition on its head.   Gender, in providing a powerful set
of symbols by which to argue over what is human and natural
and what is social and artificial, has been fed into the controversy, with the result that ideas about gender become
modified and the sexes are seen as social classes.*

set of religious symbols in place of another. What is relevant for us is the treatment of sex differences. Many feminists identify roles as instruments of oppression, equate dependency relationships with colonialism, and then point to
the present relations between the sexes as one of competition
rather than complementarity. The exploration of the basis of
sex differences in this light is akin to the search for self-
identity.

Gender is also manipulated in women's liberation writings
to create out of the sex category an interest group. The de-
marcation of a category of persons who share characteristics
such as common sex leads to a proclamation of common identity
in terms of shared interests. The "rights" which such a group
demands are claims against the world not for membership in a
social body defined in terms of "rights and duties" but for
recognition of its autonomous identity.* An outsider might
say that the analogy between the sexes and economic classes
or ethnic minorities stems not only from similarities in
their power situation, but from the initial principles by
which they are defined for the sake of the argument. If
women are identified with the oppressed classes then men become the oppressors whether they realize it or not. An equation is made between men (aggressive) and society (malevolent
in its controls) on the one hand and women (nurturant) and
the individual (whose reference points are his own feelings
and experience) on the other.

This is one kind of distinction between nature and culture, loaded with moral overtones. The load is heavy because of the different ways the terms are used in popular as
well as academic parlance. Nature may be all that is non-
human; or all that is non-cultural in the sense of non-
artificial; thus it comes to mean also those parts of culture
which are accepted unquestioningly as "normal"; and finally
there is the drive to equate what is normal with what is
legitimate, so that those who challenge present social forms
do so by saying they are artificial and by implication against
"nature".† Interest in sex differences has perhaps given new
life to the contrast between what is inevitable and immutable

---

* *Shirley Ardener (1973) links liberation concerns with those
of Bakweri women which seek the expression of "femineity",
an abstract model of what being a woman means.*

† *This was not always so. Culture used to be on the legitimate side (civilization versus animality).*

and what is artificial and alterable. Also introduced is
the idea of exploitation and Machiavellian intent on the part
of those responsible for the present "artificial" situation.
This leads to a search for the natural origins of sex differences which will provide a basic "starting point" from which
new and liberal ideas about the sexes may be forged: to ask
when the present power relations between the sexes began is
to search for the divide between nature and culture in time.*

The culture/nature dichotomy has been identified by anthropologists as a concern of peoples in many places. Our
particular (Western) contribution lies perhaps in the notion
of reform, which is linked to the contrast between legitimate
and illegitimate powers. Thus Millett (1970) is at pains to
destroy the legitimacy of "patriarchy" by showing it has no
true foundation in biological sex differences. Natural in-
stincts used to be considered primitive, properly controlled
by civilization or culture in its original sense, but culture
can no longer, in the modern extremist view, be a vehicle
for reform, because it is seen as an instrument of oppression.

> In our alienated society, to have lost touch with one's
> inner being and to efficiently enact the dictates of
> one's social roles, is to be normal (but by no means)
> ... healthy. ... It is impossible in our "split"
> society for anyone to be whole or really themselves.
> (Hamblin, 1972, p. 25.)

With the isolation of "the individual" as the legitimate phenomenon, we have an equation:

individual	: society
emotional bases for "personal" relationships	: artificial rule — bounded roles
human identity	: sex-role behaviour
self expression	: inhibited action
nature	: culture

* e.g. *"Potentially we are all whole human beings, the split
into masculine and feminine is artificially created ... How
did we become split? At some point in our history the early
communistic matriarchies were overthrown, women were reduced
to chattel status, and male supremacy was born"* (Hamblin,
1972, p. 24).

One aim of liberation politics is to adapt "society" to the
point where it allows individuals untrammelled freedom of
self expression, so everyone can interact on a personal basis.
Carried to its logical conclusion, this must mean the abolition of society. For in a context where the whole idea of
change/reform/revolution questions every assumption, and
where the very notion of society/social relationships is
under fire, the only basis for legitimacy must be in those
social forms most true to immutable biological facts. Hence
to add to the dichotomy

nature	:	culture
biological facts	:	social artifices
immutable characteristics	:	changeable characteristics
sex	:	gender

Thus the division of labour between the sexes may be regarded,
in this view, as the original oppression of one class by
another. It is not the correlation here which is suspect,
but the deliberate politicisation of the analysis. This requires that social relationships as such are seen as oppres-
sive, so that all bonds are class struggles in miniature,
which does more for the ideology of class struggle than it
does for an understanding of society.

  A clear example is Firestone's *The dialectic of sex*,
demonstrating the kind of millenial thinking described by
Douglas which is obsessed with overthrowing differentiation
and definition as such. For her the ultimate goal is the
abolition of society ("achievement of cosmic consciousness"),
explicitly following the disappearance of culture, class,
sex, race and age distinctions. In fact by the stage this
is envisaged there is no more childhood, ageing or death.
This is the place of sex in her argument:

> Culture develops not only out of the underlying eco-
> nomic dialectic but also out of the deeper sex dia-
> lectic ... The cultural revolution, like the economic
> revolution, must be predicated on the elimination of
> the (sex) dualism at the origins not only of class,
> but also of cultural division. (1971, p. 179.)

The revolution is not just to conquer male privilege (power
inequalities) but to eliminate distinction (social life):
"genital differences between human beings would no longer

matter culturally" (1971, p. 19).   It becomes impossible here
to disentangle goals from symbols.

SYMBOLS IN SCIENCE

It is revealing, as other chapters attest, that we should
feel it important to establish the relationship between innate
biological factors, and those of cultural origin.   Even if
the conclusion is an interactionist one, "biology *plus* culture
in Money's words (1973), which asserts that these elements can
not be held separately accountable for differences in behaviour but contribute to a developmental sequence of determinants
they remain indispensable distinctions.   While an insider
might say that he is interested in exploring sex differences
to which end he will bring to bear both the physical and
social sciences, the outsider might comment that this discussion symbolizes Western philosophical concern with the distinction between nature and culture.   For it is a kind of
rock-bottom test.   There are certain primary differences between the sexes; and a multitude of secondary differences,
some highly dependent on the primary ones but others more
culturally malleable.
The point of significance is that we should be aware
that some of our indices, and especially those dealing with
behavioural characteristics such as degree of aggressiveness
or intelligence, are likely to be influenced by our own cultural preoccupations.   Thus the way we define males and females, our scientific gender stereotypes, may be related to
concerns which have no direct bearing on men and women, the
point being that these concerns receive emphasis by being related to sex differences: the high evaluation our culture
places on achievement is reflected in the ascription of
stronger achievement orientation to the higher status sex,
i.e. to males.   Achievement motivation as an index for gender
discrimination in fact tells us as much about our society as
it does about sexual differences.
There is nothing trivial in the conclusion that the
search for indices of maleness and femaleness symbolises certain social values.   Attention is drawn to the manner and language, the idioms, in terms of which we think.   The European
syndrome male/aggressive/logical-minded/problem solving/
achievement oriented/purposive/ambitious brings together
several values and activities which are seen to belong to one
another and by becoming attached to "male" lead to assumptions

about the "naturalness" of men holding certain roles. Gender
associations mark out what is appropriate behaviour for men,
and such disparate notions as aggressiveness and problem-
solving capacities, are linked by being both "male-like", a
highly significant association for a career-based, technologically conscious society.

Ours is also a society very interested in change, and
the nature/culture dichotomy lends weight to this interest
when, as we have seen, the natural is often linked to the
immutable,* whereas what is cultural is considered artificial
and therefore amenable to alteration. Anthropologists, avow-
edly interested in culture, face the accusation of believing
that all is relative. Margaret Mead has been interpreted as
saying that there is an almost infinite plasticity in sexual
temperament. But it is clear that this is only arbitrariness
of a certain order. Cross-culturally, temperamental stereotypes seem concerned with certain common themes such as ag-
gressiveness/submissiveness; self-interest/interest in others;
adventurousness/lack of imagination. These are related to
how human beings are seen to behave. They bear an intrinsic
relationship to human nature, the element of arbitrariness
coming in when a culture attaches this or that quality *definitively* to one or other sex. Within the culture, this process itself loses arbitrariness when it is analysed in relation to what men and women do in the society - the kind of
social realities discussed by Rosenblatt and Cunningham
(Chapter 4) - and in relation to the symbolic use made of
gender stereotypes, which provides a means of organising
various activities and values. This symbolic usage reintro-
duces an element of the arbitrary. It is arbitrary insofar
as symbols other than gender could presumably have been used;
but non-arbitrary in that power of the symbol must derive
from a primary meaning seen to be based on reality. If a division of labour is used to symbolize the relative importance
of public and domestic life, actual work arrangements must be
of a kind to substantiate it. To say that gender is a set of
symbols is not to say it has nothing to do with physiological
differences. It does; just as earth, a symbol of what is fundamental to human nature and to sustenance, has to do with the
ecological base of our species, although as a symbol it cannot be described fully in these terms.

* *Relative to culture. Evolutionary theory of course sees
nature as under constant change.*

CONCLUSION

Dornbusch's afterword to the papers Maccoby edited on
The development of sex differences ends:

> Why are myths of masculinity and femininity believed
> and sustained – even in the face of evidence to the
> contrary? Clearly both sexes must have a fairly high
> degree of emotional interest in the current sex-role
> ideology. At the same time, however, this ideology
> does change ... (1967, p. 216).

He leaves the question unanswered, with the negative conclusion that it is difficult to separate the cultural product
from its biological base, that we do not know enough about
hormones, that there has been inadequate observation of
parent-child interaction, and so on. He ends with the hope
"that tomorrow's ideology may reflect increased understanding of the forces that shape men and women" (*ibid*). With
all respect, I think that he has missed the point. Myths
about masculinity and femininity (gender constructs) endure
and change, as language endures and changes, because of their
usefulness as symbols in the society at large. No amount of
scientific precision in investigating the make-up of the sexes will alter this. Rather, the scientific activity itself
should be considered as part of the same process in so far
as it contributes to the meaning which gender is invested
with. If other cultures, as well as our own, are anything to
go by, tomorrow's gender ideology will reflect tomorrow's
society.

Sex differences as they are moulded by culture into stereotypes are not just the end products of multivariate biological, psychological and social forces. Gender in many societies is put to work. It frequently carries a heavy symbolic
load, relevant for how men and women regard one another, but
also to how society regards itself. In the perceived attributes of males and females are likely to be mirrored general
intellectual and moral concerns. In considering the elements
of these as sex-linked ("natural"), the validity of the concerns themselves is given a boost. We are talking about the
values of achievement-orientation when we try to discover
which sex is more prone to perform best under specified conditions; similarly we are talking about the legitimacy of continuing a class struggle in identifying the sexes as classes
which should become politically conscious, or the integrity of

minority cultures, in wondering whether there are female as well as male models of society. The desire to seek a natural base for cultural institutions and values is another line of enquiry in itself. A simple point to make here is that because gender constructs are put to work, there will be constant feedback between what they are useful for and how they are built.

Acknowledgements
I have benefited considerably from discussions on various aspects of this chapter with Inge Riebe, Sue Robertson, Andrew Strathern, and Elizabeth and Neil Warren. I am also grateful for the comments made by Ruth Latukefu, Barbara Lloyd and Ann Whitehead, Paul Rosenblatt and Paula and Abe Rosman.

This chapter was first written in 1973 and does not take into account the considerable anthropological literature "on women" published since then.

REFERENCES

D'Andrade, R. (1967). Sex differences and cultural institutions. *In* "The Development of Sex Differences". (E.E. Maccoby, ed.) Tavistock, London.

Ardener, E. (1972). Belief and the problem of women. *In* "The Interpretation of Ritual". (La Fontaine, ed.) Tavistock, London.

Ardener, S. (1973). Sexual insult and female militancy. *Man,* 8, 422-440.

Callan, H. (1970). "Ethology and Society. Towards an Anthropological View". Oxford University Press.

Dornbusch, S.M. (1967). Afterword. *In* "The Development of Sex Differences". (E.E. Maccoby, ed.) Tavistock, London.

Douglas, M. (1970). "Natural Symbols, Explorations in Cosmology". The Cresset Press, Barrie and Rockliff.

Firestone, S. (1973). "The Dialectic of Sex. The Case for Feminist Revolution". Paladin, London.

Firth, R.M. (1970). The social images of man and woman. *Journal of Biosocial Science,* Suppl. 2, 85-92.

Goodale, J.C. (1973a). The Kaulong gender. Symposium on
    Gender in Oceania. Unpublished.

Goodale, J.C. (1973b). The rape of the men and the seduction
    of the women. Paper read at A.S.A.O. conference.

Greer, G. (1970). "The Female Eunuch". MacGibbon and Kee,
    London.

Hamblin, A. (1972). Ultimate goals. *Women's Liberation Review*,
    1, 23-46.

Hartley, R.E. (1964). A developmental view of female sex-role
    definition and identification. *Merrill-Palmer Quarterly*,
    10, 3-16.

Kohlberg, L. (1967). A cognitive-developmental analysis of
    children's sex-role concepts and attitudes. *In* "The Deve-
    lopment of Sex Differences". (E.E. Maccoby, ed.) Tavistock,
    London.

Maccoby, E.E. (1967). Sex differences in intellectual func-
    tioning. *In* "The Development of Sex Differences". (E.E.
    Maccoby, ed.) Tavistock, London.

Millet, K. (1971). "Sexual Politics". Hart-Davis, London.

Mitchell, J. (1971). "Woman's Estate". Penguin, Harmondsworth.

Money, J. (1973). Review of C. Hutt's "Males and Females".
    Contemporary Psychology, 18, 603-604.

Tiger, L. (1969). "Men in Groups". Nelson, London.

Turnbull, C. (1965). Wayward Servants: The Two Worlds of
    the African Pygmies". Natural History Press, Garden City,
    New York.

Van Baal, J. (1970). The part of women in the marriage-trade:
    objects or behaving as objects? *Bijdragen tot de taal-,
    land-, en Volkenkunde*, 26, 289-308.

Woodburn, J. (1964). The social organisation of the Hadza
    of North Tanganika. Ph.D thesis, University of Cambridge.

4. SEX DIFFERENCES IN CROSS-CULTURAL PERSPECTIVE

Paul C. Rosenblatt and Michael R. Cunningham

We have reached a point, in Europe and America, where the traditional notions of what is feminine and what is masculine seem no longer to be trusted. Sex differences that formerly were assumed to be immutable are now judged by many to be cultural artifacts. What previously constituted plausible explanations of sex differences are now seen by many as myths used as a means of justifying discrimination. In searching for fundamental differences between the sexes we must be more sceptical of culture-bound studies dealing solely with the behaviour of people in Europe and America. One place to which we can turn in our search for the essential sex differences is the scholarly literature on humans reared in cultures other than our own. If there are regularities in human behaviour as a result of biological sex differences, these patterns should occur across the globe.

While information from other societies can illuminate species-wide patterns of sex difference, turning to the cross-cultural literature is not without risk. The data from other cultures are largely gathered by people who have been reared in Europe and America; hence, the facts and conclusions may be biased in terms of the questions asked, the answers heard, the behaviour observed, and the behaviour reported. Moreover, the large majority of ethnographic studies carried out in other societies have been done by men and based on information gathered largely from male informants. In fact, where ethnographers have used translators, these translators, who filtered information from informants, seem to have been relatively Europeanized or Americanized males.

The cross-cultural literature is also by no means comprehensive with respect to questions concerning sex differences. There have been a relatively small number of comparative studies dealing with sex differences and a relatively small num-

ber of essays and ethnographies providing substantial detail
on sex differences. To our knowledge there have been no comparative studies of such centrally important topics as the
cultural correlates of variations in sexual dimorphism or of
cultural correlates of variations among cultures in the degree of emphasis placed on sex differences in appearance and
personality. Nor, to our knowledge, have there been comparative studies of correlates of the status of women and men as
perceived by the women and men themselves.

The cross-cultural literature does make it clear that
sex differences are generally important from a social and
behavioural standpoint. Gender seems to be a basic distinction in many languages and possibly a basic distinction of
social organization in all societies (D'Andrade, 1966, p.
181). There is, in addition, a certain cross-cultural consistency in the sexual division of labour. To an extent,
there are behaviours and activities in which men engage but
women do not and some in which women are much more likely to
engage than men (Hammond and Jablow, 1973; Murdock, 1937).
The specific domains where sex differences are found are discussed in subsequent sections of this chapter.

The recognition of cross-cultural sex differences in
behaviour does not in itself suggest that such patterns are
necessary. Nor does the establishment of a correlation between sex and certain activities provide a great deal of insight into the nature of the differences between the sexes
contributing to the differential behaviour.

Three theoretical interpretations have been offered to
provide some coherence to the overall pattern of sex differences observed in societies. Two interpretations centre on
division of labour. One of these emphasizes the linkage of
females to childcare and the restriction on female mobility
imposed by childcare functions, while the other stresses a
division of labour stemming from sex differences in strength
and aggressiveness. The third interpretation of sex differences in behaviour is grounded in an evolutionary perspective
and postulates that sex differences in bonding, hunting, and
warfare form a basis for other sex differences in social behaviour. We favour the first rather than the second interpretation, and the second rather than the third.

SEX DIFFERENCES IN WORK

Work, the behaviour which enables people to sustain and

develop themselves, their kin and their society, may be the key to understanding differences between the sexes. The requirements of work seem to us to underlie how people are brought up, what their sources of power and status are, what their skills and interests are, and even the extent of such sexual dimorphism as muscle size. We begin, therefore, by describing cross-cultural regularities in the work women and men do. It should be noted, however, that we are not implying that cross-cultural differences in work or in any other area suggest necessary or desirable differences in our society, that the anthropological data justify discrimination in any form, that any differences between the sexes except the bearing of children are inevitable, or that there are any differences in the worth of people as a result of differences in the work they do. We are merely reporting what appear to be the cross-cultural facts at this time and what may be behind these apparent facts.

DIVISION OF LABOUR

A major factor of importance in understanding pervasive differences between the sexes in behaviour related to work involves the value to a society of the division of labour. Among the gains from division of labour is the value of having tasks done by specialists. Specialists can be better trained, have more relevant knowledge, and be in better practice for their task than generalists. They can also be socialized to have appropriate dispositions and musculature. When there is a clear division of labour, less time needs to be spent allocating tasks, and people who have trouble making decisions or whose relationship might be undermined by disagreements, argument or anger can be protected from the costs of having to allocate roles themselves.

In every society there is some division of labour by sex. Though there are societies in which each sex engages in many of the work activities of the other, it seems to us that commonly there is a relatively large amount of differentiation. In addition to the functions of division of labour noted above, division of labour may have its greatest value in the social solidarity it produces (Durkheim, 1964). People who are dependent on each other can become more closely bound together. Thus, division of labour by sex may stabilize male-female relationships by making it necessary or much more comfortable to live with an opposite sex adult. In fact, where division

of labour does not serve adequately to hold men and women together, other cultural institutions (such as romantic love)
may be needed to bind the sexes together (Coppinger and
Rosenblatt, 1968). The crucial need in the species seems to
be the linking of people in social units. Role differentiation is of extraordinary value in this linking, but what seems
essential in a family or other social unit is not that males
do X or that females do Y but that different people do different things.

   Childcare. One task which may be at the root of many
other sex differences in behaviour is childcare (Brown, 1970,
1973; Chodorow, 1974; Murdock and Provost, 1973; Rosaldo,
1974; Williams, 1971). Women, of course, bear children. It
is not clear to us that a typical healthy pregnancy requires
restriction on many kinds of work. Nor is it clear to us
that even shortly after delivery a woman's having given birth
typically puts any necessary restriction on her work. However, in most societies a mother must nurse her child. Hy-
gienic containers, alternative sources of wholesome milk, and
perhaps even alternative sources of protein are often not
available. Early introduction of solid foods may be associated cross-culturally with high infant mortality rates
(Nerlove, 1974). Consequently it is desirable, in many societies, to feed children exclusively by breast throughout infancy. The need to nurse an infant means that the mother
(or some other lactating woman) must be near the infant,
which gives the mother (or other lactating woman) the option
of staying near home or transporting the child. The humour-
ist Nathaniel Benchley could have been speaking of the problems of transporting children in any society when he said,
"In America there are two classes of travel - first class,
and with children" (1954). Carrying children is tiring, reduces one's ability to carry other things, and reduces speed
and, hence, the distance one can travel in a given period of
time. Carrying a child over long distances may even reduce
the supply of milk a woman can provide. If children can and
do walk, they still may reduce speed of travel. And, of
course, children are often disposed to follow their own fan-
cies. As long as a woman nurses, it seems much more convenient for her to stay near the child than for the child to
travel with her. If we assume, using Nag's (1968, pp. 169-
172) birth data from 80 societies and estimating that roughly
20% of children die before age two, that the average woman
in the world has roughly four children which survive through

age two, and if we assume that children are breastfed for an
average of two years, a typical woman might, because of nursing, experience approximately eight years of reduced mobility.
This may be quite a powerful factor in producing sex role differentiation and physical and dispositional differences between the sexes.

Mobility restrictions still leave considerable room for
variability in work activities. Mobility may be necessary
for warfare, fishing, hunting or herding of large animals,
and long-distance trade activities. Hence, such activities
might typically be done by men. But in societies where men
are not extensively tied down to such activities, men could
easily become involved in sedentary activities such as weaving
and mat-making. In fact, as Hammond and Jablow (1973) point
out, the division of labour by sex for relatively sedentary
activities shows quite a bit of variability cross-culturally.
This pattern of variability seems to result from cross-
cultural variations in customary childcare arrangements and
in the demand for activities requiring substantial geographic
mobility.

Childcare in most societies is not solely a duty of a
child's mother. In fact it may be less so in most societies
than is true of middle class European and American families.
In other societies, older children typically have responsibilities for the care of younger siblings and cousins
(Minturn and Lambert, 1964, pp. 98, 107; Rosenblatt and
Skoogberg, 1974). In some societies, men and older people
of both sexes may also have childcare duties. Childcare arrangements free many west African women to engage in extensive trade (Mintz, 1971) and free many younger women in matri-
focal families to engage in economic pursuits (e.g. Gonzalez,
1969, pp. 51-54). Nonetheless, the heavier burden of childcare even for children beyond nursing age, seems to fall on
young and middle aged women. And it must be remembered that
in most places in the world children are not in school for
as many years as children in Europe and America are. Although
children, particularly girls, in many societies do perform
substantially more useful labour than children do in Europe
and America (Newton, 1967, pp. 156-158), they still must be
supervised. The supervision of girls and younger boys is
typically women's work. The burden of caring for and super-
vising children beyond infancy may arise from a pattern that
is founded on nursing. But whatever the source of female
responsibility for childcare, it certainly helps to magnify

whatever differences there are between adult women and men.
The temperament, musculature, and attitudes needed to care
for and supervise children undoubtedly differ from those
needed for activities engaged in by people who are doing
things other than childcare.

Food getting and food preparation.   In the search for
calories, women in societies around the world bring in an
average of roughly 30-40% of the calories people eat
(Coppinger and Rosenblatt, 1969; Heath, 1958; Sanday, 1973,
1974).   The deviation from an even split may represent the
reduced mobility of women more than anything else - mobility
reduced by child bearing and childcare and mobility reduced
by rules such as *purdah* requiring the seclusion of women.
However, in some gathering societies and in a large number
of crop growing societies lacking the plough and requiring
intensive agricultural labour, women make large contributions
to calorie-getting, frequently contributing more than men
(Murdock and Provost, 1973; Sanday, 1973, 1974).

Some may argue that the sex differences which have been
observed cross-culturally in the division of labour for food-
getting stem from a male advantage in strength.   However, the
data in the most comprehensive survey of sexual division of
labour in world cultures, a study by Murdock and Provost
(1973) of a representative sample of 185 societies, make it
difficult to maintain that strength underlies sex differences.
The work that is most frequently male work includes tasks
requiring strength, such as hunting of large aquatic and
land animals, but men also do almost all the fowling, butcher-
ing, fishing and collecting of wild honey.   Although females
generally do some tasks requiring less strength, such as the
preparation of vegetable foods, cooking, and gathering of
wild plants, they also generally fetch water.   In many societies, water containers are of such a size as to require
great strength when full.   Moreover, in any society there
are likely to be some women who are stronger than some men.
Thus, it is not at all clear that the assignment of tasks
is based solely or even partially on a difference between
the sexes in level of muscular strength.   Rather than strength
being crucial, the data at this point might more parsimonious-
ly be explained by the tendency of men's work to require
more mobility (cf. Ward, 1963).   In addition, as Brown (1970,
1973) has suggested, women's work may be work that can be
done despite interruptions from children.   Brown argues that
work such as gathering wild plant foods and hoeing tend to

be women's work because they can be done well despite interruptions due to children and because they do not require extensive excursions once one has arrived at the place of work.
Domestic labour, manufacturing, warfare. We have suggested that the division of labour can be the basis of other
sex differences in society, and we have discussed mobility,
strength, and interruptability considerations as interpretations of the sex differences which have been noted in calorie
production cross-culturally. The same factors can be examined
in work activities not directly related to food. In the
Murdock and Provost data, women, far more than men, do laun-
dering, spinning, pottery making, manufacturing of clothing,
and fuel gathering. The activities not directly related to
food that are performed more or less exclusively by men include smelting of ore, mining, metal working, stoneworking,
land clearance and housebuilding. Again women's work seems
to require little physical mobility and less freedom from in-
terruption, men's work to require perhaps more mobility and
more strength. It may also be that the division of labour
by sex is designed so that women, who are more likely to be
caring for children, do tasks which would be less likely to
endanger youthful bystanders (Sandra L. Titus, personal communication, June, 1974).

Warfare seems to be primarily an activity of men (Ember
and Ember, 1971). No major society dominated by female warriors has been documented in the scholarly literature. This
state of affairs has attracted a great deal of comment and a
variety of more and less plausible interpretations. Although
the general absence of women in combat may be a consequence
of greater strength and endurance on the part of males, it
may be wholly or in part due to the fact that females are
burdened with children. It is not clear that women would
not possess more than adequate strength in any task, given
appropriate strength-developing experiences. Further, while
mobility restrictions could prevent women with children from
participating in raids and invasions, the strength and mobility explanations alone or jointly may not be entirely adequate to account for the absence of unmarried or barren female combatants. Nor should the presence of children prevent
women from contributing militarily to the defence of their
community in the event of attack. Actually, women of the
Vietnamese National Liberation Front and of Israel have par-
ticipated in combat; the occasions upon which women in other
societies have stood on the parapets may simply have gone

unreported.

Some writers have presented speculative evolutionary interpretations for the absence of female warriors. Such interpretations suggest that males possess a biologically greater capability for military organization or action than females. Tiger (1969) has conjectured extensively on male-female differences, and has suggested that survival pressures have selected for certain traits in males based on the need for successful co-operative hunting expeditions. The exigencies of hunting, Tiger believes, have resulted in males becoming through the centuries stronger, more aggressive, more concerned with dominance and status, more capable of leadership and co-operation, more predisposed to seek unisexual group activity and more capable of forming lasting same-sex bonds of friendship and loyalty than women.

Tiger (1969) places particular weight on his controversial hypothesis of a greater male bonding capacity to account for sex role differentiation, such as male control of military, political, economic and social institutions. Male occupancy of these roles, Tiger asserts, arises from a greater ability of men to organize themselves, which is supposedly due to (a) their greater capacity to form lasting affiliative relationships and (b) other temperamental factors such as their greater concern with pecking order or status. Tiger unfortunately offers cross species analogy and cross cultural anecdote rather than valid evidence to support his claims. Relevant data such as the strength of attachment of males to males and females to females are quite scarce in the cross-cultural literature. But the work of Tiger has stimulated studies that seem to contradict him (e.g. Leis, 1974). Many of the concepts involved in Tiger's formulation lack the clear definition necessary for formal investigation. In fact, ideas concerning qualitative differences between the sexes based on the evolution of society are exceedingly difficult to test scientifically, and thus such theories may be more metaphysical than scientific (cf. Chapter 10 by Archer).

TEMPERAMENT

Margaret Mead has asserted that the sexes are quite variable on dimensions of temperament and that no sex differences in temperament are inevitable (Mead, 1950). By temperament, Mead meant a very wide range of dispositions, e.g. artistic interests, aggressiveness, jealousy, dependency,

and interest in personal adornment. Mead is probably right
that males and females are quite plastic in what is distinct-
ively masculine and feminine. However, future systematic study
of sex differences may indicate several strong leanings. In the
following section of the chapter we consider the possibility
that men and women differ in physical characteristics in aggression and attachment behaviour.

AGGRESSION AND PHYSICAL CHARACTERISTICS

Male mammals seem generally to show more physical aggression (see Chapter 10 by Archer; Archer, 1976; Moyer, 1971).
The greater physical aggressiveness of males is apparently
due in part to the presence of androgens. Male humans, like
other male primates, also seem to be bigger on the average
than the females of their species, better muscled, and with
a higher metabolic rate, higher activity level, a more powerful heart, and proportionately more red corpuscles (Crook,
1972). Although aggressive behaviour can be shaped and cur-
tailed by socialization (Archer, 1976), it seems that males
are better equipped physically and temperamentally than females for physical aggression. There is, however, need for
a great deal of research before we can specify the domains
where differences between the sexes in the expression of aggression exist cross-culturally. As one illustration of the
question of the domain of differential aggressiveness, in a
cross-cultural study of bereavement in 78 societies, males
seemed more likely than women to attack others following a
death but women were more attacking of self (Rosenblatt *et
al.* In press). The differences in behaviour in that study
suggest that men and women may not differ in aggressiveness
as much as they do in styles of aggression or in aggression
targets. We unfortunately do not have information concerning differences between the sexes in response to other types
of frustrations.

The prevalence of men in warfare has already been noted,
but it is conceivable that aggressiveness may not be important in determining male participation, since warfare may
very often be based on calculation and political interest
rather than aggression. On the other hand, androgen-related
aggressiveness when coupled with male training in use of
muscles for things like warfare, manipulation of large animals, hunting and fishing, could give males a distinct advantage in individual physical power struggles with women and

could thus markedly influence dyadic male-female relationships.

While it has not been directly demonstrated that aggressiveness on the part of the male serves as a major factor controlling the nature of male-female relationships, the data in
one study on aggression between spouses are suggestive. In
Schlegel's (1972) study of women and men in matrilineal societies, 34 out of 45 societies were reported to have tolerance
of severe aggression of husband against wife (p. 192). Severe
aggression includes "any beating that goes beyond a light
cuffing; cutting or burning; public humiliation, such as
holding up the wife to mockery or allowing one's friends or
relatives to beat or rape her (*op. cit.* p. 153)". It may be
that severe aggression between husband and wife rarely occurs
in the societies in which it is tolerated. But the fact that
aggression of husband against wife is tolerated may well have
a substantial impact on relations between husbands and wives.

It would be useful in trying to understand relations
between the sexes if factors such as strength differences,
differences in irritability, and experience using muscles in
physical combat could be separated and studied in isolation
from each other. The *Burundi*, as described by Albert (1963),
are an interesting case in point. Among the *Burundi*, women
are stronger, at least as measured by the amount people can
carry on their heads, and are thought to be less able to control their anger. Yet men generally win physical battles
with their wives, apparently because they are more agile.

ATTACHMENT

There has been a great deal of discussion in the English-
speaking countries of women's greater dependency and emotionality, but few cross-cultural studies have examined these variables. In the cross-cultural study of bereavement mentioned
above (Rosenblatt *et al.* In press), women were found to be
much more likely than men to mutilate themselves and to cry
following a death, which might suggest greater attachment
and emotionality. However, these sex differences could arise
from differences in socialization for anger. Men may generally be socialized to deal with anger, such as that arising
from a death, by attacking or being angry at others. Women
may generally be socialized to channel their anger in the
form of crying and self-mutilation. Such a difference in
socialization could be linked to hormonal differences which

make it difficult to limit some of the anger and aggression of males or to socialization which supports male dominance by encouraging males to do more attacking when disposed to feel angry or aggressive and women to do less attacking.

The sex differences in crying and self-mutilation behaviour in bereavement may actually mean that women experience a loss more strongly. Perhaps through their roles in dealing with children and through their roles in domestic groups (cf. Chodorow, 1974), they develop stronger attachments than males so that when a death occurs they experience the loss more strongly. (Such a tendency would, of course, be contrary to Tiger's aforementioned contention of a stronger capacity for bonding on the part of the male.)

STATUS AND POWER

Across the world it appears that men have higher public status than women (D'Andrade, 1966; Hammond and Jablow, 1973; Rosaldo, 1974; Stephens, 1963, Ch. 6). Men typically are the formally-recognized heads of domestic groups (Evans-Pritchard, 1965; Romney, 1965) and are more prominent in religious and judicial activities (Evans-Pritchard, 1965).

Where there are sex differences in access to desirable things, women seem to get less. Women seem to have less access to alternative sex partners (Ford and Beach, 1951). They also have less access to alcohol (Child et al. 1965) and to residence close to their own kin (Stephens, 1963, p. 290). Rosenblatt et al. (1973) report that in societies lacking scientific knowledge about the causes of childlessness women are more likely than men to be blamed for childlessness. Far more societies allow men to have multiple wives than allow women more than one husband (Stephens, 1963, Ch. 2), and even if having co-wives often works to the benefit of a woman in a polygynous household, polygyny may still be in some sense an expression of higher male status. Further, polygyny and brideprice are more likely to occur than monogany and dowry in societies where more food comes from women's work (Heath, 1958), which suggests a view of women as resources in societies with polygyny. In societies where polygyny is common, however, many women may prefer to live in households with multiple wives.

Women in many societies are defined as polluting during their menstrual periods and are required to withdraw from some normal daily activities (Stephens, 1961; Young and

Bacdayan, 1965). Whether women observing such menstrual taboos feel a lower status as a consequence of their observance
or enjoy the opportunity to escape from their domestic roles
is unknown, but being defined as polluting, being confined
to a menstrual hut, and being prohibited from having sexual
intercourse certainly do not seem to be indicators of high
status.

Public Status and Power

There seems little question that around the world the
activities of men have greater public status than the activities of women. There are, however, many complexities that
are entangled in that statement.

People around the world appear to be more or less interested in something resembling their reputation, prestige, or
status among their peers. However, who their peers are is
not always clear. It may be that in many societies men com-
pete primarily with men, and women judge themselves primarily
in relationship to other women. If that is the case, the
sex difference in apparent public status could be irrelevant
to the thinking of individuals in the societies involved.
The status of a woman, her feelings about herself, the focus
of her energies that are mustered to maintain, enhance, or
protect her reputation may be linked to interaction with
women and not to interaction with men. If this is so, the
cross-cultural sex difference in status may not have much
meaning in the lives of women and men. There is at present
no unequivocal indicator of women's status within a culture.
To conclude that women in fact have lower status within a
culture may perhaps require that the women of a society perceive themselves to be of lower status or feel exploited or
that the balance of rewards in their society seems unfair to
women. The variables which we have noted that involve access
to what we call public status and to what we assume people
desire may represent American and European ethnocentrism in
the choice of status criteria, rather than an experience of
lower status by females cross-culturally. Women may generally
feel, in contrast, that by their standards they are doing
what is right, proper and desirable. If they were asked who
has the better life, a man or a woman, they might argue that
the woman has a better life, or they might argue that the
lives of men and women are different and not comparable.

Why the public differences seem so much to favour males

is not easy to determine at present. Most of the research
that needs to be done has yet to be performed. Lebeuf (1963)
and Tanner (1974) have argued that some sex differences in
political roles that can be observed currently may stem from
the sexism of colonial authorities. If so, what we observe
cross-culturally may not be a representation of an intrinsic
human pattern but of an overlay of European colonialism on
all cultures that were governed by Europeans. There is enough
cross-cultural variability in the relative status of the
sexes for it to be possible to identify the effect of colonialism and of other factors, but compelling research has
not yet been done. The most generally applicable interpretation which can be offered at present for the sex differences in public status centres on the division of labour. This
interpretation suggests that through differences in mobility
and strength and through the actions of colonial authorities
men gain control of important economic, social and organizational resources such as animal herds, mineral deposits and
relations with other groups. Because of their involvement
with these activities and resources, men also serve in the
political and judicial roles which regulate the activities
and resources. Control of the major institutions of society
could then be the precondition for the initiation and legiti-
mization of differences in public status between the sexes
as men use their power to obtain differential access to desirable ends.

Through socialization against perceiving alternatives
and through a sense of her self interest in the structure of
her society, a woman may be as committed as any man to maintain the status quo. The status of a woman may be linked to
the status of significant males in her life in such a way
that her own status is enhanced through the sex differences
in status that seem to favour males. This may mean, first
of all, that she feels little or no loss at the discrepancy
in status between the sexes but rather sees it as part of a
system that works to her benefit. Secondly, it may mean
that the apparent sex difference in status is a result of
male competition being the visible vehicle for competition
between kin groups for prestige. For display purposes it
may be necessary, in such status competition, that males appear higher status than the females with whom they are associated. The sex difference in a public status then may to a
token difference which is tolerated by females - visible
enough to avoid undermining any male's claim to status in his

relations with other males but small enough to preserve a
balance in relations between the sexes domestically and to
give females leverage on what happens in public (cf. Rogers,
1975).

Domestic Status and Power

There is not a great deal of comparative data concerning the existence or nature of a domestic war between the
sexes, but there is evidence of some skirmishing. Cross-sex
violence seems frequent during courtship in societies with
relatively great freedom of choice of spouse (Rosenblatt and
Cozby, 1972). Violence may also be frequent in marriage,
though the topic of marital violence has been little discussed in the ethnographic literature. In any society there may
be frequent tests of strength in male-female relations. For
example, in the United States it is not uncommon for courting
and young married couples to engage in playful wrestling,
racing, and other activities that communicate to the partici-
pants that there are differences in physical ability. In
Europe and the United States, and perhaps in many other societies, the norm for married couples is that the male is taller. (We have some unpublished data from Hong Kong and Bali
that show the same pattern of difference that can be observed
in Europe and America.) When we add androgen-related aggression differences, male training in use of muscles for things
resembling attack, tests of strength, and societal tolerance
for male aggression to the tendency for the male of a couple
to be taller,it seems plausible that sex differences in domestic status and power could develop that favour the male.
Further, for first marriages, women around the world are
generally younger than men (15.5 years old versus 20.4 years
old in unpublished data compiled for Rosenblatt *et al.* In
press). This age difference may further restrict the power
of a woman in her first marriage, giving the husband the
status and experience of age as an additional factor working
in favour of his having his own way (cf. Cohen, 1971, pp. 89-
91).
Where differences in publicly recognized domestic power
exist, the tendency cross-culturally is to favour the male.
We have already noted the institution of *purdah* involving
the sequestering of women. A number of societies also demand deferential forms of address by the wife when speaking
to the husband and formal acts of submission such as washing

of the man's feet. Nonetheless, even in societies where males appear to have very great power and status relative to females, females seem often to be able to hold their own. First of all, sex segregation of work gives females spheres of autonomy and authority in which they have a great deal of control over what is done (Friedl, 1967). Second, women have many sources of power over males. Sex role differentiation forces males to be more or less dependent on women. Women in some societies have power through their capacity to do things that could embarrass the men who are related to them. Women also have power through their control of sexual relations with a mate and through the influence they have with their children and their natal kin. Despite a male's public power, he may not often be in a position to have unilateral control of domestic situations. If we assume people are inclined to use whatever power they have, we can expect males to tend to take advantage of their greater strength or agility or ability in fighting, both sexes to exploit the dependence of one spouse on the other spouse's work, sexuality, and kin relations, and women to exploit their relations with children. Thus, we believe that there is generally a much more equal division of power domestically than one would expect knowing only about public status differences.

Factors Maintaining a Balance of Power

It may be that societies could not function if one side or the other actually won a battle of the sexes, and as we have indicated with respect to domestic power a number of factors can moderate tendencies toward male dominance in a society.
       Schlegel (1972) presents data showing that in matrilineal societies women who are not under the control of a single domestic authority, whose domestic group is dominated simultaneously by both husband and brother or by neither, have substantially greater autonomy than women whose domestic group is dominated by one man, either the husband or the brother. This autonomy is manifested in reduced requirements of deference to husband or brother, increased rights to retain the residence if there is a divorce, greater freedom from male aggression, greater control of property, and freedom from punishment for adultery. One interpretation of Schlegel's data is that the ability to counteract the authority of one male with the authority of another increases

the relative status and power of women. One can speculate
more generally that having something that can influence the
other sex gives people of one sex greater status and power.
Thus, status and rewards may be a function of the importance
of warfare, the scarcity of one's sex (due to labour migra-
tion, death in warfare or childbirth, infanticide), and the
value of things produced by one's sex. For example, where
warfare is unimportant and where women produce much food and
control it or produce goods of high market value their status
may often be relatively high (D'Andrade, 1966; LeVine, 1966;
Netting, 1969; Sanday, 1973, 1974). The definitive comparative studies in this area do not seem to exist at present.

So far we have argued that there are plausible reasons
to believe both that males have more power than women in relations between the sexes and reasons to believe that the
sexes are on a relatively equal footing. We have further argued that the sexes differ markedly on measures of status,
that they may really not be comparable in status, or that
they may be equivalent in status in their own thinking. To
add to the paradoxes, we would like to point out that even
in societies in which one sex appears to be quite low in status relative to the other there are often customary practices
that get the "stronger" sex working for the "weaker" sex
without altering the apparent, public balance in status and
power. Such practices include pregnancy cravings, which produce demands that must be honoured by the husband (Obeyesekere
1963), and sick roles which can enable a woman to escape
from excessive demands and to gain some redress of difficulty
from kin and neighbours (O'Nell and Selby, 1968). Trance behaviour (Lewis, 1966) and rituals of reversal (Gluckman,
1956, Ch. V) are in some cultures approved ways of manifest-
ing feelings and wishes long pent up or of seeking gratifi-
cations that would normally be difficult or inappropriate to
seek. In certain societies in recent times some women have
been able to obtain greater status or access to roles and
pleasures that were previously unavailable to them. Examples
include a number of groups in Nigeria (LeVine, 1966; Mintz,
1971; Ottenberg, 1959) and South Asia (Tharper, 1963). A
comparative study of such "liberations of women" might be of
value in understanding the contemporary situation in Europe
and America (cf. S.G. Ardener, 1973). Factors involved may
include egalitarian ideology, economic change that provides
new roles for women, increased educational opportunities,
the acquisition of self-confidence and social skills through

dealings outside the local group, and increased income for women as a result of the advent of a cash economy, improved means of transportation, effective birth control, and inventions that allow traditional work of women to be done in less time.

SOCIAL WORLDS OF THE SEXES

One might deduce from what we have said so far that the social worlds of men and women are different. Women, for example, spend more time with other women and children, are more often at home and are less likely to engage in village-wide work activities (Young, 1965). Men spend more time with men, away from home, and engaged in formal organizational role activities of a political, ceremonial, judicial, or kin group nature. Colby (1963) reports data in support of the notion that the sexes live to some extent in different social and experiential worlds. He cites data from 75 societies showing that dream reports of women and men differ, so that women report more dreams of children and women, and men report more dreams of men.

The issue of different worlds is important in part because of the male bias in the data of the ethnographic record. E. Ardener (1972) goes so far as to argue that current theories of society in anthropology represent the thinking of male informants and that theories derived from women might differ. Goodale (1971), whose study of the *Tiwi* of North Australia is one of the few monographs done from the point of view of female informants, discusses a number of world-view differences between the sexes among the *Tiwi*. Although her specific findings may be unique to the *Tiwi*, the point is well taken that in comparing the sexes it is not only biology that differs but also social environment.

SOCIALIZATION

As might be expected from the sex differences we have discussed, there are also cross-cultural differences in the ways boys and girls are socialized. In the classic study in this area, Barry *et al.* (1957) report that during childhood girls are generally pressured toward nurturance, obedience, and responsibility while boys are generally pressured toward self-reliance and achievement. These differences seem to reflect differences in the adult work roles for which

males and females are socialized, the greater demands on
girls for work and particularly for childcare, and perhaps
the earlier age at which girls are generally expected to take
on marital roles. It is not clear at what age boys and girls
begin to receive differential treatment, though Barry and his
colleagues believe that differential treatment of infants is
uncommon (Barry *et al*. 1957; Barry and Paxson, 1971).

The importance of childhood work duties such as childcare in the socialization of children seems clear from a
fascinating study done in Kenya by C. Ember (1973). She analysed social behaviour among *Luo* girls, *Luo* boys who are required to do feminine work (because there is no girl in the
family old enough to do the work), and *Luo* boys who need not
do feminine work. Ember found that *Luo* boys who are required
to do feminine work are much more like girls in such social
behaviours as aggression, dependency, and dominance.

Whiting and Edwards (1973), discussing carefully gathered data in a comparative study of childhood sex differences,
also indicate that task assignment may be crucial to socialization differences. In their study, the sexes seem quite
malleable, with only greater insulting and rough-and-tumble
play by males and greater touching behaviour by females
yielding strong and relatively consistent sex differences in
the six cultures studied. In the ethnographic literature,
socialization for sex differences seems generally predictable
from knowledge of sex differences in work requirements for
children and adults. A puzzle in the socialization literature is the fact that some girls, through their responsibility for children and through the extra respect given first
borns in some societies, receive the socialization one would
expect dominating, strong adults to have received (Rosenblatt
and Skoogberg, 1974). Yet societies typically have no formal positions other than the maternal role that make use of
female socialization for dominance. Perhaps female dominance
also gets expressed in relations with spouse and with other
adults (cf. Goodale, 1971, p. 338), and perhaps it gets expressed in relations among females within a community.

CONCLUSIONS

This chapter offers few strong conclusions. If anything it points to the need for substantially more ethnographic and comparative research on sex differences. From
a cross-cultural perspective, and given the real limitations

in present knowledge, few sex differences in social behaviour seem inevitable. Women's status may generally seem low in public, from a Euro-American point of view. But even where their status and power seem quite low, women may still have a great deal of leverage in domestic relations. Perhaps the crucial sex differences are women's roles in child-bearing and childcare and men's aggressiveness. Any sex role revolution must deal with these, though the plasticity of the sexes seems quite enough to allow for a gender revolution of almost any sort.

Acknowledgements
The preparation of this chapter was supported by the University of Minnesota Agricultural Experiment Station. We are indebted to the editors of this volume and to Carolyn Cunningham, Anne Nevaldine, Elizabeth Skoogberg, Marilyn Strathern, and Sandra Titus for constructive comments on earlier drafts of the chapter.

REFERENCES

Albert, E. (1963). Women of Burundi: A study of social values. *In* "Women of Tropical Africa". (D. Paulme, ed.) Routledge and Kegan Paul, London.

Archer, J. (1976). The organization of aggression and fear in vertebrates. *In* "Perspectives in Ethology". (P.P.G. Bateson and P. Klopfer, eds.) Vol. 2. Plenum, London.

Ardener, E. (1972). Belief and the problem of women. *In* "The Interpretation of Ritual: Essays in Honour of A.I. Richards". (J.S. LaFontaine, ed.) Tavistock, London.

Ardener, S.G. (1973). Sexual insult and female militancy. *Man*, 8, 422–440.

Barry, H. III, Bacon, M.K. and Child, I.L. (1957). A cross-cultural survey of some sex differences in socialization. *Journal of Abnormal and Social Psychology*, 55, 327–332.

Barry, H. III and Paxson, L.M. (1971). Infancy and childhood cross-cultural codes 2. *Ethnology*, 10, 466–508.

Benchley, N. (1954). Kiddie-kar travel. *The Benchley Roundup*, Harper, New York.

Brown, J.K. (1970). A note on the division of labour by sex.

American Anthropologist, 72, 1073-1078.

Brown, J.K. (1973). The subsistence activity of women and the socialization of children. *Ethos,* 1, 413-423.

Child, I.L., Barry, H. III and Bacon, M.K. (1965). A cross-cultural study of drinking: III. Sex Differences. *Quarterly Journal of Studies on Alcohol,* Suppl. 3, 49-61.

Chodorow, N. (1974). Family structure and feminine personality. *In* "Woman, Culture, and Society". (M.Z. Rosaldo and L. Lamphere, eds.) Stanford University Press, Stanford, California.

Cohen, R. (1971). "Dominance and Defiance". American Anthropological Association, Washington, D.C.

Colby, K.M. (1963). Sex differences in dreams of primitive tribes. *American Anthropologist,* 65, 1116-1122.

Coppinger, R.M. and Rosenblatt, P.C. (1968). Romantic love and subsistence dependence of spouses. *Southwestern Journal of Anthropology,* 24, 310-319.

Crook, J.H. (1972). Sexual selection, dimorphism, and social organization in the primates. *In* "Sexual Selection and the Descent of Man". (B.G. Campbell, ed.) Aldine, Chicago.

D'Andrade, R.G. (1966). Sex differences and cultural institutions. *In* "The Development of Sex Differences". (E.E. Maccoby, ed.) Stanford University Press, Stanford, California.

Durkheim, E. (1964). "The Division of Labour in Society". (Translated by George Simpson) Free Press, New York. 1st edition published in French in 1893.

Ember, C.R. (1973). Feminine task assignment and the social behaviour of boys. *Ethos,* 1, 424-439.

Ember, M. and Ember, C.R. (1971). The conditions favouring matrilocal versus patrilocal residence. *American Anthropologist,* 73, 571-594.

Evans-Pritchard, E.E. (1965). "The Position of Women in Primitive Societies and Other Essays in Social Anthropology". Free Press, New York.

Ford, C.S. and Beach, F. (1951). "Patterns of Sexual Behaviour". Harper, New York.

Friedl, E. (1967). The position of women: appearance and reality. *Anthropological Quarterly*, 40, 97-108.

Gluckman, M. (1956). "Custom and Conflict in Africa". Basil Blackwell,'London.

Gonzalez, N.L. (1969). "Black Carib Household Structure". University of Washington Press, Seattle.

Goodale, J.C. (1971). "Tiwi Wives". University of Washington Press, Seattle.

Hammond, D. and Jablow, A. (1973). "Women: Their Economic Role in Traditional Societies". An Addison Wesley Module in Anthropology, Module No. 35.

Heath, D.B. (1958). Sexual division of labour and cross-cultural research. *Social Forces*, 37, 77-79.

Lebeuf, A.M.D. (1963). The role of women in the political organization of African societies. *In* "Women of Tropical Africa". (D. Paulme, ed.) Routledge and Kegan Paul, London.

Leis, N.B. (1974). Women in groups: Ijaw women's associations. *In* "Woman, Culture, and Society". (M.Z. Rosaldo and L. Lamphere, eds.) Stanford University Press, Stanford, California.

LeVine, R.A. (1966). Sex roles and economic change in Africa. *Ethnology*, 5, 186-193.

Lewis, I.M. (1966). Spirit possession and deprivation cults. *Man*, 1, 307-329.

Mead, M. (1950). "Sex and Temperament in Three Primitive Societies". Mentor, New York. Originally published in 1935.

Minturn, L. and Lambert, W.W. (1964). "Mothers of Six Cultures: Antecedents of Child Rearing". Wiley,New York.

Mintz, S.W. (1971). Men, women, and trade. *Comparative Studies in Society and History*, 13, 247-269.

Moyer, K.E. (1971). The physiology of aggression and the implications for aggression control. *In* "The Control of Aggression and Violence". (J.L. Singer, ed.) Academic Press, New York.

Murdock, G.P. (1937). Comparative data on the division of

labour by sex. *Social Forces*, 15, 551-553.

Murdock, G.P. and Provost, C. (1973). Factors in the division of labour by sex: A cross-cultural analysis. *Ethnology*, 12, 203-225.

Nag, M. (1968). "Factors Affecting Human Fertility in Non-industrial Societies: A Cross-Cultural Study". Yale University Publications in Anthropology, No. 66.

Nerlove, S.B. (1974). Women's workload and infant feeding practices: A relationship with demographic implications. *Ethnology*, 8, 207-214.

Netting, R. McC. (1969). Women's weapons: The politics of domesticity among the Kofyar. *American Anthropologist*, 71, 1037-1046.

Newton, N. (1967). Pregnancy, childbirth, and outcome: A review of patterns of culture and future research needs. *In* "Childbearing: Its Social and Psychological Aspects". (S.A. Richardson and A.F. Guttmacher, eds.) Williams and Wilkins, Baltimore.

Obeyesekere, G. (1963). Pregnancy cravings (*dola-duka*) in relation to social structure and personality in a Sinhalese village. *American Anthropologist*, 65, 323-342.

O'Nell, C.W. and Selby, H.A. (1968). Sex differences in the incidence of *susto* in two Zapotec villages. *Ethnology*, 7, 95-105.

Ottenberg, P.V. (1959). The changing economic position of women among the Afikpo Ibo. *In* "Continuity and Change in African Cultures". (W.R. Bascom and M.J. Herskovits, eds.) University of Chicago Press, Chicago.

Rogers, S.C. (1975). Female forms of power and the myth of male dominance: a model of female/male interaction in peasant society. *American Ethnologist*, 2, 727-756.

Romney, A.K. (1965). Variations in household structure as determinants of sex-typed behaviour. *In* "Sex and Behaviour". (F. Beach, ed.) Wiley, New York.

Rosaldo, M.Z. (1974). Woman, culture and society: A theoretical overview. *In* "Woman, Culture, and Society". (M.Z. Rosaldo and L. Lamphere, eds.) Stanford University Press, Stanford, California.

Rosenblatt, P.C. and Cozby, P.C. (1972). Courtship patterns associated with freedom of choice of spouse. *Journal of Marriage and the Family,* 34, 689-695.

Rosenblatt, P.C., Peterson, P., Portner, J., Cleveland, M., Mykkanen, A., Foster, R., Holm, G., Joel, B., Reisch, H., Kreuscher, C. and Phillips, R.A. (1973). Cross-cultural study of responses to childlessness. *Behavioural Science Notes,* 8, 221-231.

Rosenblatt, P.C. and Skoogberg, E.L. (1974). Birth order in cross-cultural perspective. *Developmental Psychology,* 10, 48-54.

Rosenblatt, P.C., Walsh, R.P. and Jackson, D.A. (In press). "Grief and Mourning in Cross-Cultural Perspective". Human Relations Area Files Press.

Sanday, P.R. (1973). Toward a theory of the status of women. *American Anthropologist,* 75, 1682-1700.

Sanday, P.R. (1974). Female status in the public domain. *In* "Woman, Culture, and Society". (M.Z. Rosaldo and L. Lamphere, eds.) Stanford University Press, Stanford, California.

Schlegel, A. (1972). "Male Dominance and Female Autonomy". Human Relations Area File Press, New Haven.

Stephens, W.N. (1961). A cross-cultural study of menstrual taboos. *Genetic Psychology Monographs,* 64, 385-416.

Stephens, W.N. (1963). "The Family in Cross-Cultural Perspective". Holt, Rinehart and Winston, New York.

Tanner, N. (1974). Matrifocality in Indonesia and Africa and among black Americans. *In* "Woman, Culture, and Society". (M.Z. Rosaldo and L. Lamphere, eds.) Stanford University Press, Stanford, California.

Tharper, R. (1963). The history of female emancipation in southern Asia. *In* "Women in the New Asia". (B.E. Ward, ed.) UNESCO, Paris.

Tiger, L. (1969). "Men in Groups". Random House, New York.

Ward, B.E. (1963). Men, women and change: An essay in understanding social roles in South and South-East Asia. *In* "Women in the New Asia". (B.E. Ward, ed.) UNESCO, Paris.

Whiting, B.B. and Edwards, C.P. (1973). A cross-cultural analysis of sex differences in the behaviour of children aged three through eleven. *Journal of Social Psychology*, 91, 171-188.

Williams, S.N. (1971). The limitations of the male-female activity distinction among primates. *American Anthropologist*, 73, 805-806.

Young, F.W. (1965). "Initiation Ceremonies". Bobbs-Merrill, Indianapolis.

Young, F.W. and Bacdayan, A.A. (1965). Menstrual taboos and social rigidity. *Ethnology*, 4, 225-240.

5. INTELLIGENCE, OCCUPATIONAL STATUS, AND ACHIEVEMENT ORIENTATION

Dorothy McBride Kipnis

There is no doubt that there are large differences between
men and women in the average status level of the occupations
they enter and in the status they eventually attain within
those occupations. In all of the nations of the Western
world, including those with active feminist movements (Sweden,
Britain, and the United States) and those in which need and
governmental effort brought women into occupations previously
conducted mainly by men (the Soviet Union and Finland), there
are status or income differentials between the occupations
performed by men and by women (Patai, 1967). Sex differences
in occupational status, all of which favour males, are much
more consistent from country to country than is the sex composition of workers in particular occupations or professions.
Medicine, for instance, is largely a female occupation in
the Soviet Union, is largely male in Britain, and is overwhelmingly male in the United States. As a profession, in
the United States medicine enjoys the highest prestige. In
the Soviet Union, where it is more frequently performed by
women, it is less honoured. There are similar international
differences in a considerable number of professional occupations. School teaching is fairly prestigious in countries
in which it is a male occupation, but is one of the least
prestigious professions in the United States, where it is
female. There are also changes over time even within the
same country. The occupation of bank teller was once a fairly high-status male occupation in the United States. It is
now a predominantly female occupation, and is viewed as a
clerical occupation little different from many others.

It seems reasonable to conclude that the nature of the
occupation itself does not necessarily determine the sex of
the individuals who will be attracted to it. The fact that
many occupations seem to be performed by individuals of

opposite sex in different countries would appear to indicate that some attribute of the occupation other than the activities it calls for brings individuals to enter it. The consistency with which male occupations seem to have superior status leads one to suspect that status itself could be that attribute. If there are sex differences in the extent to which individuals are oriented toward the attainment of status in groups which they enter, and if males are usually more desirous of the attainment of status goals, it follows that whatever occupations or professions bring status in a given society would be those which attract most males. If status goals are less salient for females, they may be more often guided by other attributes of the occupation, and they may not even begin to enter prestigious fields that lack other attractions for them. Further, if our societies share a tendency to perceive high status as inherently inappropriate for females, that perception may serve as a self fulfilling prophecy which perpetuates a lack of occupational attainment for women.

If we turn from sex differences in the occupational status of adults, which seem to be very large throughout the Western world, to sex differences in intelligence, we turn from a very large difference to a very small one. In fact, whatever sex differences in intelligence exist may be so small as to be largely undocumentable given the present technology of test construction, which emphasizes item selections familiar to both sexes.

Much of the present intense interest in the relationship between intelligence, education and occupational status stems from the conflict of interest that has developed between male and female orientations to education and to the occupational system. The historical sequence of events in most countries has been such that the formal educational system has come to serve as a selection device for the higher status occupations. It is likely that it will be increasingly used for this purpose in most industrialized nations. To the extent that intelligence is an asset in the acquisition of education, it enables individuals to qualify for more steps in the later hierarchy of occupational status.

The place of females in an educational system which serves such a function is a difficult one. As the educational process which qualifies for higher echelon occupations becomes more and more extended, it encroaches more and more on the biological functions of women, and it becomes more

and more difficult to combine marital and educational objectives and to delay child rearing responsibilities. On the
other hand, to the extent that the main qualifications for
the occupations requiring most extended preparation are intellectual ones, women may meet these qualifications as well as
men. Abandonment of educational objectives for familial ones
means for many intelligent women the long-range acceptance of
low occupational status. A woman who discontinues her higher
education before she has exhausted her capacity to succeed
forfeits her claim to higher status roles for which competence is established through education. The exclusion of
many intelligent women from higher status occupations is a
more or less automatic consequence of basing the selection
for the highest status occupations on the completion of prolonged higher education. Such an exclusion can only result
in a sacrifice of the level of competence at which the occupations are performed. It is likely that this has already
happened in the United States. Miner (1957) reported that
if occupational requirements for intelligence were to be
raised, as they could be given the actual numbers of people
at various levels of intelligence in the population, more
white males would be demoted to fill jobs commensurate with
their intelligence while women would be promoted.

The experience of the United States in education and
occupational selection in relation to intelligence is probably unique among industrial nations. For historical reasons,
American women have traditionally been entitled to free
public education for many generations. Even at the level of
higher education, almost as many upper middle class or upper
class women attended college as did men in the late nineteenth and early twentieth century (Folger and Nam, 1960).
On the other hand, relatively few members of either sex attended college prior to World War II. Even among those who
did, the rationale for higher education was considerably
different from what it is today. American women attended teachers or liberal arts colleges as a means of widening their
personal or social horizons, to establish their marital qualifications, and as a form of economic insurance against possible later misfortune, as well as for career purposes. The
same orientation appears today in many young women's choice
of field of concentration in American colleges and universities. However, these young women now face young men whose
interest in education is intensively career oriented. Furthermore, women's access to higher education in the United

States was gained in a day when relative equality of intellectual resources between the sexes was less contested. In
a day when a man's occupational success had little to do
with his intellect, many men were willing to grant intellectual equality to women in the same spirit that they presently
might allow them to excel in flower arranging. Today, they
see them as encroaching on their own territory and consuming
scarce resources.

American data on the relationship between education and
intelligence come from a system in which the values to be
attained by succeeding at the more advanced levels of education have recently changed. However, the American experience
provides a record of the impact that formal educational experience has had on the intellectual attributes and on the achievement orientations of members of both sexes.

THE MEANING OF INTELLIGENCE TEST SCORES

Any discussion of sex differences in intelligence should
begin with a clear understanding of terminology. The word
intelligence is deceptive and likely to convey an impression
of understanding with no appreciation of the technical limitations of the methodology used to measure it.

Perhaps the best known and the first well-developed intelligence test was that of Binet and Simon (1905). It was
a deliberate and successful attempt to predict the scholastic
performance of French school children. As revised by Terman,
it was used in the United States to predict the scholastic
performance of children.

The Stanford-Binet was developed from its inception in
such a way as to minimize the possibility of sex differences.
Instead, it capitalized on the fact that children are generally recognized to differ in their knowledgeability according
to their ages. Children are asked questions of increasing
difficulty (that is, questions whose answers are known to
fewer and fewer of their age-mates) until they can no longer
give correct answers. Their intelligence quotients are cal-
culated by dividing the difficulty level of the items they
are able to answer, or their mental ages, by their chronological ages.

The Stanford-Binet is still recognized and widely used
as one of the best general intelligence tests available for
children, and other tests continue to be validated by their
ability to predict Stanford-Binet scores. Nevertheless, the

Stanford-Binet has never contributed to the understanding of
sex differences. As the methods through which it was perfec-
ted called for the elimination of all items which appeared to
be easier for members of one sex than for the other, it produces total scores which show few or unreliable sex differences.
        For a better understanding of the substance of sex dif-
ferences in intelligence, it is necessary to turn away from
tests in which the procedures of test development involved
the elimination of items showing sex differences. Perhaps
the most widely used tests which did not use item by item
standardization are those developed by David Wechsler. The
Wechsler-Bellevue I (an intelligence test developed for use
with adults) (Wechsler, 1939), the Wechsler Adult Intelligence Scale (WAIS), which is a revision of the earlier
Wechsler-Bellevue I (Wechsler, 1958), and the Wechsler Intelligence Scale for Children (WISC) (Wechsler, 1949) are probably the best known alternatives to the Stanford-Binet in frequent use as individually administered intelligence tests.
Like Terman, Wechsler did not wish to build into his tests
wide differentials between the sexes as these would make necessary expensive data collection to establish separate norms
for the two sexes. Such differentials would also inevitably
initiate argument as to what attributes truly constitute intelligence. Moreover, Wechsler's main interest in developing
his tests was not in sex differences but in the growth and
decline of intellectual ability according to age. Therefore,
he too eliminated types of items which seemed to be clearly
easier or more difficult for one sex than for the other. But
Wechsler's tests are composed of subscales of items represen-
ting different types of tasks, and most individuals perform
better on some types of tasks than on others. The main evidence for sex differences in intellectual functioning stem
from tests which are composed of subscales which provide the
possibility of pattern or profile differences between the
sexes. In such tests, males and females do typically differ
in the subtest scales in which their best scores are obtained.

OBSERVED SEX DIFFERENCES IN OVERALL INTELLIGENCE

        Whether the sexes differ in general intelligence is un-
certain. In practice, whether or not sex differences in intelligence exist can only be tested through the administration of tests which were deliberately developed in such a way

as to minimize the likelihood of obtaining sex differences.
However, it is of interest to note the nature and the direction of the sex differences Wechsler obtained in the course
of his standardizations of his various tests. The Wechsler-
Bellevue I was published in 1939, together with normative
data obtained by testing some 1,700 individuals who resided
in or near New York City. They were chosen to represent the
characteristics of the United States population at that time
as described by census data. The effort represented the
first large scale attempt to obtain data which could be taken to describe the adult population of both sexes and all
ages.
      The normative data obtained by Wechsler in 1939 revealed
slight but positive differences in favour of females at all
ages. Wechsler, in fact, remarked that the consistency of
the differences had led him to the belief that it might be
possible to demonstrate a measurable superiority of women
over men in general intelligence (Wechsler, 1939). However,
by 1955 studies using the same test had failed to repeat the
earlier differences (Wechsler, 1958). When Wechsler restan-
dardized his adult test in 1955, he obtained slight differences in favour of males on the revised version of a number of
the same subscales that had shown sex differences in favour
of females in 1939. Furthermore, the age range in which individuals appeared to be at their maximum in intellectual
functioning had shifted from the 20-24 year age range to the
25-29 year period. Decrements in intellectual functions with
advancing age also appeared to be slower than they had been
in 1939, as measured by the Wechsler-Bellevue I.
      It is well know that educational attainment tends to
correlate highly with tested intelligence in adult populations. Wechsler reported a correlation of 0.64 between educational attainment (as indicated by the last grade reached
in school) and adult intelligence scores in the standardization sample for the Wechsler-Bellevue I. The same correlation was 0.68 for the WAIS. It has also been found that not
only does intellectual ability seem to lead to an increase
in ability to proceed through our formal educational institutions, but increases in schooling seem to lead to better
later intelligence test scores. Lorge (1969) reported results for a sample of males tested first in their early juni-
or high school years, then followed up and retested as young
adults in their early thirties. Those who had completed more
years of schooling obtained better retest scores than those

who completed fewer years, even when their scores as junior
high school students were identical. Most intelligence tests
devised for adults of a level of difficulty adequate to differentiate among more intelligent adults correlate with educational attainment. Terman's Concept Mastery Test, for example, which he used in an adult follow-up of his sample of the
gifted, also correlated with his subject's number of years of
education (Terman and Oden, 1959).

In view of the apparently reciprocal relationship between education and tested intelligence, it is of interest to
note the levels of educational attainment of Americans of both
sexes during the decades in which these tests were developed
and norms established, up through the most recent census.
These data are reported in Table I. In 1940, the year following Wechsler's original report of the normative data on the
Wechsler-Bellevue I, on average, in every age category females had completed more years of education than males had.
However, the median number of years education for members of
both sexes failed to reach the level of graduation from high
school. It will be remembered that Wechsler's normative data
for 1939 also showed feminine superiority at every age level.
By 1950, the beginning of the great change in American educational practice had made its appearance, initiated by a sudden increase in the number of years schooling completed by
males in the youngest age category, 25-29 years. Between
1940 and 1950, the median number of years education completed
by American males at younger ages increased almost two years,
from a level trailing women of their age to a level exceeding
them. Furthermore, the median education of both sexes included the beginning of college. Both the increase in median
level of education and the reversal in direction of sex differences in median number of years education completed are
systematically perpetuated in the 1960 and 1970 census data.
Both decades show younger males exceeding females in their
age groups in education, with older males being exceeded by
them. Both decades also show a later change in the relative
educational advantages of the sexes.

The occasion for the dramatic shift in the educational
level of the American public was undoubtedly the effort of
the United States government to reward veterans of World War
II by conferring educational advantage. Financial support
for college education was given to all individuals who had
contributed military service, whether in battle or as support
personnel. As far more war veterans were male than female,

TABLE I

Median Years of School Completed by White American
Men and Women in Four Consecutive Decades

	Decade							
	1940*		1950*		1960[†]		1970[‡]	
Age Group	Men	Women	Men	Women	Men	Women	Men	Women
25-29	10.5	10.9	12.4	12.2	12.4	12.3	12.7	12.6
30-34	9.7	10.3	11.9	12.1	12.2	12.3	12.6	12.5
35-39	8.8	9.1	10.7	11.2	12.2	12.2	12.5	12.4
40-44	8.7	8.8	9.9	10.5	12.0	12.1	12.3	12.3
45-49	8.5	8.6	8.9	9.5	10.7	11.2	12.3	12.3
50-54	8.4	8.5	8.7	8.9	9.8	10.4	12.1	12.1
55-59	8.3	8.5	8.5	8.7	8.8	9.2	11.0	11.6
60-64	8.3	8.4	8.3	8.5	8.6	8.8	10.0	10.7
65-69	8.2	8.3	8.2	8.4	8.4	8.6	8.9	9.5
70-74	8.1	8.3	8.1	8.4	8.2	8.5	8.7	8.9
75+	8.0	8.2	8.1	8.3	8.1	8.4	8.4	8.7

* *Taken from 1950 Census of Population. Vol. II: Characteristics of the Population: Part 1, United States Summary. U.S. Department of Commerce, Bureau of the Census, Washington, D.C.: U.S. Government Printing Office, 1953.*

[†] *United States Bureau of the Census. United States Census of Population: 1960 Vol. I: Characteristics of the Population. Part 1, United States Summary. Washington, D.C.: U.S. Government Printing Office, 1964.*

[‡] *United States Bureau of the Census. Census of Population: 1970. Vol. 1, Characteristics of the Population. Part 1, United States Summary, Section 2. Washington, D.C.: U.S. Government Printing Office, 1973.*

the educational advantages of the sexes were differentially affected. These support policies have been continued through the American military adventures following World War II. Draft exemptions have also been awarded to males who were enrolled in college and were able to maintain adequate performance levels. Thus, enrolment in college for males has been systematically rewarded with a series of incentives which did not apply, or applied only to a minimal extent, for females. These decades have witnessed a differential increase in higher education for the two sexes, a differential which very much favours males.

The normative data for Wechsler's tests faithfully reflect the changes which have occurred in the American population, including the direction of sex differences and the continued apparent mental growth into later and later age ranges. Nor are Wechsler's data alone. Data obtained from a careful study of New England children and adults in the early 1930's using the Army Alpha (a group intelligence test developed during World War I) found females to be superior to males in general intelligence in every age range (Conrad *et al.* 1933). They were particularly superior during early adolescence. Data obtained from longitudinal studies which were initiated in the earlier decades of the twentieth century also tend to report feminine superiority in general intelligence (Bradway and Thompson, 1962). Studies using subjects born somewhat later report no sex differences (Bayley, 1957), and studies initiated or continued into later years tend to report greater likelihood of increases in intelligence for males than for females, or at least greater increases during more recent years (Bradway and Thompson, 1962; Kagan and Moss, 1962).

The import of all these data is that whichever sex is afforded the greater educational advantage is likely to prove the more intelligent, given the testing procedures we have devised. Sex differences seem to be reversible even late in adolescence or in early adulthood. Hence, whatever genetic differences between the sexes exist must be so slight as to be readily modifiable through exposure to appropriate learning opportunity. Second, that the reversals appear to coincide with formal educational opportunity points to the conclusion that intelligence, as we know and measure it, is a result of a continuing interaction between individuals and an environment which affords opportunity to learn.

SEX DIFFERENCES IN RATES AND CONSTITUENTS
OF INTELLECTUAL GROWTH

Given the lack of consistency in results comparing the
sexes in overall intellectual performance, the question that
arises is whether or not any conclusions in relation to sex
differences have been consistently supported, and if so, what
are they? There seem to be two such conclusions. The first
is that in any investigation which studies the same individuals repeatedly, feminine superiority is most manifest early
in life. Changes in abilities which follow will bring about
male equality, or in the case of some attributes, superiority.
Secondly, the aspects of intellectual functioning in which
females equal or excel over males are verbal skills. Males
frequently excel over females in quantitative skills or skills
entailing spatial relations (Garai and Scheinfeld, 1968). The
consistency in the types of skills at which the sexes appear
to be superior and inferior is impressive, and seems to be
consistent whatever tests are used to measure them. From investigations carried out as early as 1920 (Brooks, 1921) to
the very recent past, females appear to have been found to
be superior in verbal skills and males in areas having to do
with mathematics and spatial relations.

Girl's superiority in verbal facility is manifest at an
early age. They say their first word sooner, speak more
clearly, combine words into sentences and use longer sentences
earlier, and are more fluent (Maccoby, 1966; Garai and
Scheinfeld, 1968; see Chapter 6 by McGuiness). When they enter school, they learn to read with comparative ease, are
less likely to require remedial reading instruction, are better spellers, better at grammar, and are likely to express
themselves at greater length in written compositions (Maccoby,
1966). Boys catch up in some, but not all, of these skills
at a later age. They may equal girls in vocabulary by the
time they enter school, and by the later years of primary
school boys can read as well as girls. Females remain superi-
or to males in grammar, spelling, and word fluency throughout
their school careers.

The period during which girls' measured intellectual ability first begins to predict their adult intellectual status
antedates their entrance to school. Two extensive longitudinal studies both showed that the years from three to six were
the period during which girls' rates of intellectual growth
(as measured by IO change) first began to predict their in-

tellectual status as adults (Crandall and Battle, 1970; Kagan and Moss, 1962). Boys, at this early age, show no indications of their adult status. For boys, the period of intellectual growth which is most highly related to their adult status is the age range 6-10 years. During this age period, almost twice as many boys as girls show IQ increases (Kagan and Moss, 1962; Kagan *et al.* 1958). Despite the fact that they are less likely to show increases in IQ, and gifted girls even show statistically significant declines in IQ during this age period (Terman *et al.* 1930), girls achieve better school grades than boys throughout their school years.

As Maccoby (1966) notes, girls receive better grades even in subjects in which boys score higher on standard achievement tests. There has been speculation that female teachers are unfair to boys and favour children of their own sex. However, studies that rely on observation rather than speculation do not find this to be true; teachers more often scold boys but they also more often praise them, while girls receive less attention of any kind from their teachers (Brophy and Good, 1970; Meyer and Thompson, 1956; Serbin *et al.* 1973). An alternate explanation is that the usual multiple choice, machine scored objective achievement test permits boys to express items of information which they know in a form which is acceptable and comprehensible to their teachers, and which is free from the limitations of their handwriting, spelling, grammar, and composition skills.

As for the meaning of increases and decreases in IQ, it is useful to remember that the IQ is a measure of a proportion of correct answers to a relatively fixed series of informational questions which are so selected that approximately the same proportion of each sex knows the proper response. We are often misled by the tendency to regard the IQ as a measure of intellectual capacity which will remain fixed over the individual's lifetime. The data from all of the longitudinal studies (Crandall and Battle, 1970; Kagan and Moss, 1962; Terman *et al.* 1930) are in agreement that this is not so, and that there is a sex difference in the age period during which intellectual growth is the most rapid. The method of IQ calculation consists of a division of children's mental ages by their chronological ages, which of course increase at an identical rate for both sexes. The fact that girls' IQ's decline while those of boys increase means that a growing component of girls' mental ages results from items which have been passed for some time, while boys' rates of development are slower or later.

It should not be thought that because males IQ's continue to increase over a longer period of time that males eventually become more intelligent than females. In one study reporting such long continued increases for males, the females of the sample were superior in IQ to the males at all the ages of testing, as pre-school children, as adolescents, and as young adults. The later and more prolonged growth of the males served only to reduce the difference. Despite their later growth males' absolute IQ scores remained lower than those of the females even at ages approaching 30 years (Bradway and Thompson, 1962).

The chief areas of masculine superiority are those which depend on mathematical reasoning and on spatial relations. As we would expect, this superiority is not apparent in their earlier years. Girls learn to count earlier than boys, and in the early school years they perform as well if not better than boys in arithmetic computation. Boys' superiority is observed beginning in early adolescence in tests typically labelled arithmetical reasoning. Boys also perform better than girls in tasks involving the perception of spatial relations, again beginning only during the school years and continuing into adulthood. Some studies report that males appear to continue their mental growth over a longer period of years than females, and when growth continues into later age periods, it appears that arithmetical abilities are those involved (Haan, 1963).

The attributes in which male performance generally is better than that of females are those which involve the perception of relationships among the elements of the situation immediately at hand. Thus, males show superiority in tasks involving restructuring of elements or the breaking of already established sets, and in the categorization of objects or events on the basis of some isolated attribute they have in common, usually labelled "analytic ability" (Maccoby, 1966). Males are sometimes said to be superior in "reasoning". Actually, studies which find males superior in reasoning are generally those in which the effort to eliminate the effects of past training has led the investigator to provide the elements of his problem in the immediate setting. What passes for "intuition" in females is also generally reasoning, but reasoning from some aspect of the situation which previous experience has demonstrated to be important.

There is a tendency to attach somewhat deprecatory labels
to the female verbal talents, describing them as verbal "fluency" or as the "executive" functions alone, as if mere glib-
ness were involved. However, there is considerable evidence
that for both sexes, the core intellectual abilities are verbal skills. Miner (1957) reviews evidence that of all the
components of intelligence tests, vocabulary subtests are ordinarily the best predictors of total scores. Verbal college
aptitude scores are also the best predictors of college grades.
Interest in cross-cultural research and in intellectual tasks
which are appropriate for members of all ethnic and racial
groups has led to many attempts to devise tasks less dependent on verbal behaviour. However, none of the tests so far
devised have either the reliability or the predictive validity of verbal tests such as the Stanford-Binet. As Goslin
(1963) notes, the reason is probably that verbal ability is
of critical importance in the performance of virtually every
task requiring high intelligence. Consequently, not only intelligence tests but criterion measures contain large verbal
components.

SEX DIFFERENCES IN ACHIEVEMENT ORIENTATION

As Caplow (1964) remarks, the principle device for the
limitation of occupational choice in American society is the
educational system. First, the student who embarks on a long
course of training for one career must thereby renounce all
other careers which also require extended preparation. Second,
he must prove himself to have all the necessary qualities,
including intelligence, required for the occupation.
Unfortunately, individuals are forced to make this fate-
ful choice at an age when their basis for selection can only
be ill-informed. Borow (1966) reviews data from various studies that point to the conclusion that vocational interests
in boys develop through the acquisition of a set of dislikes.
Boys in the United States as well as other nations are forced
to make educational decisions which will affect their possibilities for vocational selection as early as at the age of
twelve years. They do not select specific vocations but it
is at this time that they make the broader choice of educational direction. They choose whether or not to pursue an
academic course of study which will allow them to enter college, and they choose whether or not to expend the greater
part of their day to day expenditure of effort on academic

study. Knowing little of the actual job demands entailed by
most occupations at the time they must make their decisions,
boys eliminate fields of work on the basis of scanty information. On the positive side, boys develop an ability to rank
occupations according to the occupational prestige usually accorded them by adults (Gunn, 1964).

An extensive area of social psychological investigation
has been developed by McClelland, Atkinson, and their colleague
in their studies of achievement motivation (McClelland *et al.*
1953). By measuring fantasy about achievement on projective
tests, McClelland *et al.* hoped to differentiate achievement
motivation from the intellectual capacity more properly measured by intelligence tests. Beginning with an attempt to predict effort and success in entrepreneurial vocations, these
investigators developed a measure that has been used to predict effort and persistence in many achievement areas, from
the scholastic achievement of school children to the business
enterprize of prospective investors of capital in less industrialized nations (McClelland and Winter, 1969).

One of the more consistent findings of this programme of
research has been that male occupational choices can be treated as an instance of "risk-taking". If collegiate males are
asked what proportion of the population would be able to succeed in a given occupational field, then asked for their estimates of their own level of ability and their vocational choices, college men with high achievement motivation choose occupations which are moderate risks in their own judgment (Mahone,
1960; Weinstein, 1969). That is, they do not choose occupations in which they believe only a few will succeed unless
they also hold a very good opinion of their own abilities.
They also do not choose fields in which success is assured.
They choose fields in which success is possible but not guar-
anteed as their own vocations.

In the case of males, associations between achievement
oriented behaviours of many different kinds and projective
measures of achievement motivation have been discovered.
Occupational choice, as mentioned above, is one of these associations. A second is scholastic performance. Boys who
obtain high scores on projective measures of achievement motivation tend to do better in school than boys who demonstrate
less interest in achievement in their thinking and fantasy
(Klinger, 1966). A third association for boys and men is
that if their test scores are based on stories told under
the belief that their stories reflect on their intelligence

or leadership abilities, their stories will reflect more concern with achievement than if they are not given such an expectation (McClelland *et al.* 1953; Klinger, 1967).

One of the more puzzling aspects of this area of research
has always been that none of its predictions appear to be valid for females (Klinger, 1966). Although girls and women
obtain scores on the projective measure that are no lower
than those of males, their scores do not relate in the same
way to other variables. They also do not appear to concentrate more on achievement themes when they feel their intelligence is at stake (Veroff *et al.* 1953).

A survey of the qualities of high school seniors' ambitions provides a clue as to why this might be so (Turner,
1964). Boys and girls in their last year of high school
(secondary school) were asked to describe their ambitions or
their life hopes along several dimensions. One was their
hoped for eventual life income, a second was their educational
plans, and the third was their occupational or career goal.
Among the boys, all three dimensions were highly related.
Among the girls, monetary goals were unrelated to educational
and career goals. Girls who were highly ambitious in the
education and career sense were not particularly ambitious
in terms of the income they wished to receive, but they appeared to attach great importance to the nature of the work
itself. Girls who had high ambitions along monetary lines
did not have either educational or career goals, and from
other data, appeared to expect to satisfy their ambitions
through marriage rather than through work. The same indif-
ference to financial considerations in career oriented females is reported in other studies. Crandall and Battle
(1970) found intellectually oriented women who were most ambitious educationally and occupationally to be indifferent
to the monetary remuneration of their chosen vocations.

For American women, the nature of societal expectations
is such that ambitions are likely to be channelled into one
of two directions which have little to do with each other.
One is toward the conventional marital role. Marriage in
American society has tended to be more universal and to occur
at an earlier age than in most European nations (Bernard,
1972; Commission on Population Growth and the American Future,
1972). Furthermore, it is traditionally arranged by girls
themselves rather than by parents. As an almost universal
expectation for girls, the dating and courtship rituals that
precede marriage absorb many girls' energies almost exclu-

sively for years. These activities may be more time consuming than marital obligations, and as they are combined with
educational efforts during the adolescent years, courtship
and dating are for many girls an interest which competes
with education.

Perhaps the most thorough description of the social behaviour of American adolescents in relation to its impact on
their pursuit of intellectual goals was provided by Coleman
(1961). In a study which considered American high schools
in a variety of kinds of communities, from small towns to
affluent city suburbs, Coleman found that adolescents placed
considerably greater value on athletic (for boys) and social
(for girls) achievements than on scholastic excellence.
Girls believed, and apparently correctly so, that boys did
not wish to date scholarly, intelligent girls. At the same
time, parents wanted their daughters to achieve academically,
and the girls had somewhat higher IQ's and better school
grades than the boys. Despite all of these factors, girls
avoided being outstanding as scholars and in every school
the girl who was thought to be the "best scholar" by her
peers was less bright than the boy who was so known. In
other words, the brighter girls who were capable of doing
the best work had managed to conceal their intellectual assets
from those around them, and those who were thought to be scholars among the girls were less than the best.

The same process is traced into colleges and universities
where it is thought that female students do not do their best
in competition with males (Horner, 1972). While there are
many ambiguities in interpretation of the usual kinds of data
reported (Monahan et al. 1974), it appears that adolescent
and young adult American women refrain from flaunting their
intellectual triumphs, and that in so doing they are responding to real, not illusory social pressures.

While the interest of females in social activity was interpreted for many years as an indication that females were
motivated primarily by affiliative needs or by a need for
social approval, reviews of empirical data have recently concluded that some girls express their achievement orientation
through social striving rather than through intellectual activity (Stein and Bailey, 1973). Stein and Bailey point out
that the imagery and themes girls express in social situations
is achievement imagery, by the scoring criteria McClelland
and Atkinson used in their measures of achievement motivation
which were successful for males. Thus, feminine striving for

social approval and the behaviours it evokes is the feminine
counterpart to male achievement striving under the set to
appear "intelligent". As the uncomplicated nature of masculine ambition permits the male to strive for money, education,
and status simultaneously, no choice of objectives is elicited from him. As choice is demanded from the female, the
conventional path is the route to marriage.

Ironically, if we equate achievement with social mobility, which is essentially what we are doing when we use income
or occupational prestige as indices of accomplishment, the
social mobility of females whose "achievement" results from
marriage is more highly correlated with their measured intelligence than is that of males, whose social mobility results
from their occupational efforts (Haan, 1964).

INTELLIGENCE AND INTELLECTUAL INTERESTS IN ADULTS

Social pressures for males are such that one would expect all but the socially rebellious to attempt to enter the
highest status occupations for which they can qualify. The
more ambiguous expectation for women in the United States
and in other technologically oriented nations has produced
a residual category of females who do not conform with traditional role expectations. They either eschew the marital
role altogether or they attempt to combine marriage and occupational achievement. The antecedents and correlates of
intellectual interests in adults of both sexes have been studied intensively in a number of longitudinal studies. These
studies tell us something of the attributes of men and women
who are to be found in, or who hope to enter, the occupational
categories that entail heavy demands for intellectual performance.

In all of the studies, there is considerable difference
between the variables identified as predictors of intellectual capacity and intellectual interest for males and for
females. Crandall and Battle (1970) and Kagan and Moss
(1962) report that intellectually oriented young women were
women whose mothers had displayed distinctive orientations
toward them when they were infants and small children. The
maternal behaviours associated with intellectual competence
in females are the reverse of the stereotyped conventional
recommendations. Females who persist in problem situations
as adults had mothers who were unprotective and even hostile
toward them when they were infants and toddlers (Kagan and

Moss, 1962). The most consistent correlates of intellectual
effort in Crandall and Battle's (1970) adult females were
lack of maternal babying and protectiveness. The general
picture emerging from the results of both studies is that
the girls who persist in intellectual concern as adults are
girls who have resisted (or perhaps been excused from) the
traditional sex-role socialization of Western females.

For males, the picture is the reverse. Males who display strong effort in academic learning or achievement-
testing situations are males who have been encouraged to do
so by their mothers (Bayley and Shaefer, 1964; Crandall and
Battle, 1970) and who quite possibly are more fearful than
most of their same sex peers of rough body contact or peer
disapproval. Among males, boys whose relationships with
their mothers have been warm and affectionate (Bayley and
Shaefer, 1964) and whose mothers apparently genuinely invest
effort in their training and education are advantaged intellectually (Bayley and Shaefer, 1964; Crandall and Battle,
1970; Kagan and Moss, 1962).

The impact of socialization on intellectual functioning
and on sex-role learning is full of paradoxes. For both
sexes, the individual who succeeds best and persists the
longest in intellectual matters does not exemplify the usual
behaviour in individuals of his or her sex. Among males,
it is quite possible that intellectual facility must be encouraged by an interpersonal relationship which develops in
the earliest months (Bayley and Shaefer, 1964). For females,
the more necessary ingredient may be the acquiescence and
support of a mother who is able to allow her daughter to be
less than a perfect lady.

In addition to divergence from traditional sex-role expectations, further data indicate that males and females differ generally in the goals they expect to accomplish through
intellectual effort. For males, intellectual accomplishment
is not inherently different from other forms of status striving. Hence, the applicability of the predictions stemming
from achievement motivation theorists, which apply equally
well to business enterprise and to the most trivial of intellectual games. For females, status appears to be relatively
inconsequential. Females who invest effort in intellectual
performance appear to have internalized standards of their
parents (Kipnis, 1974). Women who have achieved distinction in intellectual fields have usually done so as a result
of intense interest in the content of the field, and the ap-

plication of intellectual effort to that content. It is also of at least passing interest that status striving in women is expressed in the behaviours related to courtship and mating, as described in the previous section, and not through intellectual achievement striving, as it seems to be in males.

OCCUPATIONAL CHOICE AND OCCUPATIONAL EFFECTIVENESS IN ADULTHOOD

McClelland (1973) has argued with considerable cogency that our tendency to perceive intelligence (at least as measured by most tests) as an unmixed asset in vocational effectiveness is rather overdone. He points out that the evidence is weak that intelligence furthers success in many occupations, and that for the most part, intelligence seems to be necessary to acquire the school grades and the academic degrees that permit entrance to the various occupations rather than to further success once occupational selections have been made. He cites as evidence various studies in Britain and the United States (Berg, 1970; Hudson, 1960) which carefully document that neither amount of education nor grades in school are related to success in a considerable number of vocations.

Intelligence tests, true to their original construction, predict primarily grades in school rather than vocational and occupational success, although it is correct that there is a slight degree of correspondence between intelligence as measured by tests and eventual occupational attainment. For a provocative discussion of the ways in which the importance of intelligence has been exaggerated for many male occupations, the interested reader may consult McClelland (1973). The present discussion will be concerned primarily with the basic occupational choice made almost universally by females, but only rarely by males – the choice of the familial, procreative role versus the selection of an extra-familial occupation or profession. In recent decades, the technologically oriented nations have been in the throes of a prolonged struggle reflecting the conflict between the ideologies perpetuating the traditional dedication of women to home and family and their increasing tendency to enter the extra-familial occupational and professional world. The implications of their choices for genetic selection and for the chances of providing subsequent generations with advantageous environments have only rarely been discussed.

If one considers the undertaking of the parental role

from a biological viewpoint, it is obvious that parental obligations impose quite different commitments of time and effort
on males and females. Although the contribution of the male
and female parent is on the average equal, it is the female
who undergoes the discomforts and inconvenience of the gestation period, whose body furnishes the prenatal environment
of the developing infant, and who is biologically equipped
for lactation.

Thus the female cannot contribute her genetic potential
without some subsequent investment. To the extent that this
investment is penalized and can be averted by appropriate action, the intelligent female may very well choose to keep her
genes to herself. The situation of the intelligent male is
entirely different; as his procreative and occupational roles
do not ordinarily infringe upon each other, he can engage in
both. In fact, his marital and parental responsibilities may
serve to furnish incentives for occupational and professional
advancement.

A recent sociological treatise concerned mainly with
American data documents the thesis that marriage is an institution which has quite different effects on the physical, emotional and occupational status of men and women.* Bernard
(1972) argues that for men, marriage tends to promote mental
and physical health, as judged by such factors as suicide
rates among the married and the unmarried, occupational pro-
motions, and visits to doctors and psychiatrists. For women,
the opposite is true; women who marry, and to a lesser extent,
women who marry but never bear children, score higher on many
indices of mental and physical health. Her data support the
thesis that marriage is good for men but bad for women. She
interprets her data with reference to the "marriage gradient",
a concept which refers to our cultural conviction that men
should be superior to their mates in such attributes as
height, age, occupational status, and presumably, intelligence. As certain of these attributes are actually fairly
evenly distributed between the sexes (and intelligence is one
of these), assortive mating becomes difficult for males at
the bottom of some dimensions - there are few if any women
lower than they - and for women who score near the top, as
there are few if any men who are superior. The never-married
man and the never-married woman come from opposite ends of
the continua of factors deemed important to married bliss,

* See also Chapter 9 by Mayo.

and those who remain single at higher ages represent the
"bottom of the barrel" and the "cream of the crop" of their
respective sexes.

The attribute of intelligence, with which we are primarily concerned, is one which demonstrates the effect Bernard
describes. .Terman's follow-up data on his sample of gifted
children reports the intelligence of the spouses of his gifted
population at mid-life (Terman and Oden, 1959). The spouses
of the gifted males were far inferior to their mates in intelligence. The spouses of the gifted females were also inferi-
or to them in intelligence, but less so. The gifted females
were also less likely to marry, especially if they had been
to college. Gifted women who did not graduate from college
were prone to personal maladjustment and to divorce, although
their marriage rates were higher than those of the college
graduates. Other studies of women who are highly selected
intellectually or professionally also show this effect.
Ginzberg (1966) reports data on a sample of women who held
fellowships at Columbia University between the years 1945
and 1951. Of these women, 28 per cent remained single (in
contrast to 6 per cent of women in their age group in the
general population). Even the women who married, married
late and did not bear children for some time.

On the opposite end of the dimension of education, demographic data from Europe disclose quite different changes in
marital and child bearing rates in recent decades. Bernard
(1972) had contrasted American and European patterns of marriage, maintaining that for much of European history, population control had been maintained through limitation of
marriage and consequent limitation of fertility. However,
trends in marital practice demonstrate that in almost all
European nations average ages of brides at their first marriage have been steadily declining. The trend has been constant throughout the twentieth century, but has been especially marked since World War II (Sullerot, 1971). Recent data
from Britain show large increases in the number of brides
under twenty (*Society* 1974). Many such brides bear children
soon after marriage, they are married to husbands who can
ill afford parenthood, and their subsequent divorce rate is
higher than that of brides who marry at a later age. But
their early pregnancy ties them into a pattern of marriage;
their own poor and interrupted education does not equip them
to both support and care for a child, and their former spouses are unable or unwilling to contribute financial support.

Thus, remarriage becomes an economic necessity.

Myrdal and Klein (1968) have described the changes being brought about by alterations in women's roles in industrialized society. They have pointed out that longevity, decrease infant mortality, fewer pregnancies per woman, and changed jo requirements in a technological society make it almost inevitable that women engage in work outside their homes. The question for all of the more highly industrialized nations is how women can combine such work with the child-bearing and child-rearing responsibilities which someone must perform if we are to perpetuate ourselves, even if at the reduced rate many of us now see as the more desirable.

From many of the data in Myrdal and Klein's book it is evident that Americans and Europeans have approached our present period of rapid social change from different directions. In the United States, marriage has traditionally been almost universal, took place at an early age, and during much of our history, was followed by child-bearing at a rapid pace Despite the close to universal rate of marriage and the fact that until recently few women worked outside their homes, American women have always been well educated as compared with the women of other nations. Education was seen as an asset in marriage and child-rearing as well as in work. Further, American institutions and the professions considered to be female in the United States are occupations which facilitate or at least make it possible to combine family and work responsibilities.

But it has become increasingly apparent that women who hope to achieve occupationally will not find it easy to bear and rear children. Accordingly, in the United States, more educated women delay marriage and child-bearing for longer, women with children less frequently work outside their homes, and childlessness is almost at its maximum rate among our most affluent families, in many of which both husband and wife are employed in positions which provide good incomes (Ritchey and Stokes, 1974). Our most "successful" women, if one judges by occupational criteria such as income or professional recognition, are women who avoid child-bearing altogether.

Most European nations have traditionally had a much larger proportion of single women, most of whom worked throughout their lives to support themselves. However, in most nations such women were neither affluent nor educated, and their circumstances confined them to low status occupations. Among more privileged women, "marriage bars" operated to prevent

women who had already attained professional status from
marrying. Married women were preoccupied with child-bearing
and child-rearing, and many of their children did not survive
childhood.

Thus, the problem of combining child-bearing and child-
rearing responsibilities with work outside the family has
been deferred to our age and the generations now living and
long term continuation of the trends now displayed both in
Europe and the United States could only be regarded as un-
fortunate. The withdrawal of intelligent, well educated
women from child-bearing and child-rearing only serves to insure that a larger proportion of the next generation does
not share in the advantages secured by this one. Increases
in rates of child-bearing by the disadvantaged, on the other
hand, amounts to the perpetuation of poverty. Intelligence
tests cannot be expected to tell us if the intellectual capacities of future generations are impaired by our strategies
of population control. The methods by which intelligence
tests are calibrated insure that the average IQ will always
be approximately 100 and cultural change always necessitates
test revisions, at least within a generation. But if we
consider intelligence to imply the capacity to profit from
experience and to solve problems through reasoning, the
dropping out of our most intelligent women from child-bearing
and child-rearing must be presumed to result in the subtraction of their assets from those transmitted to the next generation.

This is so whether one believes that intelligence is
determined primarily by genes, by environment, or by some
combination or interaction between the two. If the mechanism
is genetic, the chain of inheritance ends with the woman who
bears no children. If intelligence results from access to a
stimulating and enriched environment, Americans and Europeans
share a system in which the most advantaged environments are
procured by those who have few or no children. Last, the
alternative that mounting evidence suggests is most tenable,
the woman who bears no children withdraws both those of her
qualities which are transmitted through genetic action and
the qualities which permit her to teach her children within
the context of a close and continuous personal relationship.
Most studies find mothers to be the more salient parent in
their impact on offspring; no doubt this is the result of
the mother's larger share in child care and the closeness
of daily association (Siegelman *et al.* 1970).

Institutional arrangements which provide compensation for work in the non-familial context only, and which base their rates on a quality such as intelligence which women share, will inevitably lure more intelligent women into non-procreative functions. All of the technologically advanced countries of the West, including Britain, the Scandinavian countries, and Canada, Australia, and New Zealand share this predicament. All are countries in which knowledge of birth control techniques is widely disseminated and utilized, and in which much is made of intelligence as an asset in the occupational world. They also share the derogation of the feminine sex role, a derogation which leads to the assumption that to escape from it is surely an accomplishment. Finally, they share an increasing secularization, especially among the more educated and intelligent parts of their populations, which disqualifies religious attitudes from forming a significant basis for the formation of attitudes toward parenthood. The challenge is therefore whether or not a basis can be found to establish loyalty to a societal rather than an individual standard of well being. Such a standard is necessary to reaffirm the desirability of behaviour which goes beyond self aggrandizement, and which can look beyond immediate self interest and our own time to justify itself. Failure to meet the challenge will mean that those who inherit the earth will be the children of those who could get no better jobs.

REFERENCES

Bayley, N. (1957). Data on the growth of intelligence between 16 and 21 years as measured by the Wechsler-Bellevue Scale. *Journal of Genetic Psychology*, <u>90</u>, 3-15.

Bayley, N. and Schaefer, E.S. (1964). Correlations of maternal and child behaviors with the development of mental abilities Data from the Berkeley Growth Study. *Society for Research in Child Development Monograph*, <u>29</u>, 63-79.

Berg, I. (1970). "Education and Jobs: The Great Training Robbery". Praeger, New York.

Bernard, J. (1972). "The Future of Marriage". Bantam,New York.

Binet, A. and Simon, T. (1905). Sur la nécessité d'établir un diagnostic scientifique des états inférieurs de l'intélligence. *Année Psychologique*, <u>11</u>.

Borow, H. (1966). Development of occupational motives and roles. *In* "Review of Child Development Research". (L.W. Hoffman and M.L. Hoffman, eds.) Vol. II. Russell Sage Foundation, New York.

Bradway, K.P. and Thompson, C.W. (1962). Intelligence at adulthood: A twenty-five year follow up. *Journal of Educational Psychology*, 53, 1-14.

Brooks, F.D. (1921). Changes in mental traits with age determined by annual retests. *Teachers College Contributions to Education*, 116.

Brophy, J.E. and Good, T.L. (1970). Teachers' communication of differential expectations for children's classroom performance: Some behavioural data. *Journal of Educational Psychology*, 61, 365-374.

Caplow, T. (1964). "The Sociology of Work". McGraw-Hill, New York. (Originally published: University of Minnesota Press, Minneapolis, 1954.)

Coleman, J.S. (1961). "The Adolescent Society". Free Press, New York.

Commission on Population Growth and the American Future. (1972). "Population and the American Future". Signet, New York.

Conrad, H.S., Jones, H.E. and Hsiao, H.H. (1933). Sex differences in mental growth and decline. *Journal of Educational Psychology*, 24, 161-169.

Crandall, V.C. and Battle, E.S. (1970). The antecedents and adult correlates of academic and intellectual achievement effort. *In* "Minnesota Symposia on Child Psychology". (J.P. Hill, ed.) Vol. IV. University of Minnesota Press, Minneapolis.

Folger, J.K. and Nam, C.B. (1960). Education of the American population. *Census Monograph*, Bureau of the Census, Department of Commerce, Washington.

Garai, J.E. and Scheinfeld, A. (1968). Sex differences in mental and behavioural traits. *Genetic Psychology Monographs*, 77, 169-299.

Ginzberg, E. (1966). "Life Styles of Educated Women". Columbia University Press, New York.

Goslin, D.A. (1963). "The Search for Ability". Russell Sage Foundation, New York.

Gunn, B. (1964). Children's conceptions of occupational prestige. *Personnel Guidance Journal*, 42, 558-563.

Haan, N. (1963). Proposed model of ego functioning: Coping and defence mechanisms in relationship to IQ change. *Psychological Monographs, 77,* (No. 571).

Haan, N. (1964). The relationship of ego functioning and intelligence to social status and social mobility. *Journal of Abnormal and Social Psychology, 69,* 594-605.

Horner, M.S. (1972). Toward an understanding of achievement-related conflicts in women. *Journal of Social Issues, 28,* 157-175.

Hudson, L. (1960). Degree class and attainment in scientific research. *British Journal of Psychology, 51,* 67-73.

Kagan, J. and Moss, H.A. (1962). "Birth to Maturity". Wiley and Sons, New York.

Kagan, J., Sontag, L.W., Baker, C.T. and Nelson, V.L. (1958). Personality and IQ change. *Journal of Abnormal and Social Psychology, 56,* 261-266.

Kipnis, D.M. (1974). Inner Direction, Other Direction, and Achievement Motivation. *Human Development, 17,* 321-343.

Klinger, E. (1966). Fantasy need achievement as a motivational construct. *Psychological Bulletin, 66,* 291-308.

Klinger, E. (1967). Modelling effects on achievement imagery. *Journal of Personality and Social Psychology, 7,* 49-62.

Lorge, I. (1969). Schooling makes a difference. *In* "Intelligence: Some Recurring Issues". (L. Tyler, ed.) Van Nostrand-Reinhold, New York.

McClelland, D.C. (1973). Testing for competence rather than for intelligence. *American Psychologist, 28,* 1-14.

McClelland, D.C., Atkinson, J.W., Clark, R. and Lowell, E.L. (1953). "The Achievement Motive". Appleton-Century-Crofts, New York.

McClelland, D.C. and Winter, D.G. (1969). "Motivating Economic Achievement". Free Press, New York.

Maccoby, E.E. (1966). Sex differences in intellectual functioning. *In* "The Development of Sex Differences". (E.E. Maccoby, ed.) Stanford University Press, Stanford.

Mahone, C.H. (1960). Fear of failure and unrealistic vocational aspiration. *Journal of Abnormal and Social Psycho-*

logy, <u>60</u>, 253-261.

Meyer, W.J. and Thompson, G.G. (1956). Sex differences in the distribution of teacher approval and disapproval among sixth-grade children. *Journal of Educational Psychology*, <u>47</u>, 385-396.

Miner, J.B. (1957). "Intelligence in the United States". Springer, New York.

Monahan, L., Kuhn, D. and Shaver, P. (1974). Intrapsychic versus cultural explanations of the "fear of success" motive. *Journal of Personality and Social Psychology*, <u>29</u>, 60-64.

Myrdal, A. and Klein, V. (1956 and 1968). "Women's Two Roles". Routledge and Kegan Paul.

Patai, R. (1967). "Women in the Modern World". Free Press, New York.

Ritchey, P.N. and Stokes, C.S. (1967). Correlates of childlessness and expectations to remain childless: U.S. *Social Forces*, <u>52</u>, 349-356.

Serbin, L.A., O'Leary, D.K., Kent, R.N. and Tonick, I.J. (1973). A comparison of teacher response to the problem and preacademic behaviour of boys and girls. *Child Development*, <u>44</u>, 796-804.

Siegelman, E., Block, J., Block, J. and von der Lippe, A. (1970). Antecedents of optimal psychological adjustment. *Journal of Consulting and Clinical Psychology*, <u>35</u>, 283-289.

Society, (1974). Social science and the citizen. <u>11</u>, (5, Whole No. 91), 12.

Stein, A. and Bailey, M.M. (1973). The socialization of achievement orientation in females. *Psychological Bulletin*, <u>80</u>, 345-366.

Sullerot, E. (1971). "Woman, Society and Change". McGraw-Hill, New York.

Terman, L.M., Burks, B.S. and Jensen, D.W. (1930). "Genetic Studies of Genius: III. The Promise of Youth: Follow-up Studies of a Thousand Gifted Children". Stanford University Press, Stanford.

Terman, L.M. and Oden, M. (1959). "The Gifted Group at Mid-Life". Stanford University Press, Stanford.

Turner, R.H. (1964). Some aspects of women's ambition. *American Journal of Sociology*, 70, 271-285.

Veroff, J., Wilcox, S. and Atkinson, J.W. (1953). The achievement motive in high school and college age women. *Journal of Abnormal and Social Psychology*, 48, 108-119.

Warner, W.L. and Lunt, P.S. (1941). "The Social Life of a Modern Community". Yankee City Series, Vol. I. Yale University Press, New Haven.

Wechsler, D. (1939). "The Measurement of Adult Intelligence". Williams and Wilkins, Baltimore.

Wechsler, D. (1949). "Manual, Wechsler Intelligence Scale for Children". Psychological Corporation, New York.

Wechsler, D. (1958). "The Measurement and Appraisal of Adult Intelligence". 4th Ed. Williams and Wilkins, Baltimore.

Weinstein, M.S. (1969). Achievement motivation and risk preference. *Journal of Personality and Social Psychology*, 13, 153-172.

6. SEX DIFFERENCES IN THE ORGANIZATION OF PERCEPTION AND COGNITION

Diane McGuinness

Individual variation fascinated Victorian psychologists and
led to the development of the concept of categories of intelligence as well as producing numerous studies on sex differences. These were brilliantly summarized by Havelock Ellis
in 1896. Since this time only three major reviews have
matched his endeavour: Garai and Scheinfeld (1968), Ounsted
and Taylor (1972) and Maccoby and Jacklin (1974). It is puzzling that an interest in sex differences was not stimulated
by Ellis' efforts and there may be many reasons for this.
Apart from prejudice and fear, one major difficulty is that
the investigation of sex differences has always proceeded
in an extremely piecemeal fashion. Even psychologists currently writing in the field tend not to make sex differences
the centre of a unified experimental effort. Thus the literature abounds with findings on gender effects that are an epi-
phenomenon of a study that was measuring something else.

Secondly, a fragmentary literature lends itself to a type
of review that while informative, is often simply overwhelming.
An unselective and unbiased review of any research area is
obviously to be welcomed, but there is also a need for a deliberately selective attitude – one which searches for common-
alities across the whole range of performance. Such an induc-
tive attitude must do more than specify generalities, but must
tease data apart and discover links between certain phenomena.
This route has obvious dangers, but I feel it is the only way
to generate productive and testable hypotheses.

This chapter is, therefore, selectively concerned with
whether or not specific sex characteristics in sensory and
perceptual processes contribute to higher-order abilities.
This raises a new issue in psychology because it enables one
to determine whether there are unifying factors in all psychological processes. For example, the consistent and well-known

differences between the sexes in linguistic and visuo-spatial
ability may have their counterpart in primary or antecendent
aptitudes and biases. Note that this single fact provides a
powerful heuristic device for psychology as a whole, for it
eliminates the necessity of employing unwieldy longitudinal
techniques. The power of this paradigm has been consistently
overlooked.

In the following sections I trace the development of
sensory-motor biases.

SEX DIFFERENCES IN RESPONSE CHARACTERISTICS

Responses in Infancy

In early infancy boys are awake for significantly longer periods than girls, and are generally more active during
these waking periods (Moss, 1967). Male activity is considerably stimulated by the mother, who spends more time in
direct physical contact with her son (Moss, 1967; Lewis, 1972.
Maternal attention has been found to correlate with increased
exploratory activity in later infancy (Rubenstein, 1967).
These studies generally refer to fairly gross motor responses
Studies investigating activity levels involving both
gross and discreet actions often find no differences between
the sexes for the total duration of activity (see Maccoby and
Jacklin, 1973 for review). Differences are observed when distinct types of responses are investigated: as children develop, response differences begin to reflect more and more the
qualitative aspects of behaviour. Responses are organized
for a purpose, which is to achieve an understanding and control of the environment.

Thus by nursery school age, males are more apt to engage in rough and tumble play and aggressive acts (e.g. Smith
and Connally, 1972). Goldberg and Lewis (1969) showed that
one-year-old boys are more attracted to the unusual, and
spend more time playing with objects that are not toys, while
devising novel ways of using them. Girls' activity is generally directed to play more specifically suited to the particular toy.

No sex differences are apparent for the total amount of
vocalization, but there are qualitative differences. Males
and females show similar rates of early babbling (Moss, 1967;
Lewis, 1972), but over a period of time a much higher rate
of vocal interchange develops between mothers and daughters

(Goldberg and Lewis, 1969; McCall, 1972; Messer and Lewis, 1972). Lewis' study (1972) suggests that this occurs because of a complex interaction between the vocal behaviour of the infant and the behaviour of the mother: girls receive much less physical attention from the mother (supporting the findings of Moss, 1967), and they appear to be more comforted by "distal" stimulation, whereas boys require physical comfort, rather than speech. Although the sexes did not differ in their amount of vocalization, Lewis found that mothers actually reinforced more of the boys' vocalizations than those of the girls. When he examined his data in terms of the mother's response to the infant's vocalization, he found that 50 per cent of male, but only 37 per cent of female vocalizations elicited a maternal response. However, 67 per cent of female vocalizations occurred in *response* to maternal behaviour (despite the lower level of reinforcement which would follow these responses). Mothers do not appear to speak more "effectively" to one or the other sex: in a complex series of experiments Phillips (1973) could find no difference in the number and complexity of words each time the mother spoke to male and female infants aged 8, 18 and 28 months.

   In general there is little support for the idea that differential reinforcement by the mother could be responsible for the female's greater language ability (discussed later in this chapter). Lewis' study might even suggest the opposite. The relevant issue is the function of vocalization to the female. Girls appear to use vocalizations to communiate, to acquire information about their environment indirectly or "distally", and they also appear to respond to the emotional inflection in speech (to be discussed later). The way in which vocalizations are employed by the sexes are illustrated in Table I: Smith and Connally show that boys make more noises, whereas girls use more speech. This greater use of vocal ability for verbal communication by girls may account for findings at later ages that girls have greater clarity and quality of speech (McCarthy, 1930; Harms and Spiker, 1959; Hull *et al.* 1971; Oetzel, 1967). This finding is strongly paralleled by girls' ability to sing in tune. Male monotones outnumber females by about 8 to 1 (Bentley, 1966; Roberts, 1972).

Responses in the Child and Adult

   Garai and Scheinfeld (1968) have categorized the sex dif-

TABLE I

Distributions of Vocalizations* as a
Function of Age and Sex

	Vocalizations Boys	Girls	Talk to Child Boys	Girls	Play Noise Boys	Girls
3.9-4.9 Years	82.9	82.4	47.0	65.6	27.7	7.6
2.9-3.9 Years	52.8	54.9	24.3	36.7	19.8	8.2
Combined Means	67.9	68.7	31.8	46.0	23.8	7.9

* Means per hour based upon sampling ongoing behaviour every ten seconds.

From Smith and Connally (1972).

ferences in response characteristics as perceptual-motor
(tasks on which males perform better) and as "clerical skills"
(tasks on which females perform better). Other writers
(Tyler, 1965; Hutt, 1972a) have been content to accept this
type of categorization without assessing the part played by
perceptual components. Two basic findings emerge when considering only response parameters. Males are superior from
mid-childhood onward in speed of reaction time. As their
ability largely parallels muscular development, causing an
improvement over girls at about 10-11 years, which reaches
its asymptote at about 18 years and remains stable throughout life (Noble *et al.* 1964; Simon, 1967; Fairweather and
Hutt, 1972) it seems reasonable to assume that speed of responses may be related to increasing muscle mass and force.
    By contrast females excel in manual dexterity involving
discreet movements of the fingers and fine coordination. In
a test of manual dexterity, requiring subjects to shift a peg
along a series of holes on a board as rapidly as possible,
Annett (1970) found that females were superior over all ages
tested ($3\frac{1}{2}$-15 years), using a sample of 219 subjects. Superiority for females at all ages in most tests of manual dexterity has been well documented (see Tyler, 1965). It does appear
therefore, that males excel in speed of gross motor outflow,
while females excel in speed of more discreet or finely controlled motor responses.

Information must be processed before a response is made:
the speed of output is determined by both the type of information and the type of response required. When the information is in the form of a visual display, and the response requires large muscle units, males excel to an overwhelming
degree. Cook and Shephard (1958) found that boys are superi-
or when operating a lever to change direction of a spot of
light at ages 5, 10 and 20 years. In a similar task where
subjects had to displace a green disc to coincide with a red
ring that appeared in one of forty-nine positions, boys and
men, aged 5-70 years, consistently scored more correct matches
over all ages. Ammons *et al.* (1955) also reported that in
tracking tasks, boys' performance begins to diverge noticeably from the girls at about 11-12 and thereafter is consistently superior. In two further studies on adults (Noble and
Hays, 1966; Shephard *et al.* 1962) males were found to be
greatly superior in producing rapidly timed movement to
visual displays.

When information is in the form of symbolic or semantic
material, and the response required demands attention to detail, females are superior. Tasks such as typing, cancella-
tion tests, and others categorized as "clerical" (Garai and
Scheinfeld, 1968) are always performed more efficiently by
women (Tyler, 1965). The WISC and the WAIS coding and digit
substitution tests are consistently performed better by females (see Chapter 5 by Kipnis for a description of these
tests).

The distinction between visual figural input, and semantic and symbolic input is highly relevant in explaining sex
differences, as the sexes are found to utilize these types
of information differently. In addition to sex differences
in handling input, there are also important response differences. The tasks which favour females generally require
small and reasonably well-coordinated movement, while those
which favour males measure larger motor processes. In order
to disentangle stimulus effects from response effects a
female-typical response should be paired with a male-specific
input, or vice versa.

The nearest approach to this type of experiment is that
of Fairweather and Hutt (1972) where they varied information
in bits in a choice reaction time test. These authors found
that at ages 5-7 years, girls were faster in simple reaction
time (RT), a cross-over effect occurred where sexes were
matched at about 8-9 years, and at older ages boys were

superior. However, when information was increased (choice
reaction time: CRT), the girls were found to be superior at
all ages and this difference increased as the information
load (in bits) was increased. In their adult sample the difference largely disappeared although no details of the size
and age of this sample were given. Since we know that men
are faster in RT, this finding would mean that females process information faster across all ages. When assessing the
types of tasks that favour women, such as clerical skills,
it is important to recognize that certain of these tasks are
in fact tests of choice reaction time (CRT). An example par
excellence is typing, where information from a written or
printed sheet is rapidly transferred by pressing the appropriate keys. Speed of typing reflects both manual dexterity
and speed of information processing. As yet there are no
conclusions as to what is involved in rapid information processing. It could be that females can attend to a greater
amount of information at any one time. This is supported by
new data reported later in this chapter.

SEX DIFFERENCES IN SENSORY SENSITIVITY

Sex differences in sensory ability provide some of the
most important evidence on the development of perceptual differences. It is difficult to argue that such basic sensitivities are produced by subtle differences in social learning.
If there are consistent differences in sensory capacities between the sexes throughout life, it is then conceivable that
such differences may contribute to other more complex central
processes.

Sensory Capacity in Infancy

In the very young infant neither the ear or the eye is
functional at any level approaching that of the adult (Spears
and Hohle, 1967): thus studies on the very young infant will
probably never be particularly informative about sex differences in sensory capacity. An added difficulty is that for
the first few weeks of life the female is physically more
advanced than the male (Garai and Scheinfeld, 1968), and
where (minimal) differences in responsivity are found, the
greater sensitivity of the female is perhaps more attributa-
ble to maturity than to any particular sensory abilities.
At this early age tactile sensitivity appears to be

greater in females (Lipsitt and Levy, 1959; Bell and Costello, 1964; Wolff, 1969) but negative findings have also been reported (Lipsitt and Levy, 1959; Gullicksen and Crowell, 1964). Data on the neonate for the auditory and visual modalities show little effect of sex (Engel *et al.* 1968; Eisenberg, 1972; Korner, 1970 and 1971; Korner and Thoman, 1970): in view of the differences found subsequently this suggests that neonates are not sufficiently advanced to provide much useful information on this issue. Korner's review (1973) essentially confirms this view, particularly for the auditory and visual modalities.

Sensory Capacity in the Child and Adult

For both children and adults females show greater tactile sensitivity in the fingers and hands (Axelrod, 1959; Weinstein and Sersen, 1961; Ippolitov, 1972), often to the extent that there is no overlap between male and female scores. It seems clear that this greater sensitivity contributes in some measure to the manual skills in females described in the preceding section. The threshold for touch does not appear to be related to sensitivity for temperature: Clark and Mehl (1971) found no significant sex differences either in response to faint or to painful heat intensities. For elderly subjects, men were found to be more sensitive to heat, while being more able to tolerate pain.

Studies on auditory threshold have consistently demonstrated superior high frequency hearing for females. The sex difference increases with higher frequencies and with age (Corso, 1959; Eagles *et al.* 1963; Hull *et al.* 1971; McGuinness, 1972). The most important and consistent sex differences in auditory sensitivity are found in tests involving responses to intensity. As I consider the development of speech and reaction to differences in intensity in the final section, the evidence will be considered in some detail. Females are intolerant of loud levels of sound both in childhood (Elliott, 1971) and adulthood (McGuinness, 1972). In my own work, the level at which adult subjects set a volume of sound as just "too loud" was measured. The mean scores across all frequencies were 75 db for the females and 83 db for males. As loudness doubles subjectively at about 9-10 db, the findings suggest that by about the level of 85 db, females will hear the volume of any sound as twice as loud as males.

Greater sensitivity by females to volume is also found
in other tasks. Zaner *et al.* (1968) report that when children aged 4-8 years were asked to judge which aspect of an
auditory stimulus was varying, girls were significantly more
able to distinguish between changes in intensity. The sexes
did not differ in their ability to notice changes in frequency, duration, or number of signals. Also when Shuter (1964)
factor analysed her results on 200 male and female students
of above-average musical ability, a broad general factor of
musical ability was found. An appreciation of intensity changes was included in this factor for women, but was entirely
absent for men. Shuter also found no sex differences in
pitch discrimination between the sexes, a finding which I
have replicated (McGuinness, 1972).

Women's greater sensitivity to sound also occurs during
sleep. Wilson and Zung (1966) monitored EEG, and instructed
subjects to waken at the sound of two specific stimuli, but
to remain asleep during all other noises. The sexes behaved
similarly in the instructed condition; all awakened, but significantly more EEG activation occurred in females to the
noises that subjects were told to ignore. A further study
in which subjects were unaware of the response they were producing, showed that women habituated more slowly on an autonomic measure of digital blood flow to a series of repeated
tones (McGuinness, 1972). Slower habituation appears to be
reflected by intolerance of auditory repetition in females.
Efficiency in hearing was found not to be continuous across
a range of tasks. No significant correlations were found between tests of threshold, intensity judgment, pitch discrimination and tolerance of repetition. This suggests that
the total auditory experience results from "multiplexing" a
number of unrelated sensitivities (Lindsay, 1970). Of the
tasks investigated only pitch discrimination showed any effect of training, improving with the number of years spent
in musical study.

There are also sex differences in the visual modality,
men being more sensitive in the light, and women more sensitive in the dark. The ability of males in photopic visual
acuity is well documented both for static and moving targets (Roberts, 1964; Burg and Hulbert, 1961; Burg, 1966;
McGuinness, in press), but the sex difference does not appear until mid to late teens (e.g. Skoff and Pollack, 1969).

As there are no comparable data to those presented for
the auditory mode, I have used a series of tasks to investi-

gate threshold, intensity judgment, acuity and short-term
memory processes in vision in men and women (McGuinness, in
press). In this study the intensity judgment test reversed
the sex differences found in audition, with males significantly more sensitive. While men appeared to have superior
cone vision, women were more sensitive in the tests performed
in the dark, adapting more rapidly and to lower threshold
levels than the men. This superior performance in the dark
was also found on the test of "iconic" or very-short-term-
memory, where women had significantly longer visual "holding"
than the men. This difference disappeared entirely when the
same test was performed after light adaptation.

In a continuation of the persistence experiment,
McGuinness and Lewis (In press) investigated sex differences
in young adults in response to a Ganzfeld (a field of uni-
form brightness) and to an after-image. Men showed longer
durations of visual experience in both cases. The visual
experience of the men, during the Ganzfeld study, was significantly more variable. They reported large fluctuations in
disappearance and reappearance of colour, effects which did
not occur in the women. An important and unexpected result
in both studies was that the women were more sensitive to
the long-wave spectrum of light: in the Ganzfeld study they
held the perception of red significantly longer than green,
and during the after-image study, all of the female subjects
but only 50 per cent of the males, reported seeing red.
There were no differences in reporting other colours in the
spectrum.

Other visual phenomena have also shown sex differences.
Boys are more susceptible to experiencing rapid reversals in
a reversible figures test (Garai and Scheinfeld, 1968), and
these results have been confirmed by Immergluck and Mearini
(1969) on children aged 9, 11 and 13. Boys had higher rates
of reversals over all ages. The authors noted that in a previous study on adults a high correlation was found for rate
of reversals and performance on the Rod and Frame test (RFT).
As I shall demonstrate later, this suggests that experiencing
rapid figural reversals is related to visual-spatial ability.

Sex differences in other visual tasks are not as stable.
Pohl and Caldwell (1968) found that women had lower thresholds
for the PHI phenomenon (the apparent movement of two alternatively lit figures). Females also show less susceptibility
to the autokinetic effect, where a stationary light appears
to move in the dark (Voth, 1941; Chaplin, 1955) although in

later studies (Aranoff, 1973; Simpson and Vaught, 1973) these findings were not replicated. It is possible that many of these results are related to the apparently superior performance of females in the dark as shown above, and that where dark adaptation and room light conditions are not precisely controlled, sex differences may be exaggerated.

The evidence on sensory capacity shows that females are more sensitive to most modalities at threshold, and that they have a certain advantage in some aspects of tactile and auditory processing. Men have superior foveal vision and greater sensitivity to light, and generally greater photopic persistence.

SEX DIFFERENCES IN ATTENTION

In 1890 William James presented an extensive categorization of attentional systems in which he discussed the evidence for involuntary (reflex) and voluntary (selective) processes. Recently this type of analysis has been extended, by Pribam and McGuinness (1975) to present a comprehensive model of attention based upon both behavioural and physiological data. Three basic attentional systems are considered in the model: reflex attention, or orienting (Sokolov, 1963), a succeeding phase of vigilant readiness in which the input is coded to produce a neuronal model, and a coordinating system requiring effort. Each category is accompanied by quite distinct behavioural and physiological changes reflecting both autonomic and CNS activity.

In the quest for the organizing forces at work in sex differences in perception, the emphasis in this section is on the development of attentional systems in the infant, and how infants differ in stimulus preference. It appears from the data that at ages where infants have not as yet been affected by selective reinforcement, they nevertheless show an interest in certain stimuli and not others. Types of stimulus information are more salient to one sex than the other, and it will be shown that this relates to the way in which the developing child seeks to control and interpret his environment.

"Attention" in the infant can either be assessed by measuring an initial orienting reflex, which produces behavioural alerting (sudden change in heart rate, and an initial discharge of the sympathetic nervous system), or it can be measured by the duration of the processes which accompany sustained vigilance to new information (fixation time, and the amount of heart deceleration, smiling and babbling). In the first type of study, infants are selectively habituated to one stimulus, and then their reaction to a novel one, which is either contrasting or highly similar, is tested: the degree of similarity in responding indicates the accuracy with which the habituated stimulus was coded. In the second type of study, the infant is usually presented with a range of stimuli and the amount of time he spends attending to each of them is taken as the measure of his choice.

Several quite comprehensive programmes have investigated infant attention and as these deal with unrestricted and non-reinforced behaviours, it is possible to gain a considerable degree of understanding into how the sexes differ in their choice of stimuli in natural conditions. One of the most consistent results from this research is that females are highly attentive to auditory input, responding both to its emotional and meaningful properties. Simner (1971) found that one-week-old girls distinguished noticeably between the sound of an infant's cry and white noise played at the same volume, but that boys of the same age were significantly less discriminating although the reservations about testing neonates must again be noted. Watson (1969) investigated 14-week-old infants and found that girls could be trained to maintain visual fixation of a white circle when a tone was used as reinforcement, but not when a line drawing of a face was employed. Boys performed better with visual reinforcement. In a comprehensive study, Kagan and Lewis (1965) found that 24-week-old girls responded more to music (complex input) whereas boys reacted more to tones (a simple repetitive input). In the same infants at 13 months, girls consistently responded to verbal input with high inflection, and a significant positive correlation was found for the girls who had high attention levels to music in the first experiment, and who at thirteen months paid most attention to the verbal input with maximum uncertainty, illustrating that they noticed its novelty. It is possible that the reaction to high levels of inflection relates to the females' sensitivity to intensity differences illustrated in the preceding section. Girls were also found to vocalize significantly more to auditory input than boys (Kagan and Lewis, 1965).

The evidence on visual attention strongly suggests that the sexes respond preferentially to two different categories of input, and that this is unconnected with maturational fac-

tors affecting visual acuity (Fagan, 1972). Whereas faces
are a powerful stimulus for both sexes, females show considerably greater interest and discriminability than boys
(Lewis *et al.* 1966; Lewis, 1969; Fagan, 1972). Girls are
able to discriminate between realistic and unrealistic line
drawings and vocalize appropriately to the most realistic
(Lewis, 1969) and are able to discriminate consistently between photographs of people of different ages and sex as well
as between photographs of two very similar faces (Fagan,
1972), whereas boys do not show these abilities.

By contrast, males respond preferentially to blinking
lights, geometric patterns, coloured photographs of objects
and three-dimensional objects (Myers and Cantor, 1967; McCall
and Kagan, 1970; Pancratz and Cohen, 1970; Kagan and Lewis,
1965; Cornell and Strauss, 1973). Boys were found to habit-
uate sooner to objects and produce more consistent orienting
responses to novel objects than girls, an interesting contrast to their slower habituation to faces found by Lewis
(1969). Boys show no appearance of differentiating between
faces and objects, as measured by their amount of vocalizations. Kagan and Lewis (1965) found that boys vocalized significantly more to a blinking light, and McCall and Kagan
(1967) found that heart rate deceleration (indicating attention) to a series of random patterns was almost always accompanied by vocalization for boys, but not for girls.

These findings can be interpreted to suggest that girls
give highly appropriate and discriminating responses to
social or socially affective stimuli. This is also supported
by the finding of Moss and Robson (1968) that girls' visual
behaviour is related to the amount of social interaction
with the mother. Social responses occurred in the boys but
not to the same degree. They appear, on the other hand, especially responsive to non-social novel visual input, and
especially when it is brightly coloured or is three-
dimensional (McCall and Kagan, 1970; Pancratz and Cohen,
1970; Cornell and Strauss, 1973).

Studies on attention during childhood have concentrated
exclusively on the response to novelty. However, the interpretation of this term is misleading. In fact all children
in these experiments respond to novel input: they notice
its occurrence. It is rather what they choose to do about
it that distinguishes their behaviour. Another misconcep-
tion is that only objects are novel. This leads to a mis-
conception that because boys approach novel toys more than

girls (Smock and Holt, 1962; Mendel, 1965; Hutt, 1970), they
are more sensitive to novelty *per se*, and more imaginative
in devising ways of playing with the novel toys. Yet people
can also be novel. In an observational study of newcomers
entering a play-group, McGrew (1972) reports that girls as
young as three years of age responded to new children with
affection, interest and comforting actions and verbalizations.
The "novel" interlopers were initially ignored by the boys
and were excluded from their games.

   Novelty experiments are, therefore, often more related
to the phase of vigilant readiness rather than to the initial
orienting reaction. Both sexes orient to the stimuli, but
since the types of input (objects and people) are familiar,
the two sexes have already established preferences for responding to this type of input.

   The object-social distinction between the sexes appears
pervasive across age groups, but this dichotomy tends to be
blurred when social interaction is investigated. This leads
Maccoby and Jacklin (1974) to conclude that greater social
orientation cannot be demonstrated in females. However, we
have been able to offer clear evidence on this distinction
in an experiment in which adult subjects *must* choose between
object and social stimuli without being aware of the reason
for their reactions (McGuinness and Symonds, in press).
Photographs of objects were paired with photographs of people
and presented stereoscopically. This results in binocular
rivalry in which the most meaningful stimulus predominates.
Males reported objects more than people, while females showed
the reverse. The interaction was significant at $p < 0.001$.

   An understanding of the quality of this difference is
provided by Jastrow in 1891 (reported in Ellis, 1896). High
school and college age students were asked to produce associations to a list of words. These were categorized by
Jastrow with several surprising results. One of the most
important, was that males typically associate an *action* to
an object, whereas females associate its quality. This illustrates that objects interest males because of what they
do. The female supplies the descriptive code which is most
communicable.

COGNITIVE ABILITIES

   The evidence reviewed so far has shown some consistent
biases in perception between the sexes. The argument that

these biases arise because of differential reinforcement or
some developmental lag is difficult to support in view of
evidence such as the following: males receive significantly
more affection and direct physical contact with their mothers
but nevertheless prefer objects to people, and show poorer
speech development. We therefore have to presume that certain processes are biased by differences in neural structures present in early life. How might these biases affect
cognitive functioning?

     This section outlines very briefly the overall pattern
of cognitive differences between the sexes. The data described below have been set out under separate headings for
males and females. Females excel in a range of verbal skills,
in memory and social sensitivity. Males excel in visual and
mechanical spatial ability, certain types of mathematics,
and in problem solving tasks where restructuring is required
in the solution.

Special Abilities in Females

     Verbal and auditory skills. It was noted above that fe-
males aged 1-5 years are more proficient in linguistic skills,
and perhaps the most notable distinction between the sexes at
this age is the use of speech by females for specifically
communicative purposes (see Table I). This early aptitude
is fully documented by Maccoby and Jacklin (1974).

     During middle childhood, the female advantage is some-
what reduced. In particular vocabulary tests fail to show
differences, although females remain marginally ahead in
overall ability such as fluency, comprehension, verbal reasoning and flexibility in handling verbal symbols. This is
particularly evident in large sample surveys (see Maccoby
and Jacklin, 1974). However, females are outstandingly superior in reading skills, and it is well known that remedial
reading classes contain significantly higher proportions of
males (Ounsted and Taylor, 1972; Maccoby and Jacklin, 1974).

     In adolescence and adulthood females once again clearly
emerge as the superior sex and Maccoby and Jacklin have suggested that this may be due to different phases of development. While this must remain a possibility, it seems that
environmental factors may be more critical. Early schooling
places greatest emphasis on verbal skills, and these pressures could markedly improve male performance. Maintaining
fixed age groups might also handicap females and slow their

progress. Thus the natural ability of the female may be partially curbed to re-emerge later when mathematics and sciences siphon off male interest, and also when more complex verbal skills are necessary.

This view is supported by findings on deprived families
that show females clearly ahead on verbal ability in middle
childhood (see Maccoby and Jacklin, 1974). This suggests by
negative inference that a *good* environment can reduce the
natural differences between the sexes in language ability.
To anticipate a later discussion, it is important to emphasize that early training in visuo-spatial, or spatial-
mechanical skills might work to a similar advantage for females.

Memory. Ellis (1896) reports a study by Jastrow, showing that females were superior in delayed recall. Likewise,
Guilford (1967) found that women excelled in short-term processes such as digit-symbol substitution, as well as recall
for both visual and verbal information. Recent work upholds
these results, showing that females are superior in most
forms of visual and verbal memory. Superior verbal recall
has been reported in children (Zahorsky, 1969; Mittler and
Ward, 1970; Duggan, 1950) and in adults where higher imagery
is also found (Randhawa, 1972; Ernest and Paivio, 1971; Marks,
1973). In view of the results cited on social facility in
females, memory for socially relevant information ought to
be superior in females, and so it is. (Witryol and Kaess,
1957; Bahrick *et al.* 1975.)

Social. Girls as young as three years respond appropriately to children in need (McGrew, 1972) and Witryol and
Kaess (1957) showed that girls remember socially relevant input while boys do not. Thus girls are interested in other
people. This sex difference is apparent at one week, and at
five months (see earlier section). Goodenough (1957) has
found more sensitivity to people in girls than in boys at
2-4 years. Oetzel (1967) listed 21 studies in which girls
and women were found to have a significantly greater interest
in people and social matters than males.

One might expect that a greater interest in people would
produce a more analytic outlook in personal relationships,
and this suggestion is supported by the finding that females
use many more complex psychological categories or constructs
in describing others than males do (Livesley and Bromley,
1973; Little, 1968; Yarrow and Campbell, 1963).

Special Abilities in Males

Spatial-mechanical. The superiority of males in spatial ability is well documented (e.g. Guilford, 1967; Tyler, 1965; Garai and Scheinfeld, 1968; Hutt, 1972a).
The particular aspect of spatial and mechanical ability at which males excel seems to be the capacity to rotate or isolate visual images into new planes or combinations. It is often observed that the solution to a mechanical problem is more readily solved by looking rather than by continuous manipulation. However, if the theoretical views of Piaget (see Flavell, 1963) are correct, schemata are internalized only after a great deal of exploratory and manipulative behaviour. The saliency for boys of novel objects and their exploratory tendencies have been noted earlier. It is possible that early manipulative skill gives rise to a high degree of spatial imagery.
In studies of "cognitive style" Witkin *et al.* (1962) have investigated the performance of males and females in tests designed to reflect independence or dependence of a visual discrimination task on the surrounding background or "field". Males show greater "field independence". The most successful of their tests has been the Rod-and-Frame test (RFT) in which the subject is asked to set a rod which is surrounded by a tilted frame to the true vertical. As the RFT correlates significantly and forms a factor with block design, picture completion and object assembly on the WISC* (Witkin's own data) it seems reasonable to conclude that the RFT is measuring certain aspects of spatial ability, and that performance on the RFT has little to do with being "analytic", "global", "dependent" or "independent" of the field as Witkin suggests it does.
Thus men excel in visual-spatial ability, and this can be demonstrated in a number of tasks. What I find unacceptable, as do others (Sherman, 1967; Bock and Kolakowski, 1973), is Witkin's assumption that visual-spatial ability, and in particular performance on the RFT, is indicative of some general intellectual capacity of analytic thought. Sherman summarizes the problem succinctly:

It would seem that the empirical results of sex differences in analytic approach on field dependence might be explainable without any reference to field, without any need to infer a passive approach to the

field, globality or lack of analytic skill. The
fallacy involved is similar to concluding that
women are more analytic than men based on findings of superior female ability to decontextua-
lize the red and green figures on the Isihara
Colour Blindness Test. (Sherman, 1967, p. 292.)

A similar argument can be made concerning the female's superior performance on the Stroop word-colour Test (Peretti,
1969).

  Mathematical. While there is no difference between the
sexes in mathematical ability until the early teens (Oetzel,
1967; Maccoby and Jacklin, 1974) it appears that whereas
males improve over females at this time, girls' mathematical
ability actually declines from ages 11-15 with respect to
their previous performance (Ross and Simpson, 1971). The
available evidence suggests that this mathematical superiority in males occurs as the problems dealt with increase in
their emphasis on spatial properties. For example, Bock and
Kolakowski (1973) note that spatial ability correlates with
school geometry (rho = 0.57) and quantitative thinking (rho
= 0.69) as well as finding significant correlations with
drafting, shop mechanics and watch repair.

  Curiosity and problem-solving. The studies reviewed
earlier showing greater distractibility by novel objects and
more exploratory behaviour in boys than in girls, suggests
that "curiosity" may be the best brief description of these
types of behaviour, since it implies both awareness and activity. There is now fairly convincing evidence that this
characteristic of curiosity in boys (but not in girls) leads
to success in certain types of problem-solving tasks, usually
those which require visual or manipulative solutions.
Greenberger *et al.* (1971) found that problem-solving ability
in boys was highly correlated with two tests of curiosity,
but with verbal ability in girls. These results and those
of Kreitler *et al.* (1974) which confirm them, strongly suggest that where problem-solving involves the manipulation of
objects and the ability to break set, to try a range of approaches, boys will be superior. That boys excel in problems
which involve restructuring is now well documented (Garai
and Scheinfeld, 1968; Hutt, 1972a).

DISCUSSION

The essential findings are these: boys initially re-

spond to objects more than girls do, and most noticeably to
those which are geometric, brightly-coloured or three-
dimensional. Novel visual input produces a range of responses which extends from spontaneous vocalizations in infancy,
to direct contact, manipulation and investigation in childhood. In early childhood boys are found to be less able to
delay responses until appropriate choices are made, but eventually to be able to solve restructuring problems with greater
alacrity. From years of early experience in contact with physical objects they ultimately learn what can be done with objects and object relations. By puberty much of this ability
is internalized and visual-spatial problems can be solved
without manipulation by silent non-verbal transformations.
Nevertheless, males consistently are attracted by objects,
and enjoy the challenge of coming to grips with mechanical
problems of all types. The later manifestations of mechanical interest and aptitude are well known.

There is no doubt that these abilities result from an
interaction of cultural influences and the young infant's
initial fascination with objects. The mechanical interest
which is predominantly found in males occurs as early as 4-
5 months of age. From their early teens onwards, males possess keen visual acuity and fast efficient responses which
correspond to their increasing physical strength. All of
these attributes would interact to form an all-round superiority in exploratory and manipulative action.

Female skills can be tentatively described as "communicative", although this does not completely capture the range
of female capacities. In the youngest age group the auditory
system is predominant in girls. Before visual discrimination
is possible, girls listen and respond meaningfully to a range
of auditory inputs whether in the form of an infant's cry,
adult speech or music. By the age of 4-5 months they show
a strong preference for faces over objects, and by five
months are able to distinguish not only one person from
another, but also photographs of people. Girls also show a
very specific response pattern to auditory and visual information that captures their interest. Their motor activity
and heart-rate slows, and they smile and vocalize in response
to social stimuli. From these early and highly consistent
types of behaviour, females continue throughout life to be
more sensitive to certain categories of auditory input, in
particular intensity changes and localization of sound, and
to develop a strong interest in people and social situations.

During this developing period they also display consistent
superiority in handling speech and singing, at all levels of
perception and production.

Females also show greater tactile sensitivity from early
childhood and this is later expressed in fine digital sensitivity which finds its outlet in delicate handwork and tasks
requiring deft coordinated movements. Finally, females show
ability in remembering verbal, visual and social information
and display a greater degree of visual imagery than males.
This could mean that they process more information initially
about any stimulus input, and also that they hold onto this
information longer than males do. The data suggests that
both explanations must be adopted.

When considering possible explanations for the consistent differences between the sexes, none of the proposed
theories are really adequate or sufficiently developed to
deal with the data. For example, the hemisphere dominance
theories (Buffery and Gray, 1972; Levy, 1971; Harris, 1973)
imply that cognitive function is "pre-wired" to specific lo-
cations and determines subsequent development of sex differences. Data on the plasticity of neural function is too
overwhelming to support this theory (Lashley, 1950; Pribram,
1971; Luria, 1966), besides which the development of sex differences in certain cognitive skills cannot be attributed
solely to one hemisphere or another as many female skills
are to be found in the right non-dominant "male" hemisphere:
singing ability, intensity judgment, recognition of faces
and visual memory, as well as their facility in language, a
left-hemisphere function (Luria, 1966; Milner and Teuber,
1968). Hormone theories (see Chapter 10 by Archer) often
carry an equally implicit assumption that the hormone is
regulating or controlling perceptual or cognitive development.
But this type of theory presents a greater problem in explaining how sex differences occur so early in life, when
hormone levels only increase noticeably at or before puberty.

The data suggest, rather, that a different type of explanation be sought, and while a number of important considerations are raised by the findings, there is only space to
deal with a few of them. The first relates to the question
of how linguistic and visual-spatial abilities may be developed from initial sensory differences, and conclusions about
the impact of the environment follow from this.

The central theme is that sensitivity to intensity (produced by the amplitude of the signal) determines a perceptual

bias. It is now well documented that intensity is an important factor in deciding whether a stimulus will be registered
in the nervous system (Sokolov, 1963; Berlyne, 1970; Pribram
and McGuinness, 1975). A highly discriminable signal on one
channel will produce greater attention by allotting a greater
amount of central capacity to that input. This may in turn
draw more attention to the modality as a whole, and this is
especially likely to be true of intensity, which is highly
important biologically.

The finding that females are much more sensitive to intensity in the auditory mode has certain implications. It
was noted by Shuter (1968) in both her own data and that of
others, that females score particularly well on musical tests
involving dynamic interpretations. They are able to distinguish between subtle changes in volume, one of the components
of musical "phrasing" along with changes of timing, that give
music its emotional impact. Music performed in strict tempo,
with no dynamic alteration is static and conveys little emotion. It is quite conceivable that this facility in discer-
ning subtle changes in intensity causes the female to react
with feeling to music and explains why music has such a
distinct appeal to all females from early infancy onward.

Since females respond so overwhelmingly to music (Kagan
and Lewis, 1965) and as the only distinct difference between
the sexes in musical ability is due to a factor of intensity
(Shuter, 1968), it seems reasonable to suggest that this
same factor may be responsible for producing an emotional
reaction to intensity differences in speech. This prediction
has yet to be tested. However, if it were accurate, it would
clarify results such as the following. Simner (1971) found
that women respond quite differently from men to the sound
of an infant's cry, and this could be due to the fact that
the females are responding to the inflectional shifts (and
possibly also to the high frequency components of the sound).
Kagan and Lewis (1965) showed that female infants consistently responded to speech with high inflection, whether it had
high or low meaning. Again, this could occur because she
detects the emotional overtones in speech, and would enable
the mother to comfort her female infant "distally" as has
been observed (Lewis, 1972). This would be less effective
for the male infant who requires more physical reassurance.
Speech may then develop faster in the female infant, who
evokes more maternal verbal responses by directing babbling
to her mother.

Differences in perception of intensity would also have
other consequences. Teuber (in Milner and Teuber, 1968)
notes that the ability to localize sound is due to the detection of ,intensity differences between the ears. This occurs by a computation of the time lag of the sound arriving
at each ear. Teuber reports that intensity is the more critical variable as a louder input appears to arrive sooner,
even when the louder input actually follows the quieter signal. Thus greater sensitivity to cues of laterality (Pishkin
and Shurley, 1965) and the greater ability to locate a sound
source (Schaie *et al*. 1964) by females can be attributed to
their greater volume sensitivity.

Similarly, males respond more to levels of visual intensity (McGuinness, in press). McDonnell (reported in Berlyne,
1970), demonstrated that orienting and choice behaviour for
visual input is determined both by brightness and by contrast.
It is possible that the attraction for males of visual objects may arise from their greater perception of the contrasts between the various planes and surfaces. However,
further studies on the reaction of males of various ages to
brightness are required to test this prediction.

Visual preference also relates to cross-modality cueing
involving associative processes. If females are particularly
sensitive to verbal inflection, they will come to associate
the emotional information from verbal input with its source,
i.e. a face. Although both sexes appear sensitive to faces
initially, the fact that faces "speak" ought to increase the
interest of the female. One way to test this prediction
would be to examine sex differences in visual discrimination
in the congenitally deaf.

Early sensitivity differences might also produce subtle
differences in looking behaviours involving eye-movements.
Females may scan the environment with a greater degree of
visual axis, a type of eye-movement highly suitable for detailed visual discrimination and visual memory (Vurpillot,
1968; Luria, 1966), whereas males may use more vergence movements of the eyes. Vergence movements lead to an understanding and prediction of the relationships of objects in space.
Gibson and Walk (1960) and Bower (1964 and 1965) both show
that binocular and motion parallax (which requires vergence
information) are the basic visual processes giving rise to
accurate depth and distance perception. Thus females may
search "pictorially", producing a broader field with less
depth, while males may search "spatially", producing a nar-

rower field with greater depth. This view, along with the
data (McGuinness, in press) that females appear to have greater rod sensitivity (giving them better peripheral vision)
may contribute to their greater "field dependence" (Witkin
et al. 1962).

What are the cultural implications of these findings?
For a number of years educationalists have been criticized
for providing females with a male-based education, some going
so far as to suggest that females ought to spend more time on
arts and domestic subjects and leave scientific and technical
subjects to males. The interesting fact which has emerged
from this review is that males begin with a female education
in nearly every respect and their initial difficulties in
reading and writing are well documented (Taylor and Ounsted,
1972). The important lesson to be learned is not that the
males should give up this pursuit of linguistic excellence,
or to be taught at later ages (according to the developmental
lag theory), but precisely the opposite. The fact that boys
do learn to read and write, as well as to speak fluently,
suggests that though initial processes may be guided by certain sensory differences, there is no reason to assume that
these differences must remain. Parents insist that boys
learn to speak, read and write, but no such insistence indu-
ces the female to learn about spatial-mechanical relationships
Thus the male overcomes his initial handicap at school, but
by the time certain spatial skills are required by the cur-
riculum, the female may be too old to acquire them. Spatial
ability ought to be taught like speech and at an age which
permits an internalization of processes by the time cognitive
transformations occur in the developmental sequence (Piaget,
see Flavell, 1963). Without this early help females will be
disadvantaged at these sorts of tasks, and consistent failure
becomes defeating.

The evidence reviewed shows that females are communicative, and have a considerably greater interest in people than
males have. It was also suggested that females may be more
sensitive to certain forms of emotional communication, possibly due to a greater sensitivity to inflection. It would
seem to me that sensitivity to people, "social intelligence",
is a trait which is profoundly important in maintaining a
stable social system. Yet several authors imply that these
female characteristics render them unable to carry out logical thought. Silverman (1970) speaks of the male as "logos"
and the female as "eros", inferring as he writes that these

abilities are mutually exclusive. Broverman *et al.* (1968)
also seem to equate emotion with a lack of higher intellectual capacity. The authors support their arguments by drawing upon popular lay beliefs in sex stereotypes, largely supporting their more scientific statements by selective evidence on rat behaviour.

A further value judgment is implicit in Witkin *et al.*'s
(1962) statements concerning the passive-dependent female,
derived from evidence based almost entirely on reactions to
a visual illusion. All statements of this type carry the
implicit assumption that to be assertive, independent and
unfeeling is good, but to have characteristics of sensitivity and co-operativeness is bad. Despite these assumptions
it seems, rather, that traits of aggression, competitiveness,
coupled with a lack of empathy and sensitivity to others, are
the very characteristics that lead to the downfall of civi-
lized life.

As a final statement on this issue I would like to suggest that "social intelligence", as yet entirely neglected by
academic institutions, be given equal status with other forms
of intellectual training. The plea is concerned not so much
with the argument that men and women are equal, but that men
and women are different. What needs to be made equal is the
value placed upon these differences. To be able to understand and predict human action; to be able to sense motives
behind another's speech and behaviour; to be able to compre-
hend another's feelings, are all as important as the ability
to elaborate mechanical expertise into complex edifices and
machines. Communicative and spatial-mechanical skills, in-
telligently and logically employed, are equally necessary
for the preservation of human civilization.

These conceptualizations lead to more speculative notions about the nature of sex differences in thought processes. There are many who will deny that, in spite of the evidence, there are really any major differences between the
sexes in perceptual ability, but these same persons would
undoubtedly agree that men and women think differently.
This juxtaposition of quite incompatible beliefs is characteristic of attitudes about sex differences. If we suppose
that thinking is determined to a great extent by our experience, and experience consists of percepts and feelings combined, then it may be possible to suggest some tentative pro-
positions about the character of sex differences in thought
processes by analogy with the evidence now available on per-

ception.

If, in males, the predominant characteristic is one of exploration, internal and external structuring of non-social input, then it is conceivable that this leads to a characteristic mode of thought which is largely organizing or restructuring. One could call this type of thinking "synthetic", and it would enable structures and processes to be seen in combination, and to extend and create them. It would also imply that when dealing with social situations, the male sees largely categories or stereotypes, and that he tends to adapt to the situation by constructing rules, attitudes, laws, etc., applied externally. The woman, whose approach is more communicative and whose interest is more social, would use both direct perceptual and abstract linguistic cues to enable her to form judgments of intent. She would thus see the internal aspects of personal and social situations, asking "why" questions, rather than "what" questions. Female sensitivity to symbolic and semantic cues would enable her also to see content. She would thus be able to determine the specificities and intricacies of situations, and her type of thinking could thus be described as "analytic", the capacity both to interpret intention and to abstract the constituent elements from any type of verbal or non-verbal communication. It is interesting that this view of the data leads to the exact opposite conclusion about analytic thought to the views of Witkin *et al.* (1962), Broverman *et al.* (1968), and Silverman, (1970).

* *WISC: Wexler Intelligence Scale for Children. Discussed by Dorothy Kipnis.*

REFERENCES

Ammons, R.B., Alprin, S.I. and Ammons, C.H. (1955). Rotary pursuit performance as related to sex and age of pre-adult subjects. *Journal of Experimental Psychology,* 49, 127-133.

Annett, M. (1970). The growth of manual preference and speed. *British Journal of Psychology,* 61, 545-558.

Aranoff, D. (1973). Relationship between immobilization and autokinetic movement. *Perceptual and Motor Skills,* 36, 411-41

Axelrod, S. (1959). "Effects of Early Blindness. Performance of Blind and Sighted Children on Tactile and Auditory Tasks". American Foundation for the Blind, New York.

Bahrick, H.P., Bahrick, P.O. and Wittlinger, R.P. (1975).
Fifty years of memory for names and faces: A cross-
cultural approach. *Journal of Experimental Psychology
(General)*, 104, 54-75.

Bell, R.Q..and Costello, N.S. (1964). Three tests for sex
differences in tactile sensitivity in the newborn. *Biologia
Neonatorum*, 7, 335-347.

Bentley, A. (1966). "Musical Ability in Children and its
Measurement". Harrap and Co., London.

Berlyne, D.E. (1970). Attention as a problem in behaviour.
In "Attention: Contemporary Theory and Analysis". (D.I.
Mostofsky, ed.) Appleton Century Crofts, New York.

Bhavnani, R. and Hutt, C. (1972). Divergent thinking in boys
and girls. *Journal of Child Psychology and Psychiatry*,
13, 121-127.

Bock, R.D. and Kolakowski, D. (1973). Further evidence of
sex-linked major-gene influence on human spatial visuali-
zing ability. *The American Journal of Human Genetics*, 25,
1-14.

Bower, T.G.R. (1964). Discrimination of depth in premotor
infants. *Psychonomic Science*, 1, 368.

Bower, T.G.R. (1965). Stimulus variables determining space
perception in infants. *Science*, 149, 88-89.

Broverman, D.M., Klaiber, E.L., Kobayashi, Y. and Vogel, W.
(1968). Roles of activation and inhibition in sex differences in cognitive abilities. *Psychological Review*, 75,
23-50.

Buffery, A.W.H. and Gray, J.A. (1972). Sex differences in
the development of spatial and linguistic skills. *In*
"Gender Differences: Their Ontogeny and Significance".
(C. Ounsted and D.C. Taylor, eds.) Churchill Livingstone,
Edinburgh.

Burg, A. (1966). Visual acuity as measured by dynamic and
static tests: A comparative evaluation. *Journal of Applied
Psychology*, 50, 460-466.

Burg, A. and Hulbert, S. (1961). Dynamic visual acuity as
related to age, sex, and static acuity. *Journal of Applied
Psychology*, 45, 111-116.

Chaplin, J.P. (1955). Sex differences in the perception of autokinetic movement. *Journal of General Psychology*, 52, 149-155.

Clark, W.C. and Mehl, L. (1971). Thermal pain: A sensory decision theory analysis of the effect of age and sex on d', various responses criteria, and 50% pain threshold. *Journal of Abnormal Psychology*, 78, 202-212.

Cook, T.W. and Shephard, A.H. (1958). Performance on several control-display relationships as a function of age and sex. *Perceptual and Motor Skills*, 8, 339-345.

Cornell, E.H. and Strauss, M.S. (1973). Infants responsiveness to compounds of habituated visual stimuli. *Developmental Psychology*, 2, 73-78.

Corso, J.F. (1959). Age and sex differences in thresholds. *Journal of the Acoustical Society of America*, 31, 498-507.

Duggan, L. (1950). An experiment on immediate recall in secondary school children. *British Journal of Psychology*, 40, 149-154.

Eagles, E.L., Wishik, S.M., Doefler, L.G., Melnick, W. and Levine, H.S. (1963). "Hearing Sensitivity and Related Factors in Children". University of Pittsburg Press, Pittsburg.

Eisenberg, R. (1972). Unpublished data reviewed by Korner, 1973.

Elliott, C.D. (1971). Noise tolerance and extraversion in children. *British Journal of Psychology*, 62, 375-380.

Ellis, H. (1896). "Man and Woman: A Study of Human Secondary Sexual Characteristics". Walter Scott, London.

Engel, R., Crowell, C. and Nishijima, S. (1968). Visual and auditory response latencies in neonates. *In* "Facilitation Volume in Honour of C.C. de Silva". Kularatue and Company, Ceylon.

Ernest, C.H. and Paivio, A. (1971). Imagery and sex differences in incidental recall. *British Journal of Psychology*, 62, 67-72.

Fagan, J.F. (1972). Infants recognition memory for faces. *Journal of Experimental Child Psychology*, 14, 453-476.

Fairweather, H. and Hutt, S.J. (1972). Sex differences in a perceptual motor skill in children. *In* "Gender Differences: Their Ontogeny and Significance". (C. Ounsted and D.C. Taylor, eds.) Churchill Livingstone, Edinburgh.

Flavell, J.H. (1963). "The Developmental Psychology of Jean Piaget". D. van Nostrand Co. Inc., Toronto.

Garai, J.E. and Scheinfeld, A. (1968). Sex differences in mental 'and behavioral traits. *Genetic Psychology Monographs,* 77, 169-299.

Gibson, E.J. and Walk, R.D. (1960). The visual cliff. *Scientific American,* (April).

Goldberg, S. and Lewis, M. (1969). Play behaviour in the year old infant: Early sex differences. *Child Development,* 40, 21-31.

Goodenough, E.W. (1957). Interest in persons as an aspect of sex differences in the early years. *Genetic Psychology Monographs,* 55, 287-323.

Greenberger, E., O'Connor, J. and Sorensen, A. (1971). Personality, cognitive and academic correlates of problem-solving flexibility. *Developmental Psychology,* 4, 416-424.

Guilford, J.P. (1967). "The Nature of Human Intelligence". McGraw-Hill, New York.

Gullicksen, G.R. and Crowell, D.H. (1964). Neonatal habituation to electroactual stimulation. *Journal of Experimental Child Psychology,* 1, 388-396.

Harms, I.E. and Spiker, C.C. (1959). Factors associated with the performance of young children on intelligence scales and tests of speech development. *Journal of Genetic Psychology,* 94, 3-22.

Harris, L.J. (1973). Neurophysiological factors in spatial development. Paper read at meeting of the Society for Research in Child Development, Philadelphia.

Herzberg, F. and Lepkin, M.A. (1954). A study of sex differences on the primary mental abilities test. *Educational and Psychological Measurement,* 14, 687-689.

Hull, F.M., Mielke, P.W., Timmons, R.J. and Willeford, J.A. (1971). The national speech and hearing survey: Preliminary results. *ASHA,* 3, 501-509.

Hutt, C. (1970). Curiosity in young children. *Science Journal*, 6, 68-72.

Hutt, C. (1972a). Neuroendocrinological behaviour and intellectual aspects of sexual differentiation in human development. *In* "Gender Differences: Their Ontogeny and Significance". (C. Ounsted and D.C. Taylor, eds.) Churchill Livingstone, Edinburgh.

Hutt, C. (1972b). "Males and Females". Penguin Books, London.

Immergluck, L. and Mearini, M.C. (1969). Age and sex differences in response to embedded figures and reversible figures. *Journal of Experimental Child Psychology*, 8, 210-221

Ippolitov, F.V. (1972). Interanalyser differences in the sensitivity-strength parameter for vision, hearing and cutaneous modalities. *In* "Biological Bases of Individual Behaviour". (V.D. Nebylitsyn and J.A. Gray, eds.) Academic Press, London.

James, W. (1890). "Principles of Psychology". Routledge and Kegan Paul, London.

Kagan, J. and Lewis, M. (1965). Studies of attention in the human infant. *Merrill-Palmer Quarterly*, 11, 95-127.

Korner, A.F. (1970). Visual alertness in neonates: Individual differences and their correlates. *Perceptual and Motor Skills*, 31, 499-509.

Korner, A.F. (1971). Individual differences at birth: Implications for early experience and later development. *American Journal of Orthopsychiatry*, 41, 608-619.

Korner, A.F. (1973). Sex differences in newborns with special references to differences in the organization of oral behaviour. *Journal of Child Psychology*, 14, 19-29.

Korner, A.F. and Thoman, E.B. (1970). Visual alertness in neonates as evoked by maternal care. *Journal of Experimental Child Psychology*, 10, 67-78.

Lashley, K.S. (1950). In search of the engram. *In* "Physiological Mechanisms in Animal Behaviour". Society for Experimental Biology. (Great Britain). Academic Press, New York.

Levy, J. (1971). Lateral specialization of the human brain: Behavioural manifestations and possible evolutionary basis. Paper presented at 32nd Annual Biology Colloquium, Oregon State University.

Lewis, M. (1969). Infants'response to facial stimuli during the first year of life. *Developmental Psychology*, 1, 75-86.

Lewis, M. (1972). State as an infant-environment interaction:
An analysis of mother-infant interaction as a function of
sex. *Merrill-Palmer Quarterly*, 18, 95-121.

Lewis, M., Kagan, J. and Kalafat, J. (1966). Patterns of
fixation in the young infant. *Child Development*, 37, 331-
341.

Lindsay, P.H. (1970). Multichannel processing in perception.
In "Attention: Contemporary Theory and Analysis". (D.I.
Mostofsky, ed.) Appleton Century Crofts, New York.

Lindzey, G. and Goldberg, M. (1953). Motivational differences
between males and females as measured by the TAT. *Journal
of Personality*, 22, 101-117.

Lipsitt, L.P. and Levy, N. (1959). Electroactual thresholds
in the neonate. *Child Development*, 30, 547-554.

Little, B.R. (1968). Factors affecting the use of psychological versus non-psychological constructs on the Repetory
Test. *Bulletin of the British Psychological Society*, 21,
34.

Livesley, W.J. and Bromley, D.B. (1973). "Person Perception
in Childhood and Adolescence". Wiley and Sons, London.

Luria, A.R. (1966). "Higher Cortical Functions in Man".
Tavistock, London.

McCall, R.B. (1972). Smiling and vocalization in infants as
indices of perceptual cognitive processes. *Merrill-Palmer
Quarterly*, 18

McCall, R.B. and Kagan, J. (1970). Individual differences in
the infant's distribution of attention to stimulus discrepancy. *Development Psychology*, 2, 90-98.

McCarthy, D. (1930). "Language Development of the Preschool
Child". Institute of Child Welfare Monograph No. 4.
University of Minneapolis Press, Minneapolis.

Maccoby, E.E. and Jacklin, C.N. (1973). Stress, activity and
proximity seeking: Sex differences in the year old child.
Child Development, 44, 34-47.

Maccoby, E.E. and Jacklin, C.N. (1974). "The Psychology of
Sex Differences". Stanford University Press, Stanford.

McGrew, W.C. (1972). Aspects of social development in nursery school children with emphasis on introduction to the group. *In* "Ethological Studies of Child Behaviour". (N. Blurton-Jones, ed.) Cambridge University Press, London.

McGuinness, D. (1972). Hearing: Individual differences in perceiving. *Perception*, 1, 465-473.

McGuinness, D. (In press). Away from a unisex psychology: Individual differences in visual perception. *Perception*.

McGuinness, D. and Lewis, I. (In press). Sex differences in visual persistence: Experiments on the Ganzfeld and the afterimage. *Perception*.

McGuinness, D. and Symonds, J. (In press). Sex differences in choice behaviour: The object-person dimension. *Perceptual and Motor Skills*.

Marks, D.F. (1973). Visual imagery and differences in the recall of pictures. *British Journal of Psychology*, 64, 17-24.

Mendel, G. (1965). Children's preference for differing degrees of novelty. *Child Development*, 35, 452-465.

Messer, S.B. and Lewis, M. (1972). Social class and sex differences in the attachment and play behaviour of the year old infant. *Merrill-Palmer Quarterly*, 18, 295-306.

Miele, J.A. (1958). Sex differences in intelligence: The relationship of sex to intelligence as measured by the Wechsler Adult Intelligence Scale and the Wechsler Intelligence Scale for Children. *Dissertation Abstracts*, 18, 2,213.

Milner, B. and Teuber, H.-L. (1968). Alteration of perception and memory in man: Reflection on Methods. *In* "Analysis of Behaviour Change". (L. Weiskrantz, ed.) Harper and Row, New York.

Mittler, P. and Ward, J. (1970). The use of the Illinois test of psycho-linguistic abilities on British four-year-old children: A normative and factorial study. *British Journal of Educational Psychology*, 40, 43-54.

Moss, H.A. (1967). Sex, age and state as determinants of mother-infant interaction. *Merrill-Palmer Quarterly*, 13, 19-35.

Moss, H.A. and Robson, K.S. (1968). Maternal influences and early social visual behaviour. *Child Development,* 39, 401-408.

Myers, W.J. and Cantor, G.N. (1967). Observing and cardiac responses of human infants to visual stimuli. *Journal of Experimental Child Psychology,* 5, 16-25.

Noble, C.E., Baker, B.L. and Jones, T.A. (1964). Age and sex parameters in psychomotor learning. *Perceptual and Motor Skills,* 19, 935-945.

Noble, C.E. and Hays, J.R. (1966). Discrimination reaction performance as a function of anxiety and sex parameters. *Perceptual and Motor Skills,* 23, 1267-1278.

Oetzel, R.M. (1967). Annotated bibliography. *In* "The Development of Sex Differences". (E. Maccoby, ed.) Tavistock Publications, London.

Ounsted, C. and Taylor, D.C. (1972). "Gender Differences: Their Ontogeny and Significance". Churchill Livingstone, Edinburgh.

Pancratz, C.N. and Cohen, L.B. (1970). Recovery of habituation in infants. *Journal of Experimental Child Psychology,* 9, 208-216.

Peretti, P.O. (1969). Cross-sex and cross-educational levels performance in a colour-word interference task. *Psychonomic Science,* 16, 321-324.

Phillips, J.R. (1973). Syntax and vocabulary of mothers' speech to young children. Age and sex comparisons. *Child Development,* 44, 182-185.

Pishkin, V. and Blanchard, R. (1964). Auditory concept identification as a function of subject, sex and stimulus dimensions. *Psychonomic Science,* 1, 177-178.

Pishkin, V. and Shurley, J.T. (1965). Auditory dimensions and irrelevant information in concept identification of males and females. *Perceptual and Motor Skills,* 20, 673-683.

Pohl, W. and Caldwell, W.E. (1968). Towards an analysis of a functional deficit. *Journal of General Psychology,* 79, 241-255.

Pribram, K.H. (1971). "Languages of the Brain". Prentice-Hall, New Jersey.

Pribram, K.H. and McGuinness, D. (1975). Arousal, activation
and effort in the control of attention. *Psychological Revi*
82, 116-149.

Randhawa, B.S. (1972). A case for the uses of multivariate
analysis in concept grouping, dominance level, and sex,
as related to verbal recall. *Multivariate Behaviour Research*, 7, 193-201.

Roberts, E. (1972). "Poor Pitch Singing". Ph.D. Dissertation.
Liverpool University.

Roberts, J. (1964). "Binocular Visual Acuity of Adults".
U.S. Department of Health, Education and Welfare,
Washington.

Rosenberg, B.G. and Sutton-Smith, B. (1964). The relationship of ordinal position and sibling sex status to cognitive abilities. *Psychonomic Science*, 1, 81-82.

Ross, J.M. and Simpson, H.R. (1971). The national survey of
health and development: 1. Educational attainment.
British Journal of Educational Psychology, 41, 49-61.

Rubenstein, J. (1967). Maternal attentiveness and subsequent
exploratory behaviour in the infant. *Child Development*,
38, 1089-1100.

Schaie, K.W., Baltes, P. and Strother, C.R. (1964). A study
of auditory sensitivity in advanced age. *Journal of Geron-
tology*, 19, 453-457.

Shephard, A.H., Abbey, D.S. and Humphries, M. (1962). Age
and sex in relation to perceptual-motor performance on
several control display relations on the TCC. *Perceptual
and Motor Skills*, 14, 103-118.

Sherman, J. (1967). Problem of sex differences in space perception and aspects of intellectual functioning. *Psychological Review*, 74, 290-299.

Shuter, R.P.G. (1964). "An Investigation of Hereditary and
Environmental Factors in Musical Ability". Ph.D. Dissertation. University of London.

Shuter, R. (1968). "The Psychology of Music". Methuen, London

Silverman, J. (1970). Attentional styles and the study of
sex differences. *In* "Attention: Contemporary Theory and
Analysis". (D.I. Mostofsky, ed.) Appleton-Century Crofts,

New York.

Simner, M.L. (1971). Newborn's response to the cry of another infant. *Developmental Psychology*, 5, 136-150.

Simon, J.R. (1967). Choice reaction time as a function of auditory S-R correspondence, age and sex. *Ergonomics*, 10, 659-664.

Simpson, W.E. and Vaught, G.M. (1973). Visual and auditory autokinesis. *Perceptual and Motor Skills*, 36, 1199-1206.

Skoff, E. and Pollack, R.H. (1969). Visual acuity in children as a function of hue. *Perception and Psychophysics*, 6, 244-246.

Smith, P.K. and Connally, K. (1972). Patterns of play and social interaction in pre-school children. *In* "Ethological Studies of Child Behaviour". (N. Blurton-Jones, ed.) Cambridge University Press, London.

Smock, C.D. and Holt, B.G. (1962). Children's reaction to novelty: An experimental study of curiosity motivation. *Child Development*, 33, 631-642.

Sokolov, E.N. (1963). Higher nervous function, the orienting reflex. *Annual Review of Physiology*, 25, 545-580.

Spears, W.C. and Hohle, R.H. (1967). Sensory and perceptual processes in infants. *In* "Infancy and Early Childhood". (Y. Brackbill, ed.) Collier MacMillan, London.

Taylor, D.C. and Ounsted, C. (1972). The nature of gender differences explored through ontogentic analysis of sex ratios in disease. *In* "Gender Differences Their Ontogeny and Significance". (C. Ounsted and D.C. Taylor, eds.) Churchill Livingstone, Edinburgh.

Tyler, L. (1965). "The Psychology of Human Differences". Appleton Century Crofts, New York.

Voth, A.C. (1941). Individual differences in the autokinetic phenomenon. *Journal of Experimental Psychology*, 24, 306-322.

Vurpillot, E. (1968). The development of scanning strategies and their relation to visual differentiation. *Journal of Experimental Child Psychology*, 6, 632-650.

Watson, J.S. (1969). Operant conditioning of visual fixation in infants under visual and auditory reinforcement.

Development Psychology, 1, 508-516.

Wechsler, D. (1958). "The Measurement and Appraisal of Intelligence". Williams and Wilkins, Baltimore.

Weinstein, S. and Sersen, E.A. (1961). Tactual sensitivity as a function of handedness and laterality. *Journal of Comparative and Physiological Psychology,* 54, 665-669.

Wilson, W.P. and Zung, W.K. (1966). Attention, discrimination, and arousal during sleep. *Archives of General Psychiatry,* 15, 523-528.

Witkin, H.A., Dyk, R.B., Faterson, H.F., Goodenough, D.R. and Karp, S.A. (1962). "Psychological Differentiation". Wiley and Sons, New York.

Witryol, S.L. and Kaess, W.A. (1957). Sex differences in social memory tasks. *Journal of Abnormal and Social Psychology,* 54, 343-346.

Wolff, P.H. (1969). The natural history of crying and other vocalizations in early infancy. *In* "Determinants of Infant Behaviour". (B.M. Foss, ed.) Vol. 3. Methuen, London.

Yarrow, M.R. and Campbell, D.J. (1963). Person perception in children. *Merrill-Palmer Quarterly,* 9, 57-72.

Zahorsky, T. (1969). Short-term memory in children as a specific function of different sensory modalities. *Psychologia a Patapsychologia Dietata,* 4.

Zaner, A.R., Levee, R.F. and Gunta, R.R. (1968). The development of auditory perceptual skills as a function of maturation. *Journal of Auditory Research,* 8, 313-322.

7. MALE HORMONES AND BEHAVIOUR

Lesley Rogers

There are no hormones exclusive to the male sex, but, as a group, males do have higher concentrations of some steroid hormones, called androgens. This difference between the sexes is a statistical one, since there is overlap between the range of androgen concentrations found in males and females (Gandy and Peterson, 1968). Androgenic action produces and maintains morphological differences between the sexes. Moreover, androgens can affect behaviour. They have been traditionally associated with male sexual behaviour and aggression. This chapter will examine what evidence there is available for this in man and other animals. Androgenic effects on other behaviour, not directly related to sex and aggression, will also be discussed with critical consideration of the commonly-accepted hypothesis that human sex differences on psychophysical and more complex cognitive tasks are caused by hormonal differences between the sexes.

ACTIONS OF CIRCULATING HORMONES IN ANIMALS

Firstly, what do we know about the effect of androgens on sexual and aggressive behaviour? In many species seasonal reproduction is correlated with an increase in aggression (Archer, 1976). During the breeding season the male holds a territory, which it aggressively defends against intruders. At this time testicular activity is high and there is an increased level of sex hormones circulating in the blood-stream. Such correlations between hormonal and behavioural changes imply nothing about causation in either direction. From this data we are unable to deduce whether the changed hormonal state is producing mating behaviour and increased aggression, or vice versa. To investigate causal relationships between hormones and behaviour we must manipu-

late one of the variables and look for parallel changes resulting in the other. That is, we can change the hormonal
state and look for parallel changes in behaviour, or we can
alter the animal's behaviour and assay for changes in hormonal state. For example, castration of adult, male rats leads
to a decline in sexual and aggressive behaviour, and these
behaviours are restored by administration of testosterone,
an androgen. Therefore, in this case, increased testosterone
levels cause increased copulation and attack. And now
another question arises. Is this causal relationship due to
the direct action of testosterone on neural circuits in the
brain controlling this behaviour, or could it be due to a
peripheral effect on, say, the morphology of the genital organs?

     After castration the male rat has a reduced number of
sensory papillae on the penis, and these are restored by
testosterone treatment (Beach and Levinson, 1950). Reduction in penial sensitivity after castration could indirectly
lead to a decline in sexual activity. Beach and Westbrooke
(1968) have answered this question by administering fluoxymesterone to castrated male rats. Fluoxymesterone is an ana-
logue of testosterone which restores the number of papillae
but has no effect on sexual behaviour. Several workers (see
Whalen, 1972) have claimed to be able to produce copulation
in castrated male rats by implanting very small quantities
of testosterone, often in the form of crystals, into the hypothalamic area of the brain. These studies imply that testosterone is influencing sexual behaviour through a direct
effect on the central nervous system. Brain lesioning followed by systemic administration of hormone, electrical and
chemical stimulation of small areas of the brain and searching for localized areas of uptake of radioactive androgens
can also assist in elucidating a causal relationship from
hormone to behaviour. It must be noted, however, that there
is at present some controversy as to whether there are dis-
cretely localized "sex centres" in the brain. Difficulty in
repeating the original implantation experiments and variability in the sites found by different researchers suggest
that the neural pathways controlling sexual behaviour extend
throughout the diencephalon.

     Past experience may play a most important role in deter-
mining the behavioural response to hormonal manipulation
(Lehrman, 1971). Cats which have been allowed pre-castration
experience in mating have a more prolonged post-castration

retention of mating than do those which are inexperienced
(Rosenblatt and Aronson, 1958). (Interestingly, this does
not seem to be so for dogs, see Beach, 1970.) Michael *et al.*(1973)
have found that castration of sexually experienced, male rhesus monkeys has very little effect on the incidence of mounting behaviour, although frequencies of ejaculation decline
because the penis becomes too limp to gain intromission. Animals castrated before puberty or before they have been allowed sexual experience will never indulge in sexual activity.
In many species castration after puberty has surprisingly
little effect on sexual activity. Circulating levels of sex
hormones are necessary for the initial establishment of sexual behaviour in the animal's repertoire, and so may be in-
timately involved in a learning process about how to copulate.
However, in the previous examples, once the pattern of sexual behaviour has been established it becomes to a large extent emancipated from hormonal control (Davidson, 1972). Indeed, experience very early in life, well before puberty,
may drastically influence the behavioural response to hormones in adulthood. Male rats removed from their parents before weaning and raised by hand show marked deficits in the
amount and intensity of their sexual behaviour when they
reach sexual maturity (Thoman and Arnold, 1968). In fact
the same result can be achieved by rearing one male rat
alone with its mother without the rest of the litter (Hard
and Larsson, 1968). Adult sexual behaviour is determined by
social experience with litter-mates in very early life. This
experience does not involve practice of the sexual act *per
se*, although elements of it may be practised in play, for
example. Neither does the experience depend on watching
other individuals perform copulation; it is clearly a subtle
learning process.
     In many species aggressive behaviour can be influenced
by circulating androgens. For example, administration of
testosterone causes an increase in attack behaviour of young,
male chickens (Andrew, 1966), or restoration of aggressive
behaviour in castrated male mice and rats (Bronson and
Desjardins, 1971). However, here too learning factors can
mask the action of androgens. Guhl (1964) demonstrated this
in socially reared chickens. Androgen treatment was shown
to produce an increase in aggression when the injected bird
was matched against a total stranger, but not when it was
tested in its usual social group. Habits developed in the
peck-order of the social group were able to over-ride the

hormonal effect. In mice past experience of winning or losing fights with other animals has been found to have a greater influence on aggressive behaviour than has androgen levels
(Bevan et al. 1960). We can therefore conclude that circulating androgens can often influence the level of sexual activity in animals, but learning factors are also important,
sometimes even to the extent of over-riding hormonal effects.

Such effects of past experience may result from interaction at the behavioural level between learned patterns of
aggression and induced levels of aggressive behaviour, or
alternatively from an interaction at the hormonal level. Environmental factors such as high population density, contin-
ual defeat or prolonged subordination can affect the pituitary
adrenal system. Mice which are repeatedly defeated have an
increased output of corticosterone from the adrenal glands
(Bronson and Eleftheriou, 1965), indicating an increase in
adrenocorticotrophic hormone release from the pituitary.
Thyroid stimulating hormone is also found in increased concentration in the blood streams of defeated mice (Eleftheriou
et al. 1968). Interaction of these hormones with the gona-
dotrophic or sex hormones is completely feasible. In fact,
testicular size is smaller in subordinate than it is in dominant animals (Christian et al. 1969). Testosterone levels
in primates can be altered by manipulating the social setting
(Rose et al. 1972). In laboratory rats conditions of rearing alter the circulating levels of sex hormones (Dessi-
Fulgheri et al. 1975). Male and female rats raised in isolation have higher levels of plasma androgens than those
raised in groups of four males and four females. There is a
parallel increase in aggression in the isolated animals. Also sex steroids are higher in rats raised in heterosexual
groups than in those raised in homosexual groups. As yet,
data in this area is scanty, but it is clear that environmental stimuli can modulate hormonal systems either directly or
indirectly connected to aggressive behaviour.

Androgens are not the only hormones associated with aggression in animals. In starlings luteinizing hormone is
the hormone which causes the seasonal increase in aggression,
while testosterone acts on sexual and nesting behaviour
(Mathewson, 1961; Davis, 1964). Amongst mammals, hamsters
and gerbils are notable exceptions to the general theory linking androgens to aggression. In contrast to other rodents,
female gerbils and hamsters are just as aggressive as males.
Castration of male gerbils produces an increase in aggression

(Christenson *et al.* 1973). Castration of male hamsters produces the more usual decline in aggression towards other
males, but this behaviour is restored not only by administration of testosterone but also by administration of oestradiol or progesterone (Vandenberg, 1971; Payne and Swanson,
1972). Levels of aggression in ovariectomized females are
enhanced by progesterone, but not by oestrogen or testosterone.

In summary, support for a general theory stating that
male sex hormones promote aggressive and sexual behaviour
must be immediately qualified by exceptions where androgens
play a minimal role compared to past experience, or where
other hormones influence these behaviours.

ACTION OF CIRCULATING HORMONES IN MAN

What then do we know about the effects of circulating
androgens on sexual behaviour and aggression in man? Of the
latter we know very little. In young men Persky *et al.* (1971)
have found a positive correlation between the production rate
of testosterone and performance on the Buss-Durkee Hostility
Inventory. This test is a self-report of behaviours said to
be hostile or aggressive. But, before we place too much importance on data like this, it is best to consider what we
mean by "aggression". So far we have used the term "aggression" in animals to refer primarily to those behaviours that
ethologists might better call "agonistic", that is, behaviours which fall into a broad category of attack, threat or
defence and aimed intraspecifically. Interspecific defence,
or predation, has been deliberately avoided since, while it
may share some common ground, it is on the whole a separate
issue at least at our present state of knowledge. Aggression
is difficult, if not impossible, to define. In man it can
mean anything from physical violence (actual or intended;
self-directed or directed towards others) through verbal
abuse to warfare in all its forms. The term is often used
to cover such a wide range of complicated behaviours that it
is meaningless. Obviously no singular definition of aggression can be satisfactory, and the validity of any self-
reporting questionnaire to such behaviour in the real world
is debatable. In my opinion this difficulty in definition
precludes any attempt to tie aggressive behaviour in man to
a causal explanation based on his biology and I must stress
the dangers involved in popular attempts to do this (Ardrey,

1967; Lorenz, 1966). To push such glossy "biological" theories one step further in an attempt to explain possible differences in aggression between men and women leads us even
further into the realm of the ridiculous.

We know a shade more about sex hormones and human sexual
behaviour; just enough to allow us to make some very tentative hypotheses which humbly await further confirmation. It
is possible to define sexual behaviour more precisely than
aggressive behaviour by restricting it to the act of copulation. However, social taboos have prevented any comprehensive studies from being made, and all of the human studies
rely on the subjects themselves reporting their level of
sexual desire (i.e. libido, which is in itself a vague term).

Eunuchoids, men whose testicles have failed to become
functional, lack libido and potency, but acquire both when
treated with androgen. Swyer (1968) reports that men castrated in adulthood do not lose their secondary sex characters
and may retain relatively normal libido and potency even
though their ejaculation volume may fall off completely. He
also says that most men who are impotent show no lack of androgen and no benefit from androgen therapy, thus concluding
that almost all cases of impotence in men are caused by changes in the central effector mechanisms of sexual behaviour,
perhaps of psychological origin and not from changes in hormone secretion.

In contrast, Money (1961) has reported that, when his
male patients suffering from hypogonadalism (lowered functioning of the testes) stopped taking androgens, they had
fewer erections and less desire to masturbate or engage in
coitus. The relationship between circulating androgens and
sexual arousal in men is unclear, butperhaps we can at this
point suggest that circulating androgens are necessary for
sexual behaviour to become established in males and that the
level of sexual activity in adulthood may be to some extent
dependent on circulating androgens, although psychological
or cultural factors would seem to outweigh this in importance.
Libido in females seems to be more dependent on circulating
androgens than on either of the female sex hormones, oestrogen or progesterone (Money, 1965). These androgens are produced by the ovary and adrenal cortex. Money found that his
female patients who stopped taking oestrogen experienced no
decline in libido. Some frigid women have responded to androgen therapy with increased libido; however, placebo tests
for this sort of data are unavailable. It is possible that

the androgens are acting peripherally by increasing the vascularity and sensitivity of the clitoris, which is the primary erotic zone of the female. Androgens do not appear to affect the vagina. As in men, psychological factors can also over-ride these hormonal effects in women (Bardwick, 1971).

Androgens, therefore, seem to be the hormones most directly involved in sexual libido in humans. However, it must be stressed that all the examples showing this are from gross changes in hormonal levels (either the absence or presence of androgen, or administration of high doses). No correlation can be found between the frequency of sexual activity and androgen levels in normal males and females at any age. In extreme cases it may be possible to see the hormonal effects, which normally are superseded by psychological determinants. Also, if a correlation between androgen level and sexual activity were found for the normal population, we could not definitely conclude that androgen levels control libido because sexual activity itself may produce changes in hormone levels. In fact, an individual's attitude to the sexual act, be it one of anxiety or pleasure, may lead to production of different hormones. The hormonal constitution of the body is a symphony of interactions (alteration of one hormone causes changes in all the others) so that fluctuation in androgen level could occur directly or indirectly as a result of sexual activity. Indeed, as in animals, there is some evidence that stressful environments can produce changes in sex hormone production in man. Soldiers in Vietnam have been found to have lowered levels of testosterone excretion under conditions of training and combat (Rose *et al.* 1969), and adrenalin and cortisol, released from the adrenal gland during periods of stress, can inhibit testosterone production in men (Levin *et al.* 1967).

CIRCULATING LEVELS OF ANDROGENS AND ATTENTION

Thus far I have discussed sexual and aggressive behaviour with respect to circulating levels of androgens. What now can we say about sex differences in performance on a range of psychophysical tasks, which measure sensory thresholds, verbal ability and spatial ability, etc? (See Chapter 6 by McGuinness.) Some recent work on animals has lead us to a point where we can ask concrete questions about the possible causes of such differences; so I shall relate this work in some detail.

If a young male chicken, in the first week or two of
its life, is injected with testosterone its comb and wattles
will redden and grow, and its bone and muscle growth will be
modified so that it adopts a different body stance. In addition to these morphological changes a number of behavioural
changes will occur; attack and male copulatory behaviour can
be elicited with greater ease and the pattern of vocalization:
will alter - crowing may occur (Collias, 1950; Andrew; 1966).
Since all of these behaviours occur at low levels before
treatment with testosterone and they simply become more apparent after treatment, testosterone has been considered to
act on the behavioural mechanism by lowering the thresholds
for eliciting these behaviours. As mentioned earlier this
sort of data is available for many other species. But testosterone is now known to have an additional and entirely different effect. Andrew and Rogers (1972) have found that male
chickens treated with testosterone have altered attention.
Once they have started to respond to a given stimulus they
lock-on-to it; in other words, they show increased persistence in responding to that stimulus and resist distraction
by other stimuli (see also Chapter 10 by Archer). As an extension of this same mechanism, once they have begun to respond to a stimulus in a given place in their environment,
they persist in responding in that place and resist moving
to a new place even if the same type of stimulus is available
there.
     This was first demonstrated in tasks requiring hungry
animals to search for grains of food scattered on different
backgrounds. The chicks were trained to eat two colours of
chicken mash, red and yellow, but to prefer red food over
yellow. In the test situation red and yellow grains were
scattered over the entire floor and runs of pecking at grains
of each colour were scored, together with moving from one
area of the floor to another. At any given time the chicken
has a number of possible targets in its visual field and can
adopts a variety of different searching strategies. A peck
at a grain of one colour tends to be followed by pecking at
another of the same colour, so that pecking occurs in runs
on one colour followed by runs on the other colour. Hence
the length of runs on red and yellow food grains can give
us indication of attention switching, or persistence. Distracting stimuli could also be scattered amongst the food
grains. For example, in one test small pebbles which looked
very like the red food were stuck-down at random over the

floor. In this situation the untreated chicks pecked in
short runs at red food, their preferred food, followed by
shorter runs on yellow food, to which they switched when
red became difficult to find, with occasional very short runs
on the non-edible pebbles. After testosterone treatment runs
on red food were markedly increased in length, and yellow
food and pebbles were almost completely avoided. This implies that attention switch from red stimuli to yellow stimu-
lie was now more difficult and that irrelevant stimuli were
ignored.

When the food was given in small clusters over the floor
with no distracting stimuli, and moving from cluster to cluster was scored, the testosterone-treated chickens pecked more
times at each cluster before they moved on to a new one
(Rogers, 1974). In this test they were more reluctant to
switch their search from one area to another area. The reader can find a much more detailed discussion of the theoretical explanation for this in Andrew (1972a). Similar findings have also been obtained by Archer (1974) for food reward in a runway. Male chicks were trained to run down a
long, straight runway for a food reward. Running times in
the runway for control and testosterone-treated chicks were
investigated after altering the colour and pattern of the
runway walls. Controls were more distracted by this change
in an irrelevant cue than were testosterone treated birds,
many of which appeared not to notice it as they headed single-
mindedly towards the food-dish. They were, however, more
distracted by changes in the food-dish, a relevant cue.

Testosterone has a very similar effect on operant behaviour in which the chick is presented with two keys differing in colour. Pecks on one key are rewarded by food and
pecks on the other key are not rewarded. Changes in the non-
rewarding key go unnoticed by testosterone-treated chicks
but not by the controls (Messent, 1974). Changes in the rewarding key are noticed by both.

Archer (1973a and 1973b) has investigated the way in
which the attentional changes occurring after testosterone-
treatment influence behaviour of chicks in a novel environment. Many effects of testosterone were observed but to
mention just two; treated birds were more persistent in the
jumping attempts to escape and made fewer head movements in
scanning the new environment since they fixated each aspect
of the environment for a longer time. It is clear that
testosterone's action on attention can extend over a wide

range of behaviours within the chicken's repertoire.

The behavioural action of testosterone is limited to the male sex. Female chicks injected with the hormone show all the peripheral effects of comb growth, wattle growth and change in body stance including some changes in vocalizations, but they do not show changes in attack, copulation or attention (Andrew, 1972b).

Caution must always be used when interpreting data from experiments in which a hormone is administered, for it could be transformed into another steroid. Also, where high doses are given, as in these experiments, the hormone may be acting non-specifically. In order to ascertain that the above effects were physiological, Rogers (1974) tested adult fowls. Food search tests were given to untreated hens, untreated cocks, cocks treated with antiandrogen, cocks castrated soon after hatching, and castrates treated with testosterone. (Antiandrogens, like cyproterone acetate, block the action of androgens.) The presence of androgen in the untreated males and castrated males treated with testosterone produced the same effects on attack behaviour, crowing and, in particular, attention in the adults as had been previously found in young chickens (Fig. 1). This confirms that the previous findings apply for physiological levels of circulating hormones. The lesser degree of persistence in hens would seem to result from their lower levels of androgens.

Where do we go from here? In chickens further research is being directed to determining whether the effect on attention is specific for testosterone or whether it can perhaps be generated by other androgens or steroid hormones. The behavioural outcome of testosterone-treatment is being characterized in more detail, and a search is being made for a possible brain site for control of this behaviour.

It is now necessary to see whether a similar mechanism holds for other species, and indeed we can begin to question whether it may occur in man. When these sorts of questions are asked of the human species we are faced with immense problems. Human behaviour is greatly influenced by cultural, or learning, phenomena and it is not possible to control for these as one can in animals. Cross-cultural studies in which we attempt to isolate the effects of different cultural environments on a given piece of behaviour can be useful. However, constancy of a behaviour across cultures can never ascertain that this behaviour has a genetic or hormonal basis, since the cultural influences on that piece of behaviour could

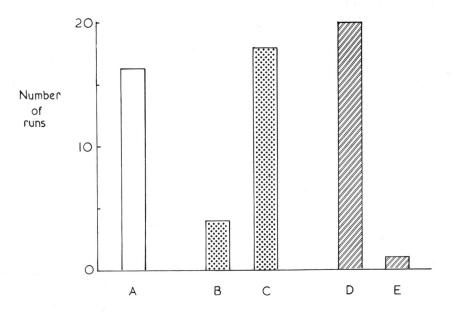

Fig. 1. Persistence in adult fowls is represented by the total number of runs on red and yellow food in the first 100 pecks on the pebbled floor. More runs means less persistence. A, females; B, males; C, males treated with antiandrogen; D, castrated males; E, castrated males treated with testosterone.

be the same in all cultures. Only variation between cultures can lead to deductions; *for* cultural influence being the main determinant, and *against* biological/genetic factors being important determinants. I stress this point because some ethologists fail to realize it (e.g. Eibl-Eibesfeldt, 1970).

When we consider sex differences in behaviour we must realize that each sex belongs to a different sub-culture, and that learning must be enormously important. To return to chickens, sex differences in the attention of adult fowls could also have been explained by differential learning had evidence for castrates, antiandrogen-treated males and, in particular, young chickens not pointed so strongly towards a hormonal explanation. In both chicks and man, males with higher levels of androgens have a different physical appearance to low androgen males and this could lead to their being reared differently.

Having said this, let us take a very tentative and cautious look at the way in which we might predict androgens to effect human attention and persistence basing our hypothesis on the evidence for chickens, as Andrew (1972) has done.

Broverman *et al.* (1964 and 1968) and Klaiber *et al.* (1967) claim to have found data indicating an effect of androgens on human cognition. We can assess this in relation to the theory for androgens and persistent attention. (Broverman's own interpretation of his data is discussed in Chapter 10 by Archer.) Males with high androgen levels were selected by physique (greater shoulder and chest width as compared to height), more extensive hair on chest and above-average 17-ketosteroid excretion, one of the breakdown products of testosterone. These subjects were found to have superior performance on simple, automatic tasks which required "sustained rapid volleys of the same responses to a limited set of stimuli". For example, tasks which tested speed of reading repeated colour names, or speed of naming three simple and very different figures repeated in a long, random sequence. Increased persistence in responding to the presented stimuli coupled with an ability to resist attention shift and distraction away from the task should be crucial to rapid performance on a simple task, particularly as the subject begins to become bored with the task and is then more likely to be distracted by other stimuli in the environment, and so to be slowed down and to make errors. Such tasks could have some similarities to the test in which chicks had to search for food on the pebbled floor (Andrew, 1972a).

However, on another test in which the subject had to examine as quickly as possible a series of unrepeated figures to find one which was a nonsense figure, not depicting anything familiar, high androgen males did not score above average. Here an ability to rapidly switch attention from one figure to the next, recognize it and move on until the nonsense figure is reached would seem to be best achieved by a lack of persistence. Increased persistence could cause interference between successive recognitions, since the subject may still be attempting to find the previous figure when a new one comes up and this could waste time. Actually, as a direct prediction from the data for chickens we would expect high androgen males to perform below average on this

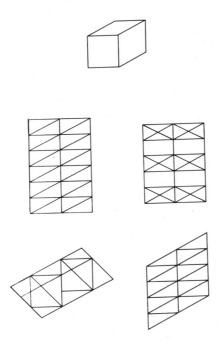

Fig. 2. An example of the Witkin Embedded Figure test. The subject is first shown one of the complex figures in the lower 2 rows, followed by the simple figure above. The simple figure is then hidden and the subject must find it embedded in the complex pattern. The time taken to do this is scored.

test.

Broverman and his co-workers have also found that high androgen males take longer to find solutions to the Gottschaldt and Witkin Embedded Figure tests, which are said to indicate "field dependence" (see Fig. 2). High androgen males may take longer because they persist in examining each part, or possible solution, of the complex pattern before they move on to another part or solution. In this manner they could

be displaying the same sort of reluctance to move from a
search area to another as shown by testosterone-treated
chicks searching for food placed in clusters on the floor
without distracting stimuli.

Another way in which poor performance on the Embedded
Figure tests could be generated, and this is the one that
Witkin himself suggested to explain "field dependence", is
by an inability to maintain memory of the simple figure
against the distracting input of the complex figure. This
would suggest increased distractibility and decreased persistence, which may possibly explain the poor performance of
women on this task. Increased distraction from the task at
hand could also lower female performance, and Boersma et al.
(1969) have found that females have a shorter mean length of
fixation on the complex figure than do males. High androgen
males and women both have difficulty on the Embedded Figure
tests, but possibly for different attentional reasons, both
stemming from a hormonal cause (Andrew, 1972a). Callaway
(1959) has shown that performance on the Witkin Embedded
Figure test bears a U-shaped relationship to a "narrowed"
and "broadened" focus of attention, these two extremes per-
forming poorly. He measures focus of attention on the
Stroop Word test, in which the subject must name the colours
of inks used to print conflicting colour names (e.g. the
word RED may be printed in green ink). A "narrowed focus
of attention" in this context means that the subject is less
distracted by the printed words. Such data supports the previous explanation for poor performance on the Embedded Figure
test in narrowly focused, high androgen men and broadly focused women.

It should be pointed out that although males can be separated into high and low androgen performance on the Witkin
test, it is the male group as a whole which has been tested
against females and has been found to score shorter times
(Bieri et al. 1958). This sex difference first appears at
an age of eight years. It is also at the age of 8-10 years
that males produce increased levels of testosterone and the
sex differences in levels of sex steroids first appear
(Gandy and Peterson, 1968). While this could add further
weight to an hypothesis of hormonal causation, it is at this
same age that differentiation between sex-roles begins to be
established (Oakley, 1972). Conditioning into the female-
role may teach women to be less persistent and more easily
distracted than males, who are oppositely conditioned. In

the same way males who have a physique most like society's
ideal image of masculinity, broad shouldered and strong because of high androgen levels, may receive even stronger conditioning into conforming to a persistent pattern of behaviour. Indeed Mead (1950) has reported a case of sex-role reversal in the *Tchambuli* tribe of New Guinea in which the women are self-assertive, practical and managing, while the men
are "skittish", wary of each other, interested in the arts
and do the shopping. She comments that, in contrast to all
other societies which she has studied, the *Tchambuli* males
had a "fitful, fleeting quality" of mind and "an inability
to come to grips with anything". Unfortunately for our present hypothesis they were not tested on the Embedded Figure
tests! However, Witkin has reported a correlation between
poor performance in his test and dependency in interpersonal
relationships, suggestibility, conformity and lack of self-
reliance, which occurred similarly for both sexes (Oakley,
1972). In a more recent study on college students Mayo and
Bell (1972) failed to find a sex difference on the Witkin
test; instead they suggested that field independence was associated with artistic ability.

Therefore, on presently existing evidence, we are unable to decide between a major contribution by hormonal or
cultural factors affecting human attentional processes. We
need more well-controlled experiments. How then are they to
be done? If we test one group of individuals and compare
them to another, be they males versus females or high androgen males versus low androgen males, we will always be caught
with the problem of separating the direct action of androgen
on attentional processes from their action on physical appearance leading subsequently to differences in cultural-
conditioning. The only way around this dilemma is to use
each individual as its own control by testing before and
shortly after administering male hormone. Testing in the
presence of elevated hormonal levels would then occur before changes in physique and conditioning could occur. Alternatively, antiandrogen could be administered. Broverman's
group has actually done one of these sorts of experiments
(Klaiber *et al.* 1971). Before and after an infusion of
testosterone male subjects were asked to serially subtract
(e.g. 17 from 981 for three minutes). The number of correct
subtractions made in the allotted time was taken as the performance score, and subjects were tested first in the morning and then again, after testosterone infusion, in the

afternoon. In the control subjects there was a decline in
performance on this task from morning to afternoon, and testosterone prevented this decline. That is, in the second test
testosterone-treated subjects made fewer errors. This test
has similarities to the one for speed of naming simple figures, since increased persistence and resistance to distraction particularly with increasing boredom could prevent for-
getting figures and so decrease errors. This sort of data
is more convincing; however, controls were a problem because
the testosterone was administered in an alcoholic vehicle,
also known to affect attention. It is well known that simul-
taneous administration of two drugs rarely produces a simple
additive or subtractive outcome. Further, testing subjects
first in the morning and then in the afternoon confounds the
results with the diurnal variation in normal performance.
Had Broverman followed his infused subjects back to their
original performance whilst monitoring return to natural
levels of testosterone, I would have been more convinced.
Future experimenters need to administer androgens in inert
vehicles more than once to the same subject so that attempts
to correlate waxing and waning of behavioural changes with
parallel changes in hormonal levels can be made. Such requirements introduce ethical problems about possible side-
effects, which explains why they have not already been done.
Indeed, I question whether the administration of testosterone by Broverman's group was an ethical procedure, since one
cannot be certain of the absence of side-effects on physiological functions. However, this is another question, which
cannot be adequately discussed here. All I suggest is that
we remain sceptical about androgenic effects on human cognition until we have the data in hand.

On the physiological side it must always be remembered
that administering one hormone can alter many other hormones
in the body so that we can never be certain of a direct effect of the administered hormone until good biochemical studies have been done. Also, the hormonal constitution of
each species varies and this must be considered when attempting to extrapolate methods and theories from one species to
another.

ORGANIZING EFFECTS OF ANDROGENS EARLY IN LIFE

Until now we have been mainly concerned with circulating
hormones in older animals. In recent years testosterone has

been found to play a critical role in prenatal and neonatal
life when it can have anatomical, physiological and psychological effects on sexual development in some species. That is,
it has an "organizational" effect on the young brain and sex
organs.

Rapid growth during prenatal and early post-natal life
makes the developing brain more vulnerable to changes in its
environment. Androgenic action during this period can per-
manently modify hypothalamic control of the production of
luteinizing hormone by the pituitary. Harris (1964) concluded that the essential difference between pituitary gonado-
trophic function in male and female rats rested upon differences in the hypothalamus, which are established by hormonal
action on this area of the brain during the first five days
after birth. The acyclic pattern of hormonal secretion from
the pituitary (lacking the ovulatory phase) characteristic
of males is established by the presence of testicular hormones
during this critical period. Absence of testicular hormones
during this period produces a cyclic hypothalamus leading in
turn to a cyclic output of luteinizing hormone from the pituitary which is characteristic of females. These females
never ovulate. In addition to the effects on their reproductive physiology, female rats so treated do not show normal
receptive behaviour in adulthood even when they are adequately supplied with ovarian hormones (Harris and Levine, 1965).
When treated again with testosterone in adulthood they show
greater amounts of mounting (male) behaviour than control females similarly treated (Harris and Levine, 1965). Both physiologically and behaviourally they appear to have been "masculinized". Male rats castrated during the critical period
showed female-like receptive behaviour when treated with female sex hormones in adulthood (Phoenix *et al*. 1968). Treatment with testosterone in adulthood did not swing them over
to a male pattern of sexual behaviour. Similar findings have
been obtained for guinea-pigs in the pioneering work of
Phoenix *et al*. (1959). Guinea-pigs have a longer gestation
period than rats and their maximally sensitive period to the
organizational action of androgen falls before birth between
days 30 and 55 of gestation (Goy *et al*. 1964). Administration
of testosterone to the maternal animal during this period produces similar responses to treatment with male and female sex
hormones in adulthood as it does in rats.

Moving on to hamsters, we find conflicting evidence for
the effects of early androgen (Beach, 1971). Nucci and Beach

(1971) obtained no effects on female offspring from androgen
treatment of pregnant hamsters at three different times during gestation (the total period of gestation is short, only
16 days). Possibly they chose the wrong times to inject.
Swanson and Crossley (1971) injected testosterone at 2 and
3 days after birth and claimed to get results similar to
those for rats. The organizational effects of androgen are
not as clear-cut for all species as they are in the rat.

It should be noted that the effects of early androgen
in the sexual behaviour of rats, guinea-pigs and hamsters is
only apparent after hormonal treatment in adulthood.

In rats motor activity (e.g. wheel-running in the home-
cage) is similarly affected by early androgen. Normal female rats have higher levels of running than normal males
and this running is further increased at oestrus. Male rats
castrated neonatally and implanted with ovaries in adulthood
show female running patterns while control males receiving
ovaries in adulthood do not (Harris, 1964). The only sexually dimorphic behaviour in rats known to be affected by early
androgen and not requiring subsequent hormonal treatment in
adulthood for its appearance is that of emergence from the
home-cage and activity, scored as the area covered in the
open-field. In contrast to normal females, females treated
with testosterone neonatally take longer to emerge from the
home-cage and are less active when they are observed in novel
situations; characteristics which are more typical of male
behaviour (Pfaff and Zigmond, 1971). The reverse is observed
in neonatally castrated males.

In dogs and primates, "masculinized" behaviour in females treated with androgen prior to birth has been found to
affect some, but not all,types of behaviour and is not depende
on subsequent hormone treatment. In dogs, Beach has produced
females which adopt the male posture for urination in adulthood (Beach, 1971). Phoenix et al. (1968) have exposed female rhesus monkeys to testosterone while in the foetal stage
by treating their mothers with testosterone. These offspring
had masculinized genitalia and their behaviour shifted towards that more typical of males in the following ways; they
were more aggressive, threatened and initiated play more frequently, mounted more often, and indulged in more rough-and-
tumble play than did control females. However, by their
third year of life the level of these behaviours had declined
in control males and the differences between androgen-exposed
females and control females had diminished along with this

(Goy and Phoenix, 1971a and 1971b). It seems, therefore, that, unlike rats and guinea-pigs, the effects of early androgen in primates may not be permanent. In view of their large dependence on learning this is not surprising (Hamburg and Lunde, 1967). One suspects a similar lack of permanence in behavioural modification by early androgen treatment in humans.

ORGANIZATIONAL EFFECTS OF ANDROGENS IN HUMANS

We can now examine what evidence is available for an organizational action of androgen in humans. For some years now Money and Ehrhardt (1972) have been studying female children exposed to excess levels of androgen before birth either because they suffered from adrenogenital syndrome, in which the adrenal gland produced too much androgen, or because their mothers took progestin to prevent miscarriage (progestin has androgenic action on the foetus).

In the first category they studied 15 girls all of whom had marked masculinization of the genitalia. All were reared as females and cortisone treatment had commenced in infancy so that the greatest exposure to androgen had been before birth (Ehrhardt et al. 1968). The 10 subjects in the progestin-exposed group had less masculinization of the genitalia; one had none at all (Ehrhardt and Money, 1967). Both groups ranged in age from about 4 to 16 at the time of testing. They were compared to a control group which had Turner's syndrome (XO genome, no gonads, feminine phenotype; Money and Ehrhardt, 1968). Compared to the group with Turner's syndrome and a group of normal girls, the androgen exposed groups are reported to indulge in more energetic play, prefer masculine clothes, prefer boy's toys and score above average on IQ tests. While these findings are interesting, no clear explanation is apparent. Money has not yet carried out controls necessary to eliminate cultural influences. Possibly, these children were reared differently by their parents, who responded to their physical virilization or who overcompensated for their abnormalities. Possibly, mothers who bothered to take progestin in order to prevent miscarriage were different in personality, or they came from a limited social stratum. Indeed three quarters of these children had at least one parent who was a college graduate, and half had a parent working at professional or business executive level. Money had not yet tested other members of these families on

the tests he·applied to his experimental subjects, and until
he can give us more information we would be wise to keep an
open-mind. He does report that one subject had a sister not
similarly exposed to progestin and she too was a tomboy, as
also had been her mother. Judging from the decline in masculinized behaviour in rhesus monkeys, as mentioned earlier,
it would seem unlikely that learning could not overlay such
an early androgen effect on behaviour. In fact, learning of
a gender-role is so strong in humans that it can occur very
successfully against hormonal constitution, as in the case
of pseudohermaphrodites (Hamburg and Lunde, 1967).

In the past, adrenogenital syndrome has often been
thought to be associated with mental retardation, psychosis
and homosexuality. Fortunately, Money has eradicated these
myths, but right now we see many more myths looming on the
psychiatric horizon. I recently heard a well-reputed psychi-
atrist, who must remain nameless, claim that transexualism
resulted (definitely "resulted", and not "possibly resulted")
from an organizing effect of androgen on the foetus. He
hastened to discuss the rat data in order to give his statement "good scientific" backing. No, he had not heard about
any work on other species and he had not considered any unanswered questions about Money's work! Others still use this
data to "explain" homosexuality or other, so called, sexual
deviations. Naive extrapolation is, I am afraid, far too
common, particularly when subsequent workers latch on to and
quote previous work without reading it carefully or without
enough knowledge in the area to properly assess it. One
fears for the psychiatric profession in this respect.

We see the same thing happening in the area of sex differences. Researchers like Dawson (1972), Reinisch (1974)
and Bardwick (1971) attempt to explain sex differences in
behaviour of rats and men by an organizational effect of androgen either fully determining them or placing a predisposition on the brain for learning different things more easily. In my opinion this is pushing the theory too far, too
soon.

Some of these researchers assume that very early sex
differences in behaviour could not have been learnt, but sex
assignment occurs at the moment of birth and from this moment
on conditioning into a sex-role commences. In some American
hospitals newborn babies are wrapped in either a blue or
pink blanket according to their sex.

There is also a conceptual difficulty in the organization effect which must be considered. Many workers (e.g. Diamond, 1968; Phoenix *et al.* 1968) assume that the same sort of differentiation process is occurring in the genitalia and the brain. When testosterone is present in the foetus, previously undifferentiated tissue, called the primitive urogenital sinus, normally develops into the male penis and seminal vesicles. In the absence of testosterone, it normally develops into the female clitoris and vagina. Except in rare hermaphroditic cases, the developmental direction adopted by the genitalia of any single individual results from a discrete choice between male and female form. That is, it must proceed in one direction or the other, and not both ways simultaneously. However, the organizational effects of androgen on behaviour work only for those behaviours that normally occur to some extent in both sexes (Goy and Phoenix, 1971a). Normal female rats show some mounting and normal males show some lordosis. The neural circuits controlling these behaviours do not make a discrete choice between development of either male or female behaviour, but instead any single individual has neural circuits for both male and female behaviour.

Hamsters are the only species so far studied in which normal males and females show no overlap in lordosis or mounting, and so have behaviour best fitting the situation for genital tissue; yet androgenic organization of their behaviour is unclear (Beach, 1971). Given this lack of parallel between the sort of differentiation process that occurs in genitalia and in the central nervous system, it seems somewhat surprising that many workers naively assume that exactly the same process is occurring at both places. The genitalia have a binary choice; the brain chooses between two overlapping distributions and must involve more factors than simply androgen organization.

SUMMARY

On available evidence the differing concentrations of androgens in males and females cannot explain human sex differences in sexual and aggressive behaviour or on psychophysical and cognitive tasks. It has been impossible to control for cultural factors. Even in animals it has frequently been possible to demonstrate that environmental factors can modify the effects of sex hormones on behaviour, and that production of sex hormones can be altered by behaviour

and environmental stimuli. Arguments using Man's evolutionary past to justify a hormonal control of human behaviour
are therefore fallacious.

Only by experimental administration of hormones to humans would it be possible to even lay claim to a hormonal
causation of sex differences. Pertinent data is accumula-
ting for many species other than *Homo sapiens*, and predictions based on this can be legitimately formulated as hypotheses to be tested on Man. Premature extrapolation should
be strenuously avoided; it is all too prevalent in this
field. Experiments on man are difficult, if not impossible
to do; yet, if our rush to explain Man leads us to danger-
ously wrong conclusions we may wind up retarding our search
rather than assisting it. Any knowledge or belief relating
to this question is not only of scientific interest, but
carries with it enormous social and political significance.
Science shapes society; society shapes science. Encompassed
by this interaction we must look at all times in all directions; to the community, to the laboratory and, if humanly
possible, at ourselves and our biases.

REFERENCES

Andrew, R.J. (1966). Precocious adult behaviour in the young
chick. *Animal Behaviour,* 14, 485-500.

Andrew, R.J. (1972a). Recognition processes and behavior
with special reference to effects of testosterone on persistence. *Advances in the Study of Behavior,* 4, 175-206.

Andrew, R.J. (1972b). Changes in search behaviour in male
and female chicks, following different doses of testosterone. *Animal Behaviour,* 20, 741-750.

Andrew, R.J. and Rogers, L.J. (1972). Testosterone, search
behaviour and persistence. *Nature,* 237, 343-346.

Archer, J. (1973a). The influence of testosterone on chick
behavior in novel environments. *Behavioral Biology,*
8, 93-108.

Archer, J. (1973b). A further analysis of responses to a
novel environment by testosterone-treated chicks. *Behavioral Biology,* 9, 389-396.

Archer, J. (1974). The effects of testosterone on the distractability of chicks by irrelevant and relevant novel

stimuli. *Animal Behaviour*, 22, 397-404.

Archer, J. (1976). The organization of aggression and fear in vertebrates. *In* "Perspectives in Ethology". (P.P.G. Bateson and P. Klopfer, eds.) Vol. 2. Plenum, New York and London.

Ardrey, R. (1967). "African Genesis". Dell, New York.

Bardwick, J.M. (1971). "Psychology of Women". Harper and Row, New York.

Beach, F.A. (1970). Coital behaviour in dogs: VI. Long-term effects of castration upon mating in the male. *Journal of Comparative and Physiological Psychology*, 70, Part 2, 1-32.

Beach, F.A. (1971). Hormonal factors controlling the differentiation, development and display of copulatory behavior in the ramstergig and related species. *In* "The Biopsychology of Development". (E. Tobach, L.R. Aronson and E. Shaw, eds.) Academic Press, New York.

Beach, F.A. and Levinson, G. (1950). Effects of androgen on the glans penis and mating behaviour of castrated male rats. *Journal of Experimental Zoology*, 114, 159-171.

Beach, F.A. and Westbrooke, W.H. (1968). Dissociation of androgenic effects on sexual morphology and behaviour in rats. *Endocrinology*, 83, 395-398.

Bevan, W.D., Daves, W.F. and Levy, F.W. (1960). The relation of castration, androgen therapy and pre-test fighting experience to competitive aggression in male C57BL/10 mice. *Animal Behaviour*, 8, 6-12.

Bieri, J., Bradburn, W.M. and Galinsky, M.D. (1958). Sex differences in perceptual behavior. *Journal of Personality*, 26, 1-12.

Boersma, F.J., Muir, W., Wilton, K. and Barham, P. (1969). Eye movements during embedded figure tasks. *Perceptual Motor Skills*, 28, 271-274.

Bronson, F.H. and Desjardins, C. (1971). Steroid hormones and aggressive behavior in mammals. *In* "The Physiology of Aggression and Defeat". (B.E. Eleftheriou and J.P. Scott, eds.) Plenum, New York.

Bronson, F.H. and Eleftheriou, B.E. (1965). Relative effects of fighting on bound and unbound corticosterone in mice. *Proceedings of the Society of Experimental Biology and Medicine,* 118, 146-149.

Broverman, D.M., Broverman, I.K., Vogel, W. and Palmer, R.D. (1964). The automatization cognitive style and physical development. *Child Development,* 35, 1343-1359.

Broverman, D.M., Klaiber, E.L., Kobayashi, Y. and Vogel, W. (1968). Roles of activation and inhibition in sex differences in cognitive abilities. *Psychological Review,* 75, 23-50.

Callaway, E. (1959). The influence of amobarbital and metamphetamine on the focus of attention. *Journal of Mental Science,* 105, 382-392.

Christenson, T., Wallen, K., Brown, B.A. and Glickman, S.E. (1973). Effects of castration, blindness and anosmia on social reactivity in male Mongolian gerbil (*Meriones unguiculatus*). *Physiology and Behaviour,* 10, 989-994.

Christian, J.J., Lloyd, J.A. and Davis, D.E. (1969). The role of endocrines in the self-regulation of mammalian populations. *Recent Progress in Hormone Research,* 14, 501-578.

Collias, N.E. (1950). Hormones and Behavior, with special reference to birds and the mechanism of hormone action. *In* "A Symposium of Steroid Hormones". (E. Gordon, ed.) Wisconsin University Press.

Davidson, J.M. (1972). Hormones and reproductive behaviour. *In* "Hormones and Behavior". (S. Levine, ed.) Academic Press, New York.

Davis, D.E. (1964). The physiological analysis of aggressive behavior. *In* "Social Behavior and Organization among Vertebrates". (W. Etkin, ed.) University of Chicago Press.

Dawson, J.L.M. (1972). Effects of sex hormones on cognitive style in rats and man. *Behaviour Genetics,* 2, 21-42.

Dessi-Fulgheri, F., Lupo di Prisco, C., Verdarelli, P. (1975). The influence of long term isolation on the production and metabolism of gonadal sex steroids in male and female rats. *Physiology and Behaviour,* 14, 495-499.

Diamond, M. (1968). Genetic-endocrine interactions and human psychosexuality. *In* "Perspectives in Reproduction and Behavior". (M. Diamond, ed.) Indiana University Press.

Ehrhardt, A.A., Epstein, R. and Money, J. (1968). Fetal androgens and female gender identity in the early-treated adrenogenital syndrome. *Johns Hopkins Medical Journal*, 122, 160-167.

Ehrhardt, A.A. and Money, J. (1967). Progestin-induced hermaphroditism: IQ and psychosexual identity in a study of ten girls. *Journal of Sex Research*, 3(1), 83-100.

Eibl-Eibesfeldt, I. (1970). "Ethology: The Biology of Behaviour". Holt, Rinehart and Winston, New York.

Eleftheriou, B.E., Church, R.L., Norman, R.L., Pattison, M. and Zolorick, A.J. (1968). Effect of repeated exposure to aggression and defeat on plasma and pituitary levels of thyrotropin. *Physiology and Behaviour*, 3, 467-469.

Gandy, H.M. and Peterson, R.E. (1968). Measurement of testosterone and 17-ketosteroids in plasma by the double isotope dilution derivative technique. *Journal of Clinical Endrocrinology and Metabolism*, 28, 949.

Goy, R.W., Bridson, W.E. and Young, W.C. (1964). Period of maximal susceptibility of the prenatal female guinea-pig to masculinizing actions of testosterone proprionate. *Journal of Comparative and Physiological Psychology*, 57, 166-174.

Goy, R.W. and Phoenix, C.H. (1971a). The development of sexual and sex-related behaviour in female mammals masculinized by early treatment with androgens. *Proceedings of the International Union of Physiological Sciences*, 7, 167-168. XXV International Congress, Munich.

Goy, R.W. and Phoenix, C.H. (1971b). The effects of testosterone proprionate administered before birth on the development of behavior in genetic female rhesus monkeys. *In* "Steroid Hormones and Brain Function". (C.H. Sawyer and R.A. Gorski, eds.) University of California Press.

Guhl, A.M. (1964). Psychophysiological interrelations in the social behavior of chickens. *Psychological Bulletin*, 61, 277-285.

Hamburg, D.A. and Lunde, D.T. (1967). Sex hormones in the development of sex differences in human behavior. *In*

"The Development of Sex Differences". (E. Maccoby, ed.) Tavistock, London.

Hard, E. and Larsson, K. (1968).Dependence of adult mating behavior in male rats on the presence of littermates in infancy. *Brain, Behavior and Evolution,* 1, 405-419.

Harris, G.W. (1964). Sex hormones, brain development and brain function. *Endocrinology,* 75, 627-648.

Harris, G.W. and Levine, S. (1965). Sexual differentiation of the brain and its experimental control. *Journal of Physiology,* (London), 181, 379-400.

Klaiber, E.L., Broverman, D.M. and Kobayashi, Y. (1967). The automatization cognitive style, androgens and mono-amine oxidase. *Psychopharmacology,* (Berlin), 11, 320-336.

Klaiber, E.L., Broverman, D.M., Vogel, W., Abraham, G.E. and Cone, F.L. (1971). Effects of infused testosterone on mental performances and serum LH. *Journal of Clinical Endocrinology and Metabolism,* 32, 341-349.

Lehrman, D.S. (1971). Experimental background for the induc-tion of reproductive behavior pattern by hormones. *In* "The Biopsychology of Development". (E. Tobach, L.R. Aronson and E. Shaw, eds.) Academic Press, New York.

Levin, J.C., Lloyd, C.W., Lobotsky, J. and Friedrich, E.H. (1967). The effect of epinephrine on testosterone produc-tion. *Acta Endocrinologica,* (Copenhagen), 55, 184-192.

Lorenz, K. (1966). "On Aggression". Harcourt, Brace and World, New York.

Mathewson, S.G. (1961). Gonadotropic hormones affect aggres-sive behavior in starlings. *Science,* 134, 1522-1523.

Mayo, P.R. and Bell, J.M. (1972). A note on the taxonomy of Witkin's field-independence measures. *British Journal of Psychology,* 63, 255-256.

Mead, M. (1950). "Male and Female". Penguin, Harmondsworth.

Messent, P.M. (1974)."Distractability and Persistence in Chicks". D.Phil. Thesis, University of Sussex.

Michael, R.P., Wilson, M. and Plant, T.M. (1973). Sexual behaviour of male primates and the role of testosterone. *In* "Comparative Ecology and Behaviour of Primates". (R.P. Michael and J.H. Crook, eds.) Academic Press, London.

Money, J. (1961). The hormones and mating behavior. *In* "Sex and Internal Secretions". (W.C. Young, ed.) Vol. 2, 3rd Edition. Williams and Wilkins, Baltimore.

Money, J. (1965). The influence of hormones on sexual behavior. *Annual Review of Medicine*, 16, 67-82.

Money, J. and Ehrhardt, A.A. (1968). Prenatal hormonal exposure: possible effects on behaviour in Man. *In* "Endocrinology and Human Behaviour". (R.P. Michael, ed.) Oxford University Press.

Money, J. and Ehrhardt, A.A. (1972). "Man and Woman: Boy and Girl". Johns Hopkins University Press, Baltimore and London.

Nucci, L.P. and Beach, F.A. (1971). Effects of prenatal androgen treatment on mating behavior in female hamsters. *Endocrinology*, 88, 1514-1515.

Oakley, A. (1972). "Sex, Gender and Society". Temple Smith, London and Sun Books, Melbourne.

Payne, A.P. and Swanson, H.H. (1972). Neonatal androgenisation and aggression in the male golden hamster. *Nature*, 239, 282-283.

Persky, H., Smith, K.D. and Basu, G.K. (1971). Relation of psychologic measures of aggression and hostility to testosterone production in man. *Psychosomatic Medicine*, 23, 265-277.

Pfaff, D.W. and Zigmond, R.E. (1971). Neonatal androgen effects on sexual and non-sexual behaviour of adult rats tested under various hormone regimes. *Neuroendocrinology*, 1, 129-145.

Phoenix, C.H., Goy, R.W., Gerall, A.A. and Young, W.C. (1959). Organizing action of prenatally administered testosterone proprionate on the tissues mediating mating behaviour in the female guinea-pig. *Endocrinology*, 65, 369-382.

Phoenix, C.H., Goy, R.W. and Resko, J.A. (1968). Psychosexual differentiation as a function of androgenic stimulation. *In* "Perspectives in Reproduction and Sexual Behavior". (H. Diamond, ed.) Indiana University Press.

Reinisch, J.M. (1974). Fetal hormones, the brain and human sex differences: a heuristic integrative review of recent literature. *Archives of Sexual Behavior,* 3, 51-90.

Rogers, L.J. (1974). Persistence and search influenced by natural levels of androgens in young and adult chickens. *Physiology and Behavior,* 12, 197-204.

Rose, R.M., Bourne, P. and Poe, R. (1969). Androgen responses to stress. *Psychosomatic Medicine,* 31, 418-436.

Rose, R., Gordon, T.P. and Bernstein, I.S. (1972). Plasma testosterone levels in the male rhesus: Influences of sexual and social stimuli. *Science,* 178, 643-645.

Rosenblatt, J.S. and Aronson, L.R. (1958). The influence of experience on the behavioural effects of androgen in pre-puberally castrated male cats. *Animal Behaviour,* 6, 171-182.

Swanson, H.H. and Crossley, D.A. (1971). Sexual behavior in the golden hamster and its modification by neonatal ad-ministration of testosterone proprionate. *In* "Hormones and Behavior". (M. Hamburgh and E.J. Barrington, eds.) Appleton-Century Crofts, New York.

Swyer, G.I.M. (1968). Clinical effects of agents affecting fertility. *In* "Endocrinology and Human Behaviour". (R.P. Michael, ed.) Oxford University Press.

Thoman, E.B. and Arnold, W.J. (1968). Effects of early social deprivation on maternal behavior in the rat. *Journal of Comparative and Physiological Psychology,* 65, 55-59.

Vandenberg, J.G. (1971). The effects of gonadal hormones on the aggressive behaviour of adult golden hamsters (*Mesocricetus auratus*). *Animal Behaviour,* 19, 589-594.

Whalen, R.E. (1972). Gonadal hormones, the nervous system and behavior. *Advances in Behavioral Biology,* 4, 1-25.

8. FEMALE HORMONES AND BEHAVIOUR

Peter R. Messent

In the preceding chapter, Lesley Rogers considered the effects
of male sex hormones, androgens, on behaviour. This chapter
provides a discussion of the relation of female hormones to
behaviour. There are two groups of sex hormones which are
found at high concentrations in most female mammals and both
are steroids of the same general structure as the androgens
of males. The two groups are called oestrogens and progestogens.
     The first major section of this chapter contains a brief
description of these hormones and their normal fluctuations
in concentration. This is necessary because female hormones
show cyclical variations in concentration at different phases
of the oestrous or menstrual cycle, unlike testosterone levels
in males which remain relatively stable from day to day.
These fluctuations provide a convenient means of studying female hormones and behaviour: thus, far more data have been
assembled for women than for men. The main focus of this
discussion involves human studies, but animal experiments are
reported when information cannot readily be obtained from human subjects.
     After briefly describing the female hormones, I then con-
sider how these influence behaviour, beginning with sexual,
maternal and aggressive behaviour, which have been most commonly investigated. Other, lesser-known behavioural influences of female hormones, e.g. on sensory thresholds, dietary
selection and activity, are then considered before I finally
review how the hormones act on the central nervous system
(CNS) and affect emotional responses. Most of the behavioural
effects have been separately reviewed in the past, but by
examining them together I shall attempt to consider their
relationship to one another and the possible adaptive significance of the various effects.

The two sex hormones present at relatively high concentrations in most adult female vertebrates are oestradiol and
progesterone. Oestradiol is a member of the group of hormones called oestrogens, while progesterone is one of the
progestogens, both groups being steroid hormones with a struc
tural similarity to testosterone and the other androgens (see
previous chapter). The three groups differ, however, in the
number of carbon atoms in the molecule, with progestogens
having 21, androgens 19 and oestrogens 18. In addition to
oestradiol, other oestrogen compounds frequently occurring
naturally are oestrone and oestriol. Of the progestogens,
progesterone is the only one of any known behavioural importance.

Synthetic compounds have been produced with actions similar to oestrogen or progesterone. Some of these, such as
diethyl stilboestrol, are not even steroids, but are similar
to steroids in their action. The synthetic compounds are
used, for example, in oral contraceptive pills since the
naturally occurring compounds would be destroyed by the di-
gestive tract.

The three groups of sex hormones, androgens, oestrogens
and progestogens are detectable in the blood plasma of female mammals, but androgen levels are comparatively low in
almost all species studied.

Oestradiol and progesterone are both produced by the
ovary, and the adrenal glands also produce some of each com-
pound, in addition to smaller quantities of androgens. When
an adult female is not pregnant, both oestradiol and progesterone show cyclical changes in the levels of production by
the ovary: these changes give rise to the oestrous cycle
(occurring in most mammals), and the menstrual cycle (occurring in primates). The latter is distinguished by the month-
ly vaginal bleeding, caused by the degeneration and slough-
ing of the uterine wall (which is much more highly developed
and vascularized in menstruating species). The hormonal
changes are fairly similar in both oestrous and menstrual
cycles, with a peak level of oestradiol occurring at ovulation. This is followed by elevated progesterone levels in
the subsequent phase, the length of which can vary considerably between species and is called "dioestrus", or the luteal phase, depending on the type of cycle; (in women, oestrogen levels are also high in this latter phase). A detailed
description of the hormonal changes in the human menstrual
cycle is given by Vandewiele *et al*. (1970), and for the oest-

rous cycle of rats by Butcher *et al.* (1974).

During pregnancy, progesterone levels are often enormously higher than at any stage of an oestrous or menstrual cycle, while oestradiol levels are generally not elevated, although other oestrogens may be (e.g. oestriol in humans). These different hormone fluctuations provide many "natural experiments" which can be utilized in studying behaviour changes in relation to hormones.

SEXUAL, AGGRESSIVE AND MATERNAL BEHAVIOUR

The relationship of sex hormones to female reproductive behaviour has been well documented for many mammals. In the previous chapter, Lesley Rogers described how in many species continued sexual activity of males is dependent on androgen, although in others (particularly primates) there is less hormonal dependence for continued sexual activity. For females, the situation is a little different because in most species except Man, sexual behaviour ceases almost immediately in the absence of circulating sex hormones (e.g. following ovariectomy). This in itself strongly suggests an important role of female hormones in controlling sexual behaviour, which has been confirmed by a number of animal studies. These are not described in detail here as there are several recent reviews of the topic to which the reader is referred for further information (e.g. Kane *et al.* 1969, for humans; Davidson, 1972, Lisk, 1973 and Michael, 1973, for other mammals).

In most mammals, oestrogens seem to be the most important hormones concerned with female sexual behaviour. Michael (1973) has outlined how oestrogen increases both the sexual receptivity and sexual attractiveness of female rhesus monkeys to males. Progesterone, on the other hand, tends to have the opposite effect on both these features, since a decline in sexual activity is seen both in the luteal phase of the menstrual cycle, and following progesterone treatment.

In mammals with oestrous cycles, it is generally the case that either oestrogen alone, or oestrogen plus progesterone provide the hormonal basis for sexual behaviour. Lisk (1973) concluded that in long-cycle species such as the ewe, pig and cow, the receptive period seems to be induced by oestrogen alone, although a previous fall in progesterone levels may also contribute. In short-cycle species such as the rat, hamster, guinea-pig and rabbit, oestrogen priming and then a surge of progesterone is the usual combination that stimulates oestrous behaviour. However, the continued presence of progesterone then becomes inhibitory to the maintenance of heat, so it has a biphasic effect.

Although receptivity of females is apparently increased by female hormones, there is little evidence that female mammals will ever actively seek males. Drewett (1973a) found that approach behaviour of female rats directed to males was uninfluenced by ovarian hormones sufficient to produce sexual receptivity. However, Eliasson and Meyerson (1975) obtained a slight but significant choice in a runway situation by female rats during oestrus and proestrus for an intact rather than an impotent male.

The behavioural effect of these hormones would appear to be almost entirely a central one since lesioning the sensory nerves to the genital area has little effect in a variety of species (e.g. Ball, 1934; Brooks, 1937). In rats, there are several brain areas with specific oestrogen receptors, the most notable being the hypothalamus (Stumpf, 1970). Localized hypothalamic implants of oestrogen also elicit female sexual behaviour in cats and rats at concentrations which do not affect peripheral tissues (Harris et al. 1958; Lisk, 1973). Generally, progesterone is not specifically retained in particular brain areas, and it has been suggested that its effects may be through a more broad based action on the entire central nervous system.

Sexual interest and behaviour is not abolished following removal of the ovaries in women, but this does not mean that female hormones are without some influence. There is evidence (Udry and Morris, 1968) of peak incidences of coitus and/or orgasm in women around midcycle, with a trough in the premenstrual and menstrual phases. This could be taken to represent a residuum of the peaks in coitus found around ovulation in many species (including sub-human primates). Davidson (1972) has suggested that the decrease in libido in the late luteal phase could result from peak progesterone secretion, known to inhibit sexual behaviour in female rhesus monkeys. However, Kinsey et al. (1953) took the alternative view that there are no specific effects of gonadal hormones on female sexual behaviour. The evidence for humans is still insufficient to support or refute the direct role of hormones in the sexual behaviour of women.

One researcher, Money (1965), has suggested that testosterone, produced by the adrenals, may be important for libido in women. Female rhesus monkeys will become more recep-

tive, but not more attractive, to males following small testosterone injections intracerebrally or intramuscularly (Michael,
1971), and female rabbits can be made more receptive following
testosterone injections (Kawakami and Sawyer, 1959). These
findings contain a warning against the dichotomous separation
of hormones, or indeed of sexual behaviour, into male and female, since both sexes of most species studied also display
behaviour normally considered more appropriate to the opposite
sex. However, bearing in mind this warning, it may be more
convenient to consider the two sexes and their hormones separately.

In males, sexual and aggressive behaviour have been
shown to have similar hormonal bases (see previous chapter).
Female mammals generally show much less aggressive behaviour
than their male counterparts (e.g. Conner, 1972) although
there are some exceptions (e.g. the hamster; Vandenburgh,
1971). It has been suggested that oestrogen may inhibit aggression in females, but Conner (1972) has argued that the
data are conflicting. Increased aggression towards both
male and female intruders has been reported during lactation
in female mice (Dennis St. John and Corning, 1973; Gandelman,
1972). This aggression declines either as the pups get older, or 5 hours after their removal. Gandelman (1972) has
suggested that hormones, possibly prolactin (a gonadotrophin
released from the pituitary), may be important.

Maternal behaviour has long been thought to be dependent on female sex hormones simply because males of many species fail to show it. Maternal behaviour is complex in that
it may involve a variety of activities such as nest building,
aggression and care of the young, which may be required to
change as the young become older. Zarrow *et al.* (1972) have
provided a comprehensive review of the evidence for hormones
controlling these behaviours in the rabbit, mouse, hamster
and rat. They have concluded that there are wide species
differences in the degree and type of hormonal control, but
that oestrogens, progestogens and prolactin are implicated.
These differences have been confirmed by more recent work.
For example, Siegel and Rosenblatt (1975) showed that oestrogen plays a major part in stimulating maternal care in preg-
nancy-terminated and virgin rats. Progesterone delayed or
inhibited this behaviour. In the hamster on the other hand,
Siegel and Greenwald (1975) found that neither progesterone
nor oestradiol administration interfered with the onset of
pre- and postpartum maternal behaviour.

SENSORY THRESHOLDS

A less well known hormonal influence is on the level of sensory thresholds. This may be viewed functionally as complimenting the changes in reproductive behaviour. In addition there is evidence of human sex differences in sensory discrimination (which are described in the chapter by Diane McGuiness). Garai and Scheinfeld (1968) have concluded that women generally have higher thresholds for hearing, pain, touch and taste, but lower visual thresholds than men.*

Stronger evidence for hormones as substances which can alter sensory thresholds has come from studies on sensory changes during the menstrual cycle. Le Magnen (1950 and 1952) pioneered this work with reports of changes in the ability to smell musk (exaltolide) during the menstrual cycle. Detection threshold was lowered during the ovulatory phase, and greatest during menstruation; oestrogen replacement therapy to ovariectomized women restored to normal levels their lowered sensitivity to musk. Vierling and Rock (1967), also using exaltolide, confirmed these changes in olfactory sensitivity during the menstrual cycle, while Schneider and Wolf (1955) found a reduced ability to detect citral during the menstrual phase of the cycle.

Schneider *et al.* (1958) followed this up by showing that oestrogen injections to women with lowered ovarian function would increase olfactory acuity to citral. However, Glanvill and Kaplan (1965) found that sensitivity to the taste of quinine and thiouracil increased during menstruation, compared with post-menstruation, indicating that the direction of olfactory change differs between compounds.

There is some evidence of menstrual changes in other modalities. Semszuk *et al.* (1967) found acoustic sensitivity to be greatest around ovulation. Pitch estimation however, was found to change in a different way, with lower frequency estimates at both around ovulation *and* around menstruation, i.e. a bimensual cycle (Wynn, 1971 and 1972). For vision, Diamond *et al.* (1972) found that sensitivity, measured by the ability to detect a patch of light in a slightly less illuminated background, was greatest at midcycle and then remained high until it declined abruptly at the onset of menstruation. Pain threshold changes have been measured by Buzzelli *et al.* (1968) who found that sensitivity was lowest around ovulation. For temperature, Kenshalo (1970) found that the detection threshold fell at ovulation, and

rose again at the onset of menstruation. The adaptive significance of these changes has been described by Diamond *et
al*. (1972), who concluded that they might result in a higher
incidence of coitus at ovulation since sensitivity to arousing stimuli would be greater but pain sensitivity reduced.
There is insufficient evidence to properly assess this theory
but it is attractive, and no alternative has been proposed.
It is, however, quite possible that the changes are merely
incidental to other functions of these hormones.

The generality of these human threshold changes has recently been demonstrated by Pietras and Moulton (1974) working with rats. They designed a device to measure odour thresholds and looked specifically at sex differences and hormonal
effects, concluding that androgens and oestrogens increased
detection for certain odours, while progesterone depressed
it. Adult female rats showed fluctuations in odour detection
during their oestrous cycles paralleling the hormonal fluctuations. A possible adaptive value of this type of change
was suggested by an experiment of Doty (1972). He showed
that females of one species of mouse would only show a significant response to the odour of a male from their own species, compared to the odour of a related species, during oestrus but not dioestrus. Such odour discrimination, it was
suggested, would help to prevent interbreeding between the
two species.

DIETARY SELECTION, FEEDING AND MOTOR ACTIVITY

The sensory changes described above must be viewed in
the context of their interaction with other hormonal effects
on behaviour. The improvement in visual sensitivity at the
time of ovulation could enhance the effects of visual courtship signals from males at this time, while olfactory improvement could have a similar effect on olfactory cues from
the male. The olfactory changes might also relate to hormonal influences on food intake and dietary selection, which
have been well-studied for rats, and for which there is some
data from human work.

In studies with humans, Wright and Crow (1973) showed
that there are variations in the pleasantness of sugar solutions at different stages of the menstrual cycle. The sugar
was least pleasant in the post-ovulatory phase, but pleasantness returned to normal levels premenstrually. The reduction in the pleasantness of sugar occurred when progesterone

and oestrogen levels were at a higher level after ovulation.
Other changes in food preference have also been reported during human pregnancy and menstrual cycles by Smith and Sauder
(1969) and Thorn et al. (1938).

Valenstein et al. (1967) have shown that female rats
will consume a significantly greater quantity of both glucose and very sweet saccharin solutions than will males.
Zucker (1969) showed that ovariectomy reduced the female preference to that of males. However, combined injections of
oestradiol and progesterone were able to restore saccharin
preferences to female levels (Zucker, 1969). Whether this
is a direct hormonal effect or not has recently been questioned by Marks and his co-workers (Marks and Hobbs, 1972;
Marks, 1974) who have suggested that the taste preference is
a consequence of body weight changes (discussed below), thus
being only indirectly a hormonal effect.

In addition, male and female rats differ in their normal dietary self-selection patterns, males consuming a significantly higher proportion of protein in their diet
(Leshner and Collier, 1973). While castration has no effect
on male food intake, ovariectomy led to females adopting
male type dietary self-selection patterns, suggesting that
oestradiol or progesterone is the important hormone regulating the female dietary self-selection.

Selection for salt in the diet is a further example of
apparent taste changes caused by female hormones. Covelli
et al. (1973) found that there is an increased salt appetite
in rabbits during pseudopregnancy, and that oestradiol injection (but not progesterone) had a similar effect. Increased
salt preference has also been shown to occur in the luteal
phase of the oestrous cycle of sheep (Michell, 1975).

In addition to these studies of food preference, there
is a much greater body of literature showing that overall
food intake is related to hormonal changes in females of
several species.

Feeding and also motor activity show cyclical fluctuations during the oestrous cycle as well as changing during
pregnancy in rats (and possibly in other species). These
two types of behaviour will be discussed together as their
functional significance is clearly linked and in general
both fluctuate at similar times in the oestrous cycle, although it has been possible to dissociate the two changes
by hypothalamic lesions (Wade, 1972). Early reports (e.g.
Wang, 1923; Brobeck et al. 1947) indicated that changes in

motor activity and feeding coincide with oestrus and early
stages of pregnancy in rats. More recent studies confirm
these findings (see Wade, 1972). Typically, an increase in
eating during dioestrus and a large increase in feeding during pregnancy and pseudo-pregnancy are shown, while motor
activity (generally measured by wheel-running) shows associated decreases at these times. On the other hand, during
proestrus, or after ovariectomy with oestrogen therapy, there
is a reduction in eating and an increase in motor activity.
On the basis of these and related findings, Wade (1972) concluded that oestrogens are the most important hormones for
controlling food intake and motor activity.

     In addition to these findings, Rodier (1971) showed that
large doses of progesterone to female rats decrease wheel-
running activity and increase body weight (through higher
food intake), provided that a minimum level of oestradiol is
present. Thus, the combination of progesterone and oestradiol exerted the opposite effect to that shown by oestradiol
alone (Zucker, 1969). Wade (1972) attributed Rodier's findings to a high progesterone level blocking the effect of
oestradiol, which he termed "functional ovariectomy". This
corresponds to the increase in eating and fall in wheel-
running activity, found by Wade and Zucker (1969a and b) in
ovariectomized rats, and to the similar findings of Wang
(1923) and Slonaker (1925) for pregnant rats. Ross and
Zucker (1974) have tried to clarify the nature of the effect
of progesterone, and suggested it could either increase food
intake by a central effect blocking oestradiol or (if present
alone) by changes not involving the brain, e.g. in metabolism.

     Although other species provide relatively few findings
relating hormonal changes to feeding and activity, it is evident from these that there are species differences. Fluctuations in wheel-running activity with reproductive state are
similar in the hamster and rat (Richards, 1966), but hormonal
control of food intake and body weight may be different. The
absence of neonatal and prenatal androgens rather than the
presence of oestrogens in the adult have been said to be the
controlling hormones in the hamster (Swanson, 1968). But
Gerall and Thiel (1975) found that oestradiol and progesterone injections would reduce body weight gain after ovariectomy, an effect they attributed to oestradiol.

     In female baboons and rhesus monkeys, food consumption
is reported as being less during the follicular phase than
during the luteal phase of their menstrual cycles, a behavi-

oural finding comparable to that for the rat (Gilbert and
Gillman, 1956; Krohn and Zuckerman, 1938). Following up
this work, Czaja (1975) found a significant increase in food
rejection around midway through the menstrual cycle in a
large sample of rhesus monkeys.

There are no detailed published studies on the relationship between food intake and the human menstrual cycle, although weight is known to increase by about 1 per cent in
the mid-luteal phase (Russell, 1972), and Watson and
Robinson (1965) found a minor peak apparently around ovulation. These may be due to water retention rather than increased eating, however. In contrast, there have been two
recent studies on motor activity in relation to the human
menstrual cycle. Morris and Udry (1970) found that a significant increase in activity (as measured by a pedometer) took
place at midcycle, with lesser peaks menstrually and premenstrually. These three phases were associated with low progesterone or high oestrogen levels. The effect was small,
with the authors adjusting to a standard 28 day cycle, and
averaging several cycles of 34 subjects.

Stenn and Klinge (1972) recorded the daily arm movements of both men (over five periods of 28 days) and women
(for 17 menstrual cycles). Two out of seven women showed
peaks of activity during the premenstrual phase, while activity peaks were least likely during the menstrual phase.
Just four men were tested, none of whom showed any regularities in activity. Unfortunately, these two studies fail to
provide a firm basis for comparison with the rat results:
there was only a very small change in Morris and Udry's experiment, and too small a sample was used in the other study.
However, the possibility that female hormones exert some control over activity and feeding in humans is one that requires
further exploration.

Drewett (1973b) has discussed the possible adaptive significance of the relationships reviewed in this section in
terms of the oestrogenic inhibition of food intake by rats.
He has argued against the suggestion that reduced food intake has evolved to allow more time for courtship activities
during oestrus, claiming that this was unlikely because one
would then expect food intake to be controlled by an
oestrogen-progesterone synergism in the same way as sexual
receptivity and ovulation. In support of his contention,
it is certainly true that all the behavioural changes mentioned here (food intake, wheel-running activity and oestrous

behaviour), although showing highly correlated fluctuations with hormonal state, have nevertheless been dissociated by various hormonal manipulations (Wade, 1972). Drewett (1973b) also showed that food intake in ovariectomized rats could be suppressed by oestradiol levels too low to affect sexual receptivity. It is thus unlikely that all the behavioural effects are controlled by a single neural system, and this has been confirmed by studies using hormone implants in different regions of the brain (e.g. running activity was induced by implants in the preoptic region, and food intake depressed by ventromedial hypothalamic implants: Colvin and Sawyer, 1969; Wade and Zucker, 1970).

Drewett (1973b) suggested an alternative function for the oestrogenic inhibition of food intake. He has claimed that the important feature is not the contrast between the oestrous and dioestrous phases of the cycle, but that between the oestrogen-dominated oestrous cycle and progesterone-dominated pregnancy. The increased food intake of early pregnancy is thus essentially an anticipatory behavioural response preceding the extreme changes of food intake necessitated by the energy demands of pregnancy and lactation. To support this contention, he cited evidence that female rats eat more not only when pregnant (e.g. Richter and Barclare, 1938) but also during pseudo-pregnancy (e.g. Kennedy and Mitra, 1963), thus indicating that the energy demands of the offspring were not the important factor.

FEMALE HORMONES AND THE CENTRAL NERVOUS SYSTEM

Observations of specific behavioural effects resulting from oestradiol implants in the brain indicate the importance of considering central nervous actions of female hormones for understanding the behaviour changes. Vernikos-Danellis (1972) has recently provided a comprehensive review of the effects of all hormones on the CNS, so that only a few examples of the relevant studies need to be considered here.

One important finding is that large doses of progesterone have a potent anaesthetic effect in rats and mice (Selye, 1941), and a soporific effect in humans at smaller doses (Merryman, 1954). Oestradiol has a similar but less pronounced effect (Selye, 1941). At lower dose levels, combined oestradiol and progesterone injections in ovariectomized female rats, or neonatally castrated male rats, resulted in a reduction in Rapid Eye Movement (REM) sleep and non-REM

sleep (Branchey *et al.* 1971 and 1973). Oestradiol alone resulted in a reduced REM sleep only. The combined hormonal
effect closely·resembles the reduction of sleeping observed
on the night of behavioural oestrus in rats (Colvin *et al.*
1968) and also guinea-pigs (Malven and Sawyer, 1966), this
reduction apparently being compensated for the next day.
The evidence that sleep is reduced at oestrus is consistent
with the theory mentioned earlier that the changes are adaptive for giving the female more time for copulatory activity
during the ovulatory phase. However, Drewett's theory (1973)
is not contradicted and it has been observed that sleep in
rats is altered during pregnancy (Branchey and Branchey, 1970)
     Using a different experimental approach to hormones and
CNS function, Woolley *et al.* (1961a and b) showed that the
minimal strength of electroshock needed to produce convulsions was lower in female than male rats, and fluctuated with
phases of the oestrous cycle, reaching its lowest level at
the time of ovulation. There is also a finding in humans
consistent with these results suggesting an excitatory effect
of oestrogens and a possible inhibitory effect of progesterone on brain function. This is a study on epileptic patients
quoted by Hamburg (1966) showing that seizures were precipi-
tated by oestrogen injection, and that they were reduced during the luteal phase of the menstrual cycle (when progesterone levels are high). Generally, progesterone has been shown
to have an inhibitory effect on brain function in line with
its anaesthetic effect. Progesterone had a depressant effect on the reticular formation greater than that of some
short-acting barbiturates, and also the posterior hypothalamus and the limbic midbrain area (Gyermek *et al.* 1967;
Kobayashi *et al.* 1962).
     Lisk (1973) considered that progesterone has generally
a broad action on the entire CNS, while the effects of oestrogen are usually specific. This view takes account of the
work described earlier showing how oestrogen implants in
certain brain areas will cause specific patterns of behaviour
such as feeding, activity or sexual behaviour, while most of
the effects of progesterone can be explained from its anaesthetic effects. This is probably too simple a view to take,
as there is now evidence that progesterone is specifically
retained in some midbrain areas so that the possibility of
specific effects on behaviour is thus raised.

EMOTIONAL, AUTONOMIC AND LEARNING EFFECTS

I have already suggested that the human menstrual cycle
can provide a natural situation where hormone levels fluctuate regularly, and fluctuations in sexual behaviour and sensory thresholds have already been discussed in this context.
Another type of behavioural response which appears to change
with the stage of the menstrual cycle is related to mood or
emotion. It is not clear that hormones are a prime cause of
these changes, and indeed there has been argument to the contrary recently, but the evidence is worth considering.
    Feelings of anxiety, irritability, tiredness and depres-
sion have commonly been reported on the day or so before menstruation starts (e.g. Ivey and Bardwick, 1968; Moos *et al.*
1969) and also in the period immediately after birth when
oestrogen and progestogen levels also fall rapidly, but to
a much greater degree than premenstrually (Hamburg *et al.*
1968; Yalom *et al.* 1968). Yalom *et al.* reported that many
women become depressed, some seriously so, after giving
birth, and that this was not related to previous mental illness (others have claimed that it could be a factor: e.g.
Gordon *et al.* 1959).
    Several studies have related phases of the menstrual
cycle to the occurrence of more specific activities associated with mood changes. The premenstrual and menstrual phases are associated with a greater tendency to commit violent
crimes (Dalton, 1961; Morton *et al.* 1953), to attempt suicide or to think seriously about it (Dalton, 1959; MacKinnon
and MacKinnon, 1956; Tonks *et al.* 1968), and to have accidents (Dalton, 1960b). Women are also more likely to be admitted to hospital with psychiatric illness at this time
(Dalton, 1959; Janowsky *et al.* 1969) and to take their children to see a doctor. Tuch (1975) confirmed this latter
finding with a sample of women taking their children to hospital, but found that the children were considered to be
less ill than children brought by women at other stages of
their menstrual cycles.
    Self-report mood questionnaires have indicated that
feelings such as irritability, tiredness and depression occur
most frequently during the premenstrual phase (e.g. Moos *et
al.* 1969; Silbergeld *et al.* 1971).
    Hamburg (1966) and others (e.g. Little and Zahn, in
press) have interpreted these findings as showing a relationship between progesterone withdrawal and the various behavi-

oural disturbances, since the premenstrual phase is associated with a sudden drop in progesterone levels, and an even more dramatic drop occurs at childbirth. Alternative hypotheses have been suggested, such as water retention (Reeves *et al.* 1971) and changes in aldosterone levels (Janowsky *et al.* 1973). Evidence to support the implication of sex hormones is derived from studies of women taking the oral contraceptive pill, where hormone levels are steadier and mood changes much less pronounced (e.g. Grant and Pryse-Davies, 1968; Herzberg and Coppen, 1970).

Attempts to relate measured changes in hormone levels to changes in mood have so far met with no success, although Persky (1974) reports an unfinished analysis of an experiment of this type. Looking at more cbjective psychological measures, Landauer (1974) found that choice reaction time was slower in the four days preceding menstruation than at other times in the cycle. However Messent (unpublished) was unable to find any correlations in 20 young women between plasma levels of oestradiol and progesterone and performance on a choice reaction time and other tasks (e.g. addition, serial subtraction, time estimation, visual acuity and rod and frame test).

As an alternative to the physiological explanations of premenstrual symptoms, Parlee (1973 and 1974) and Sommer (1973) have recently argued that social and psychological factors have received too little emphasis as possible explanations. Both have criticized some of the earlier studies on statistical grounds, and claim that negative results have been ignored or have not been published. For example, Buckle *et al.* (1965) and Holding and Minkoff (1973) both failed to find an excess of suicide attempts in women during the premenstrual phase of the cycle, in contrast to the positive relationship found in other studies mentioned above. Other negative results may not have been reported, simply because of the known bias of journals towards positive results (see Lloyd, Chapter 1). Sommer (1973) criticized the report of Dalton (1960a) that English schoolgirls showed a decline in exam performance during the premenstrual and menstrual phases of the cycle as lacking firm statistical backing, and she failed to replicate Dalton's finding when she tested American college students at regular intervals. Sommer concluded that responses mediated by social and psychological factors are more likely to show changes related to the menstrual cycle, but when social or psychological expectations

of menstrual debilitation are altered, the effect disappears.
Despite these criticisms, the problem is still open.
In a recent contribution, Little and Zahn (in press) looked
at changes in autonomic function rather than behaviour during the menstrual cycle. They found that during the luteal
phase of the cycle, heart rate and respiration increased,
whereas resting skin conductance decreased, although Koppell
et al. (1969) had previously found no variation in skin potential during the menstrual cycle. Little *et al.* (1974)
also injected progesterone (10 mg/day for 6 days) into men
and measured similar functions, but found only the decrease
in skin conductance, other measures showing no significant
alterations. They considered that this result only partially
supported the progesterone-withdrawal hypothesis of premenstrual tension, and suggested that oestrogen or another hormone might be important.

The evolutionary significance, if any, of these behavioural changes during the human menstrual cycle seems obscure.
Diamond *et al.* (1972) have suggested that the evidence from
studies of emotional changes indicates that there is a tendency for greater stability, self-satisfaction and feelings
of pleasure at about the time of ovulation. The "premenstrual
syndrome" on the other hand, confers no apparent advantage.
It should be remembered that in the past, the more "normal"
state was pregnancy, favoured by selective pressures for
fertility. There would thus be no need to account for any
features of the premenstrual phase as being of adaptive significance. Animal studies are unfortunately of little help
for resolving the problem of whether hormones influence human emotionality, as it is not possible to measure emotion
in animals comparable with the meaning of the terms in humans. However, there are several studies observing the
"open field" behaviour of rats and mice - often considered
to be a test of "emotionality" (review: see Archer, 1973),
although not with the same meaning as might be applied to
humans. It is generally considered that a decrease in the
number of faecal boluses deposited in a given period of time
after an animal is first placed in an open field (usually
an open arena larger than the home cage) is indicative of a
lower "emotionality" (e.g. Hall, 1934) which might be considered to most closely resemble "fear" in human terms. On
this basis, female rats are said to be less emotional at
oestrus or following oestrogen injections (Gray and Levine,
1964; Burke and Broadhurst, 1966). Drewett (1973b) has argued

against this conclusion, stating that despite a claim that
changes in food intake do not affect open field defecation,
there is recent evidence (Tarttelin and Gorski, 1972; Drewett,
1973b) that the two processes may be related. It would follow
from this that the changes in open field defecation with oestrogen levels, may represent nothing more than a secondary
consequence of the oestrogen induced reduction in feeding
already described.* Nevertheless, aside from Drewett's views,
there is an interesting parallel between the supposed reduced
emotionality at oestrus in rats, and the mood changes in the
human menstrual cycle where the mid-cycle is a time of low
levels of emotional disturbances. However, this can be regarded as no more than a parallel in view of the impossibili-
ty of comparing emotion in humans with animals, especially
where, even for animals, a unitary concept for "emotionality"
is not acceptable (Archer, 1973).

GENERAL DISCUSSION

Of the various types of behaviour that are modified by
oestrogen and progesterone, sexual behaviour is clearly of
the greatest evolutionary importance, since without it pro-
pagation of the species would cease. The corollary adaptation, of attractiveness to the male, has not been considered
here, since the behavioural effect is an indirect one on the
male rather than on the female. In many ways, the human female is exceptional with regard to hormones and sexual behaviour, since the effect exerted is at best very small. This
might be viewed as the end-point of an evolutionary process,
starting from the typical oestrous cycle, with a definite
oestral peak of sexual activity, and leading to the primate
menstrual cycle, with a tendency for sexual behaviour to
occur over a longer period of time.
If the relative importance of male and female hormones
on mammalian behaviour is compared, the androgenic effect in
males could possibly be considered as the more powerful. In
early development, androgens act on the sexually undifferentiated organism to make it male-like while female hormones
play no positive role at this time. In adults, androgens
influence a range of behaviour concerned with changes in
aggression, mating, and attention (see Chapter 7 by Rogers).

* A recent study by Birke and Archer (1975) provides results
more consistent with Drewett's viewpoint.

These tend to behaviourally differentiate males more from
the immature state than perhaps is true of females, where
behavioural effects are generally more subtle and transient,
and do not involve neonatal effects (see Chapter 7).

Nevertheless, a wide range of actual or possible hormonal actions has been described here. In addition to sexual
and maternal behaviour, the most obvious effect is on food
intake and activity (in animals with oestrous cycles). Two
possible theories were presented to explain why these changes should occur. One suggested that they arose because
less eating at oestrus allowed more time for coitus, while
greater activity made contact with a male more likely.

A good reason why increased activity is restricted to
such a short space of time is that the likelihood of predation would be increased in highly active animals (as shown
experimentally for mice by Glickman and Morrison, 1969).
The evidence is still insufficient to decide between this
idea and that of Drewett (1973b) who has claimed that evolution may have favoured hormonally induced feeding and activity changes for the anticipation of energy demands during
pregnancy and lactation.

In our own species, the main behavioural changes associated with the menstrual cycle are in sensory thresholds
and emotional responses. The sensory changes are particularly interesting as so many modalities appear to be affected.
The suggestion of Diamond et al. (1972) that these allow an
increased likelihood of coitus at mid-cycle by increasing
sensitivity to arousing stimuli and reducing pain sensitivity
is the most plausible evolutionary view that has been presented. It would be interesting if such findings were duplica-
ted in other mammals that show greater variation in sexual
activity: the recent studies of olfaction in rats by Pietras
and Moulton (1974) form a basis for this. The emotional changes documented during the human menstrual cycle provide much
greater difficulty in interpretation despite the large number
of studies. Even now, no hormonal involvement has been con-
clusively demonstrated, and recent reviews have stressed the
importance of psychological and social factors in the production of such changes.

A great deal of further research is required to confirm
female hormone involvement in bringing about changes in human
behaviour. Even if this work does indicate important hormonal involvement, the adaptive significance of the hormonal
effects would be far from clear, and there is unlikely to be

a unitary evolutionary explanation for all aspects of behaviour discussed above. One major problem lies in deciding which behaviour changes are the primary ones and which are secondary consequences of other physiological changes and the extent to which some changes are evolutionary vestiges of the time when the human menstrual cycle was associated with changes in sexual receptivity.

* *For central and daytime vision; see Chapter 6 by McGuinness for a different sex difference when vision in the dark is measured.*

REFERENCES

Archer, J. (1973). Tests for emotionality in rats and mice. A review. *Animal Behaviour,* 21, 205-235.

Ball, J. (1934). Sex behavior in the rat after removal of the uterus and vagina. *Journal of Comparative and Physiological Psychology,* 18, 419-422.

Birke, L.I.A. and Archer, J. (1975). Open field behaviour of oestrous and dioestrous rats: Evidence against an "emotionality" interpretation. *Animal Behaviour,* 23, 509-512.

Branchey, L., Branchey, M. and Nadler, R.D. (1973). Effects of sex hormones on sleep patterns of male rats gonadectomized in adulthood and in the neonatal period. *Physiology and Behavior,* 11, 609-611.

Branchey, M. and Branchey, L. (1970). Sleep and wakefulness in female rats during pregnancy. *Physiology and Behavior,* 5, 365-368.

Branchey, M., Branchey, L. and Nadler, R.D. (1971). Effects of oestrogen and progesterone on sleep patterns of female rats. *Physiology and Behavior,* 6, 743-746.

Brobeck, J.R., Whaatland, M. and Strominger, J.L. (1947). Variations in regulation of energy exchange associated with estrus, diestrus, and pseudopregnancy in rats. *Endocrinology,* 40, 65-72.

Brooks, C.McC. (1937). The role of the cerebral cortex and of various sense organs in the excitation and execution of mating activity in the rabbit. *American Journal of Physio-*

Buckle, R.C., Linnane, J. and McConacky, N. (1965). Attempted suicide presenting at the Alfred Hospital, Melbourne. *Medical Journal of Australia*, 1, 754–761.

Burke, A.W. and Broadhurst, P.L. (1966). Behavioural correlates of the oestrous cycle in the rat. *Nature (London)*, 209, 223–224.

Butcher, R.L., Collins, W.E. and Fugo, N.W. (1974). Plasma concentration of LH, FSH, prolactin, progesterone and estradiol 17-β throughout the 4-day estrous cycle of the rat. *Endocrinology*, 94, 1704–1708.

Buzzelli, B., Voegelin, M.R., Prozacci, P. and Bozza, G. (1968). Modificazioni della soglia del dolore cutaneo durate il ciclo mestruale. *Bolletino della Societa Italiana Biologia Sperimentale*, 44, 235–236.

Colvin, G.B. and Sawyer, C.H. (1969). Induction of running activity by intracerebral implants of estrogen in ovariectomized rats. *Neuroendocrinology*, 4, 309–320.

Colvin, G.B., Whitmoyer, D.I., Lisk, R.D., Walter, D.O. and Sawyer, C.H. (1968). Changes in sleep-wakefulness in female rats during circadian and estrous cycles. *Brain Research*, 7, 173–181.

Conner, R.L. (1972). Hormones, biogenic amines, and aggression. *In* "Hormones and Behavior". (S. Levine, ed.) Academic Press, New York.

Covelli, M.D., Denton, D.A., Nelson, J.F. and Shulkes,A.A. (1973). Hormonal factors influencing salt appetite in pregnancy. *Endocrinology*, 93, 423–429.

Czaja, J.A. (1975). Food rejection by female rhesus monkeys during the menstrual cycle and early pregnancy. *Physiology and Behavior*, 14, 579–587.

Dalton, K. (1959). Menstruation and acute psychiatric illness. *British Medical Journal*, 1, 148–149.

Dalton, K. (1960a). Effect of menstruation on schoolgirls' weekly work. *British Medical Journal*, 1, 326–328.

Dalton, K. (1960b). Menstruation and accidents. *British Medical Journal*, 2, 1425–1426.

Dalton, K. (1961). Menstruation and crime. *British Medical Journal*, 2, 1752–1753.

Dalton, K. (1966). The influence of mother's menstruation on her child. *Proceedings of the Royal Society of Medicine*, 59, 1014.

Davidson, J.M. (1972). Hormones and reproductive behavior. *In* "Hormones and Behavior". (S. Levine, ed.) Academic Press, New York.

Dennis St. John, R. and Corning, P.A. (1973). Maternal aggression in mice. *Behavioral Biology*, 9, 635-639.

Diamond, M., Diamond, A.L. and Mast, M. (1972). Visual sensitivity and sexual arousal levels during the menstrual cycle. *Journal of Nervous and Mental Diseases*, 155, 170-176.

Doty, R.L. (1972). Odor preferences of female *Peromyscus maniculatus bairdi* for male mouse odor of *P.m. bairdi* and *P. leucopus noveboracensis* as a function of estrous state. *Journal of Comparative and Physiological Psychology*, 81, 191-197.

Drewett, R.F. (1973a). Sexual behaviour and sexual motivation in the female rat. *Nature (London)*, 242, 476-477.

Drewett, R.F. (1973b). Oestrous and dioestrous components of the ovarian inhibition on hunger in the rat. *Animal Behaviour*, 21, 772-780.

Eliasson, M. and Meyerson, B.J. (1975). Sexual preference in female rats during estrous cycle, pregnancy and lactation. *Physiology and Behavior*, 14, 705-710.

Gandelman, R. (1972). Mice: Postpartum aggression elicited by the presence of an intruder. *Hormones and Behavior*, 3, 23-28.

Garai, J.E. and Scheinfeld, A. (1968). Sex differences in mental and behavioral traits. *Genetic Psychology Monographs*, 77, 169-299.

Gilbert, C. and Gillman, J. (1956). The changing pattern of food intake and appetite during the menstrual cycle of the baboon (*Papio ursinus*) with a consideration of some of the controlling endocrine factors. *South African Journal of Medical Science*, 21, 75-88.

Glanville, E.V. and Kaplan, A.P. (1965). Taste perception and the menstrual cycle. *Nature (London)*, 205, 930-931.

Glickman, S.E. and Morrison, B.J. (1969). Some behavioral
and neural correlates of predation susceptibility in mice.
Communications in Behavioral Biology, 4, 261-267.

Gordon, R.E., Gordon, K.K. and Englewood, N.J. (1959). Social
factors in the prediction and treatment of emotional disorders of pregnancy. *American Journal of Obstetrics and
Gynaecology,* 77, 1074-1083.

Grant, E.C.G. and Pryse-Davies, J. (1968). Effect of oral
contraceptives on depressive mood changes and on endomet-
rial monoamine oxidases and phosphatases. *British Medical
Journal,* 3, 777-780.

Gray, J.A. and Levine, S. (1964). Effect of induced oestrus
on emotional behaviour in selected strains of rats. *Nature
(London),* 201, 1198-1200.

Gyermek, L., Genther, G. and Fleming, N. (1967). Some effects
of progesterone and related steroids on the central nervous system. *International Journal of Neuropharmacology,*
6, 191-198.

Hall, C.S. (1934). Emotional behavior in the rat. I. Defecation and urination as measures of individual differences
in emotionality. *Journal of Comparative Psychology,* 18,
385-403.

Hamburg, D.A. (1966). Effects of progesterone on behavior.
*Research Publications of the Association for Research into
Nervous and Mental Diseases,* 43, 251-265.

Hamburg, D.A., Moos, R.H. and Yalom, I.D. (1968). Studies of
distress in the menstrual cycle and the postpartum period.
In "Endocrinology and Human Behaviour". (R.P. Michael, ed.)
Oxford University Press.

Harris, G.W., Michael, R.P. and Scott, P.P. (1958). Neurological site of action of stilboestrol in eliciting sexual behaviour. *In* "The Neurological Basis of Behaviour".
(G.E.W. Wolstenholme and C.M. O'Connor, eds.) Churchill,
London.

Herzberg, B. and Coppen, A. (1970). Changes in psychological
symptoms in women taking oral contraceptives. *British
Journal of Psychiatry,* 116, 161-164.

Holding, T.A. and Minkoff, K. (1973). Parasuicide and the menstrual cycle. *Journal of Psychosomatic Research,* 17, 365-

368.

Ivey, M. and Bardwick, J.M. (1968). Patterns of affective
fluctuation in the menstrual cycle. *Psychosomatic Medicine,*
30, 336-345.

Janowsky, D.C., Berens, S.C. and Davis, J.M. (1973). Correlations between mood, weight and electrolytes during the
menstrual cycle. *Psychosomatic Medicine,* 35, 143-154.

Janowsky, D.S., Gomey, R., Castelnuovo-Tedesco, P. and Stone,
C.B. (1969). Premenstrual-menstrual increase in psychiatric hospital admission rates. *American Journal of Obstetrics and Gynaecology,* 103, 189-191.

Kane, F.J., Lipton, M.A. and Ewing, J.A. (1969). Hormonal
influences in female sexual response. *Archives of General
Psychiatry,* 20, 202-209.

Kawakami, M. and Sawyer, C.H. (1959). Induction of behavior
and electroencephalographic changes in the rabbit by hormone administration or brain stimulation. *Endocrinology,*
65, 631-642.

Kennedy, G.C. and Mitra, J. (1963). Spontaneous pseudopregnancy and obesity in the rat. *Journal of Physiology,* 166,
419-424.

Kenshalo, D.R. (1970). Psychophysical studies of human temperature sensitivity. *In* "Contributions to Sensory Physiology". (W.D. Neff, ed.) Vol. 4. Academic Press, New
York.

Kinsey, A.C., Pomeroy, W.B., Martin, C.E. and Gebhard, P.H.
(1953). "Sexual Behavior in the Human Female". Saunders,
Philadelphia.

Kobayashi, T., Takeyama, S., Oshima, K. and Kawamura, H.
(1962). Electrophysiological studies on the feedback mechanism of progesterone. *Endocrinologia Japonica,* 9, 302-
320.

Kopell, B.S., Lunde, D.T., Clayton, R.B. and Moos, R.H. (1969)
Variations in some measures of arousal during the menstrual
cycle. *Journal of Nervous and Mental Disease,* 148, 180-
187.

Krohn, F.L. and Zuckerman, S. (1938). Water metabolism in relation to the menstrual cycle. *Journal of Physiology,* 88,

369-378.

Landauer, A.A. (1974). Choice decision time and the menstrual cycle. *The Practitioner*, 213, 703-706.

Le Magnen, J. (1950). Nouvelles donnes sur les phenomene de l'exaltolide. *Comptes Rendus Hebdomaines des Seances de l'Academie des Sciences sec. C*, 26, 1100-1105.

Le Magnen, J. (1952). Les Phenomene olfactosexuels chez l'homme. *Archives des Sciences Physiologiques (Paris)*, 6, 125-160.

Leshner, A.I. and Collier, G. (1973). The effects of gonadectomy on the sex differences in dietary self-selection patterns and carcass compositions of rats. *Physiology and Behaviour*, 11, 671-676.

Lisk, R.D. (1973). Hormonal regulation of sexual behavior in polyestrous mammals common to the laboratory. *In* "Handbook of Physiology". Section 7, Endocrinology, Vol. 2. Female Reproductive System. Part 1. American Physiological Society, Washington.

Little, B.C., Matta, R.J. and Zahn, T.P. (1974). Physiological and psychological effects of progesterone in man. *Journal of Nervous and Mental Disease*, 159, 256-262.

Little, B.C. and Zahn, T.P. (In press). Changes in mood and autonomic functioning during the menstrual cycle. *Psychophysiology*.

MacKinnon, P.C.B. and MacKinnon, I.L. (1956). Hazards of the menstrual cycle. *British Medical Journal*, 1, 155.

Malven, P.V. and Sawyer, C.H. (1966). Sleeping patterns in female guinea pigs: Effect of sex hormones. *Experimental Neurology*, 15, 229-239.

Marks, H.E. and Hobbs, S.H. (1972). Changes in stimulus reactivity following gonadectomy in male and female rats of different ages. *Physiology and Behavior*, 8, 1113-1119.

Marks, H.E. (1974). Body weight as a determinant of saccharin consumption in the orchidectomized male hamster. (*Mesocricetus auratus*). *Bulletin of the Psychonomic Society*, 3, 11-13.

Merryman, W. (1954). Progesterone "anaesthesia" in human subjects. *Journal of Clinical Endocrinology*, 14, 1567-1587.

Michael, R.P. (1971). Neuroendocrine factors regulating pri-
mate behavior. *In* "Frontiers in Neuroendocrinology". (L.
Martini and W.F. Ganong, eds.) Oxford University Press,
New York.

Michael, R.P. (1973). The effects of hormones on sexual behavior in female cat and rhesus monkey. *In* "Handbook of
Physiology". Section 7, Endocrinology, Vol. 2. Female Reproductive System. Part 1. American Physiological Society,
Washington.

Michell, A.R. (1975). Changes of sodium appetite during the
estrous cycle of sheep. *Physiology and Behavior,* 14, 223-
226.

Money, J. (1965). Influence of hormones on sexual behavior.
Annual Review of Medicine, 16, 67-82.

Moos, R.H., Kopell, B.S., Melges, F.T., Yalom, I.D., Lunde,
D.T., Clayton, R.B. and Hamburg, D.A. (1969). Fluctuations
in symptoms and moods during the menstrual cycle. *Journal
of Psychosomatic Research,* 13, 37-44.

Morris, N.M. and Udry, J.R. (1970). Variations in pedometer
activity during the menstrual cycle. *Obstetrics and Gynaecology,* 33, 199-201.

Morton, J.H., Additon, H., Addison, R.G., Hunt, L. and Sulliva
J.J. (1953). A clinical study of premenstrual tension.
American Journal of Obstetrics and Gynaecology, 65, 1182-
1191.

Parlee, M.B. (1973). The premenstrual syndrome. *Psychological
Bulletin,* 80, 454-465.

Parlee, M.B. (1974). Stereotypic beliefs about menstruation:
A methodological note on the Moos menstrual distress questionnaire and some new data. *Psychosomatic Medicine,* 36,
229-240.

Persky, H. (1974). Reproductive hormones, moods, and the men-
strual cycle. *In* "Sex Differences in Behavior". (R.C.
Friedman, R.M. Richart and R.L. Vande Wiele, eds.) John
Wiley, New York.

Pietras, R.J. and Moulton, D.G. (1974). Hormonal influences
on odor detection in rats: Changes associated with the
estrous cycle, pseudopregnancy, ovariectomy, and administration of testosterone propionate. *Physiology and Behavi-
or,* 12, 475-491.

Reeves, B.D., Garvin, J.E. and McElin, T.W. (1971). Premenstrual tension, symptoms and weight changes related to potassium therapy. *American Journal of Obstetrics and Gynaecology*, 109, 1036-1041.

Richards, M.P.M. (1966). Activity measured by running wheels and observation during the oestrous cycle, pregnancy and pseudopregnancy in the golden hamster. *Animal Behaviour*, 14, 450-458.

Richter, C.P. and Barclare, B. Jr. (1938). Nutrition requirements of pregnant and lactating rats studied by the self-selection method. *Endocrinology*, 22, 15-24.

Rodier, W.I., III. (1971). Progesterone-estrogen interaction in the control of activity-wheel running in the female rat. *Journal of Comparative and Physiological Psychology*, 74, 365-373.

Ross, G.E. and Zucker, I. (1974). Progesterone and the ovarian-adrenal modulation of energy balance in rats. *Hormones and Behaviour*, 5, 43-62.

Russell, G.R.M. (1972). Premenstrual tension and "psychogenic" amenorrhea: Psychophysical interactions. *Journal of Psychosomatic Research*, 16, 279-287.

Schneider, R.A. and Wolf, S. (1955). Olfactory perception thresholds for citral utilizing a new olfactorium. *Journal of Applied Physiology*, 8, 337-342.

Schneider, R.A., Sustiloe, J.P., Howard, R.P. and Wolf, S. (1958). Olfactory perception thresholds in hypogonadal women - changes accompanying administration of androgen and estrogen. *Journal of Clinical Endocrinology and Metabolism*, 18, 379-393.

Semszuk, B., Przesmycka, S. and Pomykalski, M. (1967). O zmianack wrazliowsci w okresie cykla menstruacyjnego (On the changes of acoustic sensitivity during the menstrual cycle). *Polski Tybodnik Lekarski*, 22, 586-588.

Selye, H. (1941). Anaesthetic effect of steroid hormones. *Proceedings of the Society of Experimental Biology and Medicine*, 46, 116-121.

Siegel, H.L. and Greenwald, G.S. (1975). Prepartum onset of maternal behavior in hamsters and the effects of estrogen and progesterone. *Hormones and Behavior*, 6, 237-245.

Siegel, H.I. and Rosenblatt, J.S. (1975). Hormonal basis of hysterectomy-induced maternal behaviour during pregnancy in the rat. *Hormones and Behavior*, 6, 211-222.

Silbergeld, S., Brast, N. and Noble, E.P. (1971). The menstrual cycle: A double blind study of symptoms, mood and behavior, and biochemical variables using Enovid and placebo. *Psychosomatic Medicine*, 33, 411-428.

Slonaker, J.R. (1925). The effect of copulation, pregnancy, pseudopregnancy and lactation on the voluntary activity of the albino rat. *American Journal of Physiology*, 71, 362-394.

Smith, J.L. and Sauder, C. (1969). Food cravings, depression and premenstrual problems. *Psychosomatic Medicine*, 31, 281-287.

Sommer, B. (1973). The effect of menstruation on cognitive and perceptual-motor behavior: A review. *Psychosomatic Medicine*, 35, 515-534.

Stenn, P.G. and Klinge, V. (1972). Relationship between the menstrual cycle and bodily activity in humans. *Hormones and Behavior*, 3, 297-305.

Stumpf, W.E. (1970). Estrogen-neurons and estrogen-neuron systems in the diencephalon and amygdala. *American Journal of Anatomy*, 129, 207-218.

Swanson, H.H. (1968). Effect of progesterone on the body weight of hamsters. *Journal of Endocrinology*, 41, xiii.

Tarttelin, M.E. and Gorski, R.A. (1972). Variations in food and water intake in a normal and acyclic female rat. *Physiology and Behavior*, 7, 847-852.

Thorn, G.W., Nelson, K.R. and Thorn, D.W. (1938). Study of mechanism of edema associated with menstruation. *Endocrinology*, 22, 155-163.

Tonks, C.M., Rack, P.H. and Rose, M.J. (1968). Attempted suicide and the menstrual cycle. *Journal of Psychosomatic Research*, 11, 319-323.

Tuch, R.H. (1975). The relationship between a mother's menstrual status and her response to illness in her child. *Psychosomatic Medicine*, 37, 388-394.

Udry, T.R. and Morris, N.M. (1968). Distribution of coitus in the menstrual cycle. *Nature* (*London*), 220, 593–596.

Valenstein, E.S., Kakolewski, J.W. and Cox, V.C. (1967).
Sex differences in taste preference for glucose and saccharin solutions. *Science*, 156, 942–943.

Vandenburgh, J.G. (1971). The effects of gonadal hormones on
the aggressive behaviour of adult golden hamsters (*Mesocricetus auratus*). *Animal Behaviour*, 19, 589–594.

Vandewiele, R.L., Bogumil, J., Dyrenfurth, I., Fain, M.,
Jewelewiez, R., Warren, M., Rizkallah, T. and Mikhail,
G. (1970). Mechanism regulating the menstrual cycle in
women. *Recent Progress in Hormone Research*, 26, 63–103.

Vernikos-Danellis, J. (1972). Effects of hormones on the central nervous system. *In* "Hormones and Behavior". (S.
Levine, ed.) Academic Press, New York.

Vierling, J.S. and Rock, J. (1967). Variations in olfactory
sensitivity to exaltolide during the menstrual cycle.
Journal of Applied Physiology, 22, 311–315.

Wade, G.N. (1972). Gonadal hormones and behavioral regulation of body weight. *Physiology and Behavior*, 8, 523–534.

Wade, G.N. and Zucker, I. (1969a). Hormonal and developmental influences on rat saccharin preferences. *Journal of
Comparative and Physiological Psychology*, 69, 291–300.

Wade, G.N. and Zucker, I. (1969b). Taste preferences of female rats: Modification by neonatal hormones, food deprivation and prior experience. *Physiology and Behavior*, 4,
935–943.

Wade, G.N. and Zucker, I. (1970). Modulation of food intake
and locomotor acitivity in female rats by diencephalic
hormone implants. *Journal of Comparative and Physiological
Psychology*, 72, 328–336.

Wang, G.H. (1923). The relation between the "spontaneous"
activity and estrous cycle in the white rat. *Comparative
Psychology Monographs*, 2, 1–27.

Watson, P.E. and Robinson, M.F. (1965). Variations in body
weight of young women during the menstrual cycle. *British
Journal of Nutrition*, 19, 237–248.

Woolley, D.E., Timiras, P.S., Rosenzweig, M.R., Krech, D.
and Bennett, E.L. (1961a). Sex and strain differences in

electroshock convulsions of the rat. *Nature* (*London*),
190, 515-516.

Woolley, D.E., Timiras, P.S., Srebnik, H.H. and Silva, A.
(1961b). Threshold and pattern of electroshock convulsions during the estrous cycle in the rat. *Federation
Proceedings*, 20, 198.

Wright, P. and Crow, R.A. (1973). Menstrual cycle: Effect
on sweetness preference in women. *Hormones and Behavior*,
4, 387-391.

Wynn, V.T. (1971). Absolute pitch: A bimensual rhythm.
Nature (*London*), 230, 337.

Wynn, V.T. (1972). Measurement of small variations in "absolute" pitch. *Journal of Physiology*, 220, 627-637.

Yalom, I.D., Lunde, D.T., Moos, R.H. and Hamburg, D.A. (1968).
"Postpartum blues". *Archives of General Psychiatry*, 18,
16-27.

Zarrow, M.X., Denenberg, V.H. and Sachs, B.D. (1972). Hormones and maternal behavior in mammals. *In* "Hormones and
Behavior". (S. Levine, ed.) Academic Press, New York.

Zucker, I. (1969). Hormonal determinants of sex differences
in saccharin preference, food intake and body weight.
Physiology and Behavior, 4, 595-602.

9. SEX DIFFERENCES AND PSYCHOPATHOLOGY

Peter Mayo

The term psychopathology is used in this chapter to cover those mental disorders which people find distressing and which lead them to seek help. Common examples are incapacitating anxiety or long-lasting subjective feelings of depression. Sometimes, however, the person concerned does not complain, but sufficient distress is caused to other people for them to take some action. The person in question may then agree to see a doctor or, as sometimes happens, he may object to the unsolicited intervention. Such situations may arise where people show psychopathic, schizophrenic, or manic behaviour.

In this review, I shall consider the main forms of psychopathology using such conventional categories of mental disorder as the neuroses, psychosomatic disorders and the schizophrenias. Whilst not above criticism these categories are used widely by research workers, clinicians and the general public, and they do provide the only generally acceptable framework against which the complexities of sex differences in this area can be viewed.

Many more women than men have neuroses, and to a lesser degree this is probably true of the psychosomatic disorders. In the first part of this chapter, studies are reviewed which demonstrate this, and the possible explanations in terms of genetically-based differences between the sexes, differences in willingness to admit to personal distress, and differences in stress are considered. Men and women may also express psychopathology in different ways, and with this in mind, childhood disorders, psychopathy, alcoholism, drug addiction and suicide, are examined. In the final section, explorations of sex differences in both the schizophrenias and the affective disorders are discussed.

THE NEUROSES

Neuroses can be viewed as maladaptive behaviour which frequently involves disturbed interpersonal relationships. On the basis of patterns of symptoms, they are divided into anxiety states and phobias, neurotic (reactive) depression, obsessional states and hysteria. Usually a combination of symptom patterns are found, and a mixture of anxiety and depressive symptoms is particularly common.

Over half of all psychiatric disorders seen by general practitioners are neuroses (Shepherd et al. 1966), and many more women than men report neurotic symptoms. Shepherd and his research team obtained records for a twelve month period from a sample of general practitioners in London. They found that for every 1,000 women registered with the G.P.s, 175 had seen their doctor and been given some form of psychiatric diagnosis, and 117 of these were classed as neurotic. For men, only 98 in every 1,000 were given a psychiatric diagnosis, and neuroses accounted for only 56 of these.

Most neuroses are treated by general practitioners, but some are referred to psychiatrists and a certain number of these, presumably the most severe, become in-patients. Again the same picture is given by figures for new admissions to psychiatric units in England and Wales during 1971. For the neuroses category women outnumber men by two to one (Department of Health and Social Security, 1973).

Many people with neurotic symptoms keep well away from official medical help (Gurin et al. 1960). Several large scale surveys covering entire populations have also found that women report more psychological distress than men (Dohrenwend and Dohrenwend, 1969).

Questionnaires given to non-psychiatric populations provide a different type of evidence, but also underline the same male/female difference. Measures of "Anxiety", "Emotionality", or "Neuroticism" give higher scores for women than men (e.g. Eysenck and Eysenck, 1964). Fear Survey Schedules ask subjects to indicate those objects (spiders, snakes, blood, etc.), and those situations (personal failure, confined spaces, etc.), which make them feel afraid. Women report both more fears and greater intensity of fear (Hannah et al. 1965; Manosevitz and Lanyon, 1965), and these differences for reported fears and anxiety apply to children as well as adults. Studies of 9-12 year old children (Scherer and Nakamura, 1969) and 15-17 year olds (Ekehammer 1974)

give essentially the same results. More girls of 10 or 11
years receive psychiatric treatment for neurotic symptoms
than boys of the same age, but the difference is not as
marked as in adults (Rutter *et al.* 1970). In adolescence
the gap begins to widen to the disadvantage of women (Baldwin,
1968), and probably continues that way throughout the life-
span. When Bergman (1970) studied a large group of English
people aged between 65 and 80 years, he found that propor-
tionally, neurotic symptoms were commoner amongst women.

  Not every type of neurosis, however, shows the clear-
cut sex difference described above. It is doubtful whether
this difference applies to obsessional states – the condition
in which a person feels compulsion towards certain patterns
of thinking and actions. Black (1974), reviewing recent research, concludes that on the available evidence there is no
reason to suppose that women are more disposed to obsessional
disorders than men.

THE PSYCHOSOMATIC DISORDERS

  Psychosomatic disorders are those physical illnesses
where psychological factors are thought to play a causative
role. Among the best known are asthma, peptic ulcer, rheu-
matoid arthritis, essential hypertension and some forms of
neurodermatitis. It is not easy to obtain a valid estimate
of the prevalence of psychosomatic disorders because research
workers vary in the stringency of their criteria. However,
Kessel and Munro (1964) reviewed the studies that were available. They pointed out that while the famous study of
"Stirling County", a rural area in Canada, (Leighton *et al.*
1963) showed no difference between the sexes for physiological symptoms, women outnumbered men (by ratios of 2 to 1 and
3 to 2) in two other investigations of psychosomatic disorders. Although the figures vary, in no studies did men outnumber women. Sex differences exist, but they are probably
not as great as for the neuroses.

  Peptic ulcers are an interesting exception. Until the
end of the nineteenth century they were almost certainly
more common in women, but since World War I, 90 per cent of
ulcer perforations have been in men (Arie, 1970). The reasons for this change are obscure, but Rosenbaum (1967) suggests they are psychological and social. He considers that
increasing social and economic pressures on men in the twentieth century have meant they are less free to express both

aggressive and dependent feelings. Women in contrast have
been more able to be both dependent and independent. A psy-
chodynamic view of this kind might fit with the stereotype
of the tense, over-conscientious executive who is ulcer prone,
but the relation between personality characteristics and psychosomatic disorders remains very unclear at the present time
and must be treated with caution (Claridge, 1973). Furthermore, ulcer mortality rates have been declining since the
1930's in Britain, particularly amongst men. To further com-
plicate the picture Susser (1967) points out that after the
menopause the difference between the sexes for duodenal ulcers is reduced and considers that endocrine factors may be
protecting women until then.

    With this exception, and perhaps also in the case of
obsessional states, women outnumber men in the types of psychopathology described so far. In attempting to account for
these differences, the possible reasons will be discussed
under the headings of biologically-based differences, willingness to admit to personal distress, stress,and sex differences in the expression of psychopathology. These approaches
are not mutually exclusive, and probably all play some part
in explaining the sex differences described above.

CONTRIBUTING FACTORS TO SEX DIFFERENCES

Biologically Based Differences

    It has been suggested that men are less "emotional" or
"fearful" than women because of hormonal differences (Gray,
1971). Elsewhere Gray and Buffery (1971) suggest that the
neural structures involved in submissive and fearful behaviour overlap with those involved in verbal behaviour and hy-
pothesize that women have a "more highly reactive behavioural
inhibition system". Archer (1971) has criticised these views
as giving a one-sided biological explanation which uses an
unsatisfactory concept of fearfulness derived from research
on rodents. Instead he thinks that a more realistic approach
would be to consider both hormonal and cultural determinants.
    Marks (1969) also believes that both biology and cul-
ture have to be considered when trying to explain why most
phobias are reported more frequently by women. He has suggested an interaction between biological differences (men
being stronger, more aggressive, and less "fearful"), environmental pressures and willingness to admit to fears. There

are certainly strong reasons for believing that the origin
of the consistently more aggressive behaviour of men is biological (Maccoby and Jacklin, 1974) and although it does not
logically follow that they should therefore be less fearful,
it might well be that these two emotional states are connected, in a reciprocal manner.

That genetic factors play some part in the neuroses
(Slater and Cowie, 1971) seems very likely but in the present
state of knowledge I would agree with the cautious opinion
of Rosenthal (1970), who concluded from the few studies available on the issue of heredity and neuroses, that polygenic
systems are probably involved in a low-keyed way. Rosenthal's
opinion is that environmental factors are important in the
development of clinical neuroses, but at the same time they
do interact with heredity.

Willingness to Admit to Personal Distress

Another possibility is that men are as distressed as
women, but do not admit to this distress so readily either
to themselves or others. Certainly the expectations of sex
role behaviour would seem to encourage such attitudes on the
part of men. Recent research by Bem (1974) supports the argument that a man appears to have more to lose in self-esteem
and in the esteem of others if he cannot cope and has to admit to psychological disturbance. Bem asked 100 people to
rate the desirability (in American Society) of 400 personality
characteristics "for a man" or "for a woman". The final 20
masculine items which emerged as highly desirable included
"acts as a leader, assertive, forceful, independent, self-
reliant and strong personality". In contrast, the 20 feminine items included "affectionate, gentle, shy, understanding and yielding". The raters, who showed high agreement
with one another, were presumably presenting their perception of the stereotypes held by most people in that society,
and the differences that emerge are striking and significant
for the present argument.

An illustration of the differences between men and women
when asked about their fears is found in a study by Wilson
(1967). He asked 120 men and 120 women to report what they
considered to be their "unreasonable" fears, i.e. those that
were out of proportion to the real danger involved. When the
elicited fears were subsequently rated by six judges, (three
men and three women), for degree of silliness, the most silly,

e.g. worms and moths, were reported exclusively by the women,
and the most reasonable, e.g. sharks and heights, significantly more frequently by the men.

The work of Jourard (1964) is also relevant. He has
suggested that men have lower "self-disclosure" than women,
i.e. that they are less willing (or less able) to reveal
highly personal matters to others. There have been problems
in validating measures of self-disclosure, but Jourard's hypothesis of sex differences in such inter-personal behaviour
is in the same direction as the other evidence.

Reviewing children's anxieties, Maccoby and Jacklin
(1974) suggest that sex differences on anxiety scales may be
related to boys' higher scores on Lie and Defensiveness Scale

My own view is that a willingness to admit to personal
distress does play a part in the issue under discussion, but
it is difficult to determine to what degree. Some men are
willing to admit to feeling anxious and depressed, furthermore severe symptoms can become virtually undeniable, and
recent changes in sex role behaviour in Western society may
include a greater willingness on the part of men to admit to
personal distress.

Stress

It has often been asserted that women's lives in
Western society are more stressful than mens' and that this
alone is sufficient to account for sex differences in psychological distress. Those who disagree can be equally dogma-
tic. It should be pointed out that such arguments frequently
forget that the concept of stress is not a simple one, involving as it does both the demands being made on the individual
and his or her individual response to those demands.

Stressful life events. In a community survey Taylor and
Chave (1964) interviewed men and women living in a new town
built since the 1939-45 war. There was no difference between
the sexes on an item relating to boredom, but the women reported experiencing significantly more loneliness than the
men. When those who reported neurotic symptoms were asked
what they considered had led to the symptoms, men emphasized
work, including the journey to work, worry about the job and
the responsibility involved. Women, in contrast, emphasized
pregnancy, childbirth and the care of children. Not surprisingly there was an overlap in the answers given by the two
sexes, both agreeing, for instance, that constitution (being

a "natural worrier") was one factor.

The care of children is central to Bart's (1971) interesting study of depression in middle-aged women. Included
in her research was an examination of the case-records of
533 women aged between 40 and 50 years who, for the first
time in their lives, had been admitted to hospital because
of mental illness; she also interviewed 20 of these women.
Amongst Jewish mothers in particular, it was clear that the
departure of their children from the home was often central
to the development of depression. Bart describes some of
these mothers as "overprotective, conventional, martyrs"
whose self-esteem was severely affected by the loss of their
role as mother to their children. A similar point was made
by Carstairs (1962) who suggested that neurosis in young and
middle-aged women may occur when their children are growing
up, household duties lighten and the lack of a constructive
role leads to a sense of uselessness.

The work mentioned so far in this section has depended
on the use of interviews and case-records. Another way forward in this uncertain area has been research into "stressful
life events". Holmes and Rahe (1967) have attempted to provide an objective and quantifiable measure of the intensity
of recent stressful life events, and to relate these to both
physical and mental illness. Life events include not only
those conventionally thought of as stressful and undesirable,
e.g. death of a family member, personal injury, divorce, or
losing one's job, but also birth of a child, expanding one's
business, changing one's job, moving house, and other such
items. Each of these requires adaptive or coping behaviour
on the part of the individual. A scale of such events was
quantified by asking judges to estimate the amount of tur-
moil and readjustment related to each item. Close agreement
was found among judges in the United States and other countries. Having established such a scale, Rahe (1968) was able
to demonstrate that those people having high "Life Change"
scores were more likely to become ill during a subsequent
period of observation, and also that those with most illness
had the greatest number of stressful life events.

Recently, this approach has been used by Dohrenwend
(1973) to study a representative sample of men and women in
one area of New York. People were interviewed and answered
a checklist of "Life Events" they had experienced in the
past twelve months, these being used to calculate a measure
of the amount of life change. They also completed a psycho-

logical symptom measure which included items relating to
headaches, poor appetite, low spirits, worrying and other
similar items. Dohrenwend found that women reported somewhat higher life change scores than men, and also that these
higher scores were associated with more psychological symptoms. She was able to show that this result was not merely
a response set on the part of the women. An interesting
point emerged when the life change events were divided into
those probably under the person's own control and those probably not under his control (as agreed upon by independent
coders). Examples of events probably not controlled by the
respondents were a death, physical illness, the marriage of
a friend or relative, and the job change of a friend or relative other than the spouse. The association with symptoms
for women was highest for those events not controlled by
themselves. In contrast, psychological symptoms in men related highly to all events, both those controlled and those
not controlled by themselves. Dohrenwend has suggested that
psychological distress for women tends to be associated with
a lack of power to control their lives, whilst for men it
has been associated with their need to provide for their
families. This study is interesting, but should be accepted
with caution and requires replication. Research into stressful life events is still in its infancy (Dohrenwend and
Dohrenwend, 1974).

In this area of research not enough attention has been
paid to the effect of positive events in people's lives.
The range of such events is no doubt very wide but might include living near a helpful parent, visits to the cinema,
local club or pub, or having money to spend on luxuries.
Some of these could neutralize the effects of the stressful
events described above. Many men are certainly under stress
in their work, but there may be psychological gains from the
money earned, the companionship at work, or the daily change
from the home environment. From this point of view, a study
such as that by Dohrenwend could be extended to include a
division between those people who are employed and those not
employed, and also a measure of the degree of personal satisfaction gained from employment and other areas of life. For
example, in a study of women with neurotic symptoms who were
coping without seeking medical aid, it was evident that some
of the group were gaining considerable satisfaction from
going to work (Mayo, 1969). It seemed very likely that if,
for some reason, these women had been forced to give up work,

then at that point they might have felt unable to cope and sought help from their doctor. For a smaller number of women in this study, the positive aspect of their life appeared to be a highly satisfactory relationship with their husbands. Here the ability to cope rested perhaps on obtaining something similar to psychotherapy within the home situation. The idea that positive as well as negative events should be considered is similar to Bradburn's (1969) proposition that psychological well-being is the outcome of both negative and positive affect. Lewinsohn (1974) in studying both depression and the aging process from a behaviourist standpoint has developed a Pleasant Events Schedule which might prove useful in this area of research.

The family and stress. Another aspect of the study of stress is the effect that the married state has on the mental health of men and women. As Rutter (1970) has pointed out, there are noteworthy differences: men who are married have less physical and mental illness and a lower death rate than single men. That this is not a simple result of differential selection is suggested by similar findings when married men are compared with those who are divorced or widowed. If marriage is associated with better physical and mental health for men, it does not appear to be so for women. Married women are usually found to have similar rates of psychiatric disorder to those of single women (Shepherd *et al.* 1966). Indeed, there is research which suggests that marriage may put women at greater risk. One well-known study related health to life stresses over a large number of years (Hinkle and Wolff, 1957). The authors found that the healthiest group on their measures were those women, then in middle age, who had chosen not to marry and who had worked out for themselves a relatively non-stressful style of living.

The differential effects of marriage carry on into widowhood. The mortality rate for spouses following the death of their husband or wife is significantly higher than the rate for others of the same age, and this is particularly so in the first six months after bereavement. The advantages of marriage for men are reflected in the significantly higher risk of death for bereaved men than for women (Rees and Lutkins, 1967). An attempt to explain the increased mortality rate of surviving spouses was made by Young and his associates (1963). The possibilities they suggested included common infection, a joint unfavourable environment previously shared with the deceased, and the effects of loss of care by the spouse. However, these authors believe that the most important factor is what they termed the "desolation effects" of being widowed, and hold that it is usually greater for men than for women. They may well be right in suggesting that men are more "desolated" than women at this time, but it does seem very likely that loss of care is important. If men are inexperienced at cooking, or if they cannot be bothered to cook for themselves, then their diet could be altered radically and their resistance to infection be lowered.

Stress and physiology. There are three physiological stresses which only women experience: the menstrual cycle, pregnancy and childbirth, and the menopause. Fluctuations of mood associated with the menstrual cycle were shown in a study of twenty-six college students (Ivey and Bardwick, 1968). At ovulation, when the oestrogen level is high, anxiety and hostility were low and the students exhibited "high levels of self esteem". During the pre-menstrual period, the reverse was the case. Bardwick (1971), commenting on this type of study, stated that "women may cope or not cope, become anxious, hostile or depressive, appear healthy or neurotic, due as much to menstrual cyclice phase as to core psychological characteristics".

Coppen and Kessel (1963) found that in a group of 465 women representative of the general population, pre-menstrual symptoms were frequently reported. Six per cent reported symptoms of depression, anxiety, nervousness or tension, over eleven per cent admitted to severe irritability, and a further twenty-four per cent had headaches or pains of some kind. However, a note of caution is needed since Moos (1968) found that fifty per cent of his sample did not report mood swings when they completed a Menstrual Distress Questionnaire. Kimmel (1974) is right to emphasize an interaction between biological, psychological and social factors in seeking to account for pre-menstrual tension (see Chapter 8 by Messent for a more detailed discussion of these issues).

Pregnancy itself does not involve any increased risk of mental illness, but the period immediately after childbirth is associated, in a minority of women, with varying forms of mental disorder. A mother has to adjust both physiologically and psychologically to the birth of her child. During labour and immediately after birth, there are major changes in circulating hormone levels (see Chapter 8). It has been estima-

ted that the risk of mental illness is increased four or
five-fold during the first three months after delivery. Approximately one third of those who are affected have some
form of neurotic reaction, often with depressive and anxiety
symptoms, whilst over half experience psychotic reactions
which can include auditory and visual hallucinations, rest-
lessness, agitation, confusion and depressive symptoms.
Again, an interaction of biological and social factors is
the only realistic viewpoint. Some expectant mothers may
be predisposed to these types of reaction on physiological
grounds, others for more psychological reasons. The dependent, immature woman, those who fear the responsibilities of
motherhood, or perceive the new baby as a rival for their
husband's affection are likely to be under high stress at
this particular time (Slater and Roth, 1969).

During the menopause, many women find that they have
depressive moods with weeping, palpitations and attacks of
dizziness, and their ability to tolerate frustration is reduced. According to Greenblatt (1955), symptoms at this
time can be linked with the rate of decline of oestrogen
production. Greenblatt hypothesizes that autonomic nervous
system functioning is closely linked with the oestrogen level and a swift decline in the latter disturbs the balance
of the autonomic nervous system, thus promoting the various
unpleasant symptoms. It is probable, however, that the physiological changes at the menopause have been emphasized to
the exclusion of psychological factors (Freedman and Kaplan,
1967). For some women the menopause is a poignant reminder
of undeniable disappointments, of the inevitability of aging
and loss of physical attractiveness. For many it is also
the time when children are leaving home. On the other hand,
there are studies which have found that many women do not
find this time of life as disturbing and unpleasant as is
commonly supposed (Neugarten *et al.* 1963).

Sex Differences in the Expression of Psychopathology

Some writers have suggested that there is a tendency
for men and women to express psychopathology in different
ways (Chesler, 1974). Phillips (1968), for instance, has
noted that men more frequently exhibit reactions which involve destructive behaviour towards others and a pathological self-indulgence, whereas women react in a more inhibited,
self-critical manner. This idea does accord with men's

greater predisposition to physical aggression (Maccoby and Jacklin, 1974) but there are very few studies in which it has been specifically investigated. Sex differences in patients' behaviour consistent with Phillips' hypothesis have been reported by Zigler and Phillips (1960) but their conclusions were based upon case histories of former in-patients and involved tabulation of symptoms from these records. One cannot be sure that the clinicians who produced the case histories some years earlier were consistent in the questions they asked their patients, or in their methods of recording.

A number of research areas do, however, provide evidence of sex differences which might be held to support Phillips' view. These will be considered under the headings: childhood disorders, alcohol and drug addiction, psychopathic behaviour and suicide.

Childhood disorders. Studies from child guidance clinics and population surveys show that more girls than boys have neuroses, but that the difference between the sexes is not as marked as it is for adults (Baldwin, 1968; Marks, 1973). Apart from neuroses, the other main category used in child psychiatry is that of anti-social behaviour or conduct disorders. The latter includes truanting, stealing, destructive and highly aggressive behaviours. Not all such behaviour can be considered psychopathological, and only a proportion of children showing these behaviours are thought to need specialized treatment. Within this group of children it is clear that boys outnumber girls.

An indication of psychopathology in children is given in a carefully conducted study of all 10 and 11-year-old children on the Isle of Wight (Rutter *et al.* 1970). Anxiety disorders (which in this case included phobias), formed the large majority of the neuroses in both sexes and girls outnumbered boys 26 to 17. Specific animal phobias were found exclusively in girls, a difference which continues into adult life where ninety-five per cent of such phobias are found in women (Marks, 1969). Boys outnumbered girls 34 to 9 in anti-social behaviour and a further category of mixed conduct and neurotic disorders also showed boys exceeding girls by 17 to 3. The overall picture given by these figures is that more boys had childhood disorders than girls, due to the larger number of boys with marked anti-social behaviour.

An earlier study in Camberwell, London (Rutter, 1970) investigated children from families where one parent had a psychiatric disorder. Parental discord and disruption in these families was associated with anti-social behaviour in the boys, but not in the girls. Wolkind (1974) has suggested that where relationships within a family are very disturbed, young boys are less psychologically damaged if they are removed to residential care. In Wolkind's own study, girls were more damaged if they had been taken away from their disturbed families to spend a prolonged period early in life in residential care.

Psychopaths, alcoholics and drug addicts. It is convenient to consider these three categories together since they all appear to involve the destructive behaviour and pathological self-indulgence which Phillips considered typical patterns of male psychopathology. In each instance, men probably outnumber women.

Psychopaths are described as being impulsive, markedly egocentric, lacking in concern for others, but without anxiety or guilt. The term "primary" psychopath is sometimes used to distinguish one small group of people from "secondary" or "symptomatic" psychopaths (Trasler, 1973). The main distinction is that primary psychopaths appear unable to acquire social avoidance responses. The anxiety which promotes avoidance learning seems to be absent. Primary psychopaths form only a small section of the criminal population.

It is not easy to obtain reliable statistics about psychopaths because of the reluctance of many to become involved with mental health agencies. However, most writers assume that there are many more men than women and research studies support this assumption. Robins (1966), for instance, followed up a group of 436 adults who had attended a child guidance clinic. Thirty years later, of the 321 men, 25 per cent were diagnosed as sociopathic (psychopathic) personality, compared with 12 per cent of the 115 women. The rates for the neuroses were just the reverse, 10 per cent of the men and 44 per cent of the women.

The causes of psychopathy are still not understood, (McCord and McCord, 1964; Craft, 1966; Hare, 1970), but social, psychological and neurological factors probably all contribute. The extent of their involvement may vary from person to person but McCord and McCord (1964) have suggested three causal patterns. Thus, psychopathy could be the result of severe childhood rejection, or of mild rejection together with a psychopathic parent model, erratic punitive discipline and an absence of adult supervision. Another possibility is that mild rejection inter-acting with brain dam-

age might be responsible for some psychopathic behaviour.
Craft (1966) has also pointed out that early brain damage,
because of infection or injury, could lead to later behaviour disorder. He added that the severity of the damage and
the site of the lesion were very important, together with
the environmental circumstances after the occurrence of the
damage.

There are two possibilities here which might help to explain the excess of male psychopaths. First of all, boys appear to be more disturbed by family discord than do girls;
such discord must sometimes include psychological rejection.
Secondly, it is known that boys are more likely to suffer
early brain damage than girls, and this, together with their
higher predisposition to aggression, may be partly responsible for the larger number of male psychopaths.

The sex differences for alcoholism and drug addiction
are summarized in Table I, and again the higher incidence in
men, in contrast with the neuroses, is clear.

TABLE I

*Admissions by Sex and Diagnostic Group: Mental Illness
Hospitals and Units under Regional Hospital Board and
Technical Hospitals (England and Wales)*

Diagnosis	Male	Female
Psychoneuroses	8,593	17,406
Alcoholics	5,483	1,470
Drug Dependence	1,105	622

*Extracted from: In-patient statistics from the Mental Health
Enquiry for the year 1971.*

The sex-ratio for alcoholism varies with different studies, but a fairly representative statement is given by
Willis (1973), who has suggested a 4 to 1, male:female ratio
for Western societies. There are some who do not accept
these figures. Block (1962) expressing perhaps a minority
view, has argued that there are as many women as male alcoholics, but they are not so easy to detect. Women, he has
suggested, drink in the privacy of the home and so manage to

avoid the social disapproval of excessive drinking in public.

However, psychiatric statistics for alcoholism, such as those in Table I, do emphasize a male dominance and it is not difficult to find social reasons to explain this result. There are still double standards with regard to drinking in Western societies. In many social situations men are encouraged to drink freely in public, while there are social pressures against excess drinking by women.

Phillips' (1968) suggestion that male psychopathology tends towards destructive behaviour and pathological self-indulgence is really too simple when considering the complexities of alcoholism. Many men start drinking heavily in an attempt to cope with excessive anxiety. If their drinking becomes unmanageable, they can become depressed and their problem then involves both neurosis and alcoholism.

In Britain men outnumber women by 5 to 1 for serious form drug addiction (Willis, 1973) but unlike the alcoholic, who is typically middle-aged, the morphine or heroin addict is frequently a young man. His first encounter with these drugs has been described as usually pleasure-seeking in character, and the environment in which he becomes addicted appears to be more readily accessible to men than to women. In a well-known study of serious drug addiction, Chein *et al.* (1964) have pointed out that since women are less involved in most forms of delinquency, they are less likely to come into contact with the drug culture.

In the case of some other drugs, however, the sex ratio is reversed. Oswald (1970) has noted that a quarter of all Scottish middle-aged women regularly take drugs to help them sleep. He also pointed out that insomnia was most frequently found as a complaint among people who complained of neurotic symptoms.

Suicide and attempted suicide. In countries where reliable data is available, the statistics indicate that more women than men attempt suicide, but that more men than women actually commit suicide. Most studies of actual suicide show a male:female ratio varying between 2:1 and 4:1 (Sainsbury, 1955; Stengel, 1964; Farberow and Shneidman, 1961; Maris, 1969). These overall ratios hide the fact that men are most vulnerable in old age. A study in Chicago for example showed that men outnumbered women by 2 to 1 in the younger age groups, but this figure changed to 3 to 1 in middle age, and 4 to 1 in the late sixties. However, Stengel (1964) noted that in England and Wales, between 1951 and 1961, the gap be-

tween men and women had been narrowing and other research
workers have since confirmed this.

Men not only kill themselves more often, they also use
more violent means. In Los Angeles, Farberow and Shneidman
(1961) found that 41 per cent of male suicides used guns,
compared with 18 per cent of the women. In contrast, 46 per
cent of the women poisoned themselves using barbiturates,
but only 13 per cent of the men. Hanging and the use of cutting and piercing instruments, although not frequently employed, are also more likely in male suicides. Several observers have found that male suicide is more likely to be related to work problems, including unemployment, downward
social mobility and retirement. Suicide in women is more
frequently related to domestic difficulties. However, a recent review of suicide in England and Wales (Whitlock, 1973)
has suggested that in the elderly, suicide in men, but not
in women, is connected with loneliness and isolation.
Whitlock also considered that physical and mental illness
were probably the most important determinants of suicide in
old age for both sexes. It is worth noting at this point
that very few children commit suicide, but a survey covering
suicides over a seven-year period in Britain found that twice
as many boys as girls in the 12-14 age group committed suicide (Shaffer, 1974).

Although actual suicide is particularly associated with
the middle-aged and the elderly, the commonest age for attempted suicide is in the late teens and early twenties.
Whether it is always justified to use the term attempted suicide is questionable, since many who come under this category
have no intention of killing themselves. There are many reasons why people attempt suicide including the notion that it
is a "cry for help". Stengel's (1964) view is that women in
particular use suicidal acts in both an aggressive and defen-
sive manner, and as a way of manipulating relationships with
men. He views this as an alternative to the predominantly
male use of physical aggression.

Attempted suicide by poisoning was studied in Edinburgh
over a one-year period (Messel, 1965). During this time,
314 women and 151 men were admitted to a special unit in the
Edinburgh Royal Infirmary and 19 per cent of both men and
women died in the hospital. When the circumstances surrounding the taking of an overdose were investigated, including
the amount taken and the potential help available, it was
found that 49 per cent of the women and 40 per cent of the

men were certain to have survived, despite their so-called "attempted suicide". The largest group of people poisoning themselves in this study were women in their twenties. It has been suggested that the relatively large number of women attempting suicide at this age is the counterpart of delinquency in young men, but Kessel does not subscribe to this view. His clinical impression was that many of these women were "emotionally isolated". From interviews it was apparent that most of them lacked close contact with other people and also had a poor relationship with a key person in their lives. A typical situation, according to Kessel, was that unhappiness mounted and reached such intensity that at a moment of special crisis the individual took an overdose. An additional finding showed that men, more than women, were likely to have been drinking at the time they poisoned themselves.

THE SCHIZOPHRENIAS

Research into the schizophrenias has been handicapped by a lack of agreement over the criteria for diagnosing schizophrenia. While this does not nullify the research discussed here, the few available studies in this area should be treated with caution. It is clear that replication and extension of work into sex differences and schizophrenia is needed.

At some time during their lifetime, 1.064 per cent of all men and 0.988 per cent of all women are diagnosed as schizophrenic in the United Kingdom (Gottesman and Shields, 1972). The commonest age for men to develop a frank schizophrenia disorder is in the early twenties, whereas for women it is after the age of thirty.

Why men tend to develop schizophrenia earlier than women is not known. It could be a genetically determined difference, but an equally plausible possibility is that male schizophrenics are particularly vulnerable because of sex-role expectations in their late teens and early twenties. Men are usually expected to find and keep employment and also to take the initiative in relationships with women. Such expectations could be highly stressful for those who feel completely unable to meet them.

One of the major divisions within schizophrenia is that between the paranoid and non-paranoid forms of the disorder (Johannsen et al. 1963). Shakow (1962) has described the paranoid form as "an over-reaction to the underlying trend towards disorganization which exists in the psychosis. The

hebephrenic gives way to the trend whereas the paranoid or-
ganizes his resources to fight the disruption".

Shakow's distinction between paranoid and non-paranoid
schizophrenia is given here because it has been asserted that
many more women than men show paranoid forms of schizophrenia,
particularly in middle age (Tyhurst, 1957; Swanson *et al.*
1970). If this is so, it may be that those who develop
schizophrenic symptoms in their late teens and twenties have
not built up any stable personality organization, and therefore give way to the threatened disorganization. By middle
age, however, there has been time to develop some degree of
personality organization. The paranoid response to the
threatened psychotic disorganization can be seen as an attempt to organize and control the environment as far as is
possible.

There are very few studies of schizophrenia and sex-
role behaviour. Cheek (1964) analysed the interaction of
mothers, fathers and their formerly hospitalized schizophrenic son or daughter. Using an observation system which analysed speech interaction it was found that the schizophrenic
sons had low total activity rates and low dominance behaviour; the women in contrast were more active and dominating
than a comparison group of normal women. Cheek does point
out that the interaction findings could be a function of selective hospitalization, since overactive men and underactive
women might more easily stay in society.

Sex-role alienation in schizophrenia was investigated
by McClelland and Watt (1968) using a variety of tasks to
investigate sex-role alienation in schizophrenia. Male patients, when asked which of two sex-typed roles they would
like to play, tended to choose the more female roles, whereas the female patients frequently chose the male roles. The
controls did not show this pattern. When asked about satisfaction with various parts of their bodies, the women schizophrenics showed a seeming lack of concern about their bodies
generally, whereas the men showed more concern with what the
authors describe as "female body parts". They concluded that
this supported their hypothesis that both sexes showed an
avoidance of or alienation from sex-role identity. It remains unclear whether disturbances in sex-role identity contribute to the development of schizophrenia, or whether these
unusual responses to various psychological tests are consequent upon the schizophrenic process.

Studies of family relationships and sex differences are

limited both in number and scope. One group of workers has
made an intensive study of 17 families (Fleck *et al.* 1963).
The sons or daughters were all young schizophrenics and it
was suggested that the inappropriate behaviour of the parents
had led to distorted identity formation and thus contributed
to the development of schizophrenia. In the case of the
girls, there was parental schism. This term implied chronic
discord in the family, recurrent threats of separation, and
the parents competing for the loyalty of their daughter,
each constantly trying to undercut the other in the process.
The mothers in such families were described as being cold
and aloof. For boys who developed schizophrenia the authors
described a skewed family pattern. The home in this case was
overshadowed by the pathology of a dominating mother; the
father was passive and inadequate and the boy's closest relationship was with his mother.
    This work, which has a strong psychoanalytical orienta-
tion, is open to criticism on a number of grounds. The sample of families studied was very small and we have no guaran-
tee that they were representative of the larger population of
families with a schizophrenic child. In addition there were
no control families and there was a lack of reliable objective measuring instruments. Despite these shortcomings, more
recent work in this area suggests that some of the ideas are
worth pursuing. For instance, Gardner (1967) used child guidance centre records to study the early lives of adult schizophrenics. For the women, but not for the men, schizophrenia
was related to serious psychopathology in the patient's mother. Mishler and Waxler (1968) were careful to include control groups. They studied the verbal interaction of mother,
father, and schizophrenic child, using multi-channel tape
recordings. The conversations were categorized according to
a number of validated coding systems. They found that mothers and their sons took relatively high power positions
and tended to defer to each other in family discussions.
The fathers exerted little influence. Daughters, in contrast,
were isolated particularly from their mothers, and little respect was accorded to them by either parent. Mishler and
Waxler concluded that neither sons nor daughters had suitable
parental models for identification.
    Jacob (1975) has reviewed all family interaction studies
in schizophrenia and points out that the majority have ignored sex difference and summed scores across sex. It is
quite possible that future research will show that certain

patterns of family interaction are particularly stressful for
males, and different patterns especially stressful for females. Such stresses interacting with a varying, biologically based predisposition to develop schizophrenia might be
sufficient to precipitate psychotic behaviour.

This research area is full of problems and the interpretation of results is often unclear. Either heredity or environment, or an interaction between the two could explain
the results. Furthermore, it seems possible that in some
respects the parents may be reacting to their schizophrenic
child rather than the other way round (Liem, 1974).

THE AFFECTIVE DISORDERS

The affective disorders include the severe form of depression, usually referred to as endogenous depression or
melancholia, mania, and manic-depression which is a combination of the two. A recent review has indicated that this
group of disorders are genetically related to one another
and are a separate form of psychopathology from the schizophrenias (Rosenthal, 1970).

The distribution of affective disorders shows a clear
contrast with that of the schizophrenias. Figures for
England and Wales show that the lifetime expectancy for developing an affective disorder is 2.4 per cent for men and
3.9 per cent for women. The mean age of onset is earlier
for women, 50.6 years, than for men, 53.2 years. In the
twenties and thirties, almost twice as many women as men
suffer affective disorders, but after 50 this difference reduces until virtual parity is reached.

Various explanations have been put forward for these
differences. One suggestion is that women, when young, tend
to have affective disorders whereas men tend to have schizophrenic reactions. However, the fact that the schizophrenias
and the affective disorders are genetically distinct does not
support this line of argument. Slater and Roth (1969) have
suggested that a diagnosis of affective disorder may, at
times, be more difficult to make in men, the illness sometimes
being masked, for instance by alcoholism. They also suggest
that higher rates of suicide in men could forestall diagnosis.
The other point made by Slater and Roth was that for women
the menstrual cycle provided what they termed a spontaneously
rhythmic constitution; if there was any disturbance on top
of this, then the peaks and troughs of mania and depression

were more readily reached. Some support is given to this
argument by the fact that the sex ratio returns to parity
after the cessation of menstruation.

It should also be pointed out that psychiatrists have
disagreed amongst themselves as to the relation between reactive (neurotic) depression and the more severe endogenous
(psychotic) depression. Some authorities place these along
a continuum, others view them as distinct disorders (Kendell,
1968). Whatever the outcome of this disagreement, I believe
that some of the factors discussed in relation to the neuroses may also be relevant, although in lesser degree, to some
depressions diagnosed as endogenous and thus may partly help
to explain the sex difference in the affective disorders.

CONCLUSION

Sweeping generalizations concerning sex differences and
mental illness are likely to be over-generalizations and can
scarcely do justice to the complexities involved in studying
psychopathology. Clearly, there are important differences,
but research workers have been slow to pay attention to them,
sometimes not even mentioning the sex of their subjects and
on other occasions simply adding together findings for the
two sexes. The situation is changing and the gain may prove
considerable. Batchelor (1969) suggested that if we knew
more about the reasons why men and women differed in their
psychopathology, then we would be well on the way to understanding the causes of many of the mental disorders.

REFERENCES

Archer, J. (1971). Sex differences in emotional behaviour:
A reply to Gray and Buffery. *Acta Psychologica*, <u>35</u>, 415-
429.

Arie, T. (1970). The decline of duodenal ulcer. *In* "Modern
Trends in Psychosomatic Medicine". (O.W. Hill, ed.) Vol.
2. Butterworths, London.

Baldwin, J.A. (1968). Psychiatric illness from birth to maturity: An epidemiological study. *Acta Psychiatrica Scan-
dinavica*, <u>44</u>, 313-333.

Bardwick, J.M. (1971). "Psychology of Women: A Study of Bio-
Cultural Conflicts". Harper and Row, New York.

Bart, P.B. (1971). Depression in middle-aged women. *In* "Woman in Sexist Society". (V. Gormick and B.K. Moran, eds.) Basic Books, New York.

Batchelor, I.R.C. (1969). "Henderson and Gillespies' Textbook of Psychiatry". 10th Edition. Oxford University Press, London.

Bem, S.L. (1974). The measurement of psychological androgyny. *Journal of Consulting and Clinical Psychology*, 42, 155-162.

Bergmann, K. (1970). Sex differences in the neurotic reaction of the aged. *Journal of Biosocial Science*, Suppl. No. 2, 137-145.

Black, A. (1974). The natural history of obsessional neurosis. *In* "Obsessional States". (H.R. Beech, ed.) Methuen, London.

Block, M.A. (1962). "Alcoholism: Its Facets and Phases". Oxford University Press, London.

Bradburn, N.M. (1969). "The Structure of Psychological Well-Being". Aldine, Chicago.

Carstairs, G.M. (1962). The changing role of women. *The Listener*, LXVIII, 947-950.

Cheek, F.E. (1964). A serendipitous finding: Sex roles and schizophrenia. *Journal of Abnormal and Social Psychology*, 69, 392-400.

Chein, I., Gerard, D.L., Lee, R.S., Rosenfeld, E. and Wilner, D.M. (1964). "The Road to H: Narcotics, Delinquency and Social Policy". Basic Books, New York.

Chesler, P. (1974). "Women and Madness". Allen Lane, London.

Claridge, G. (1973). Psychosomatic relations in physical disease. *In* "Handbook of Abnormal Psychology". (H.J. Eysenck, ed.) Pitman Medical, London.

Coppen, A. and Kessel, N. (1963). Menstruation and personality. *British Journal of Psychiatry*, 109, 711-721.

Craft, M. (1966). The causation of psychopathic disorder. *In* "Psychopathic Disorders". (M. Craft, ed.) Pergamon, Oxford.

Department of Health and Social Security, Welsh Office. (1973) Statistical and research report Series No. 6. Psychiatric hospitals and units in England and Wales. In-patient statistics from the mental health enquiry for the year 1971. Her Majesty's Stationery Office, London.

Dohrenwend, B.P. and Dohrenwend, B.S. (1969). "Social Status and Psychological Disorder: A Causal Inquiry". Wiley, New York.

Dohrenwend, B.S. (1973). Social status and stressful life events. *Journal of Personality and Social Psychology*, <u>28</u>, 225-235.

Dohrenwend, B.S. and Dohrenwend, B.P. (1974). "Stressful Life Events: Their Nature and Effects". Wiley, New York.

Ekehammar, B. (1974). Sex differences in self-reported anxiety for different situations and modes of response. *Scandinavian Journal of Psychology*, <u>15</u>, 154-160.

Eysenck, H.J. and Eysenck, S.B.G. (1964). "Manual of the Eysenck Personality Inventory". University of London Press, London.

Farberow, N.L. and Shneidman, E.S. (1961). (Eds.) "The Cry for Help". McGraw-Hill, New York.

Fleck, S., Lidz, T. and Cornelison, A. (1963). Comparison of parent-child relationships of male and female schizophrenic patients. *Archives of General Psychiatry*, <u>8</u>, 1-7.

Freedman, A.M. and Kaplan, H.I. (1967). (Eds.) "Comprehensive Textbook of Psychiatry". Williams and Wilkins, Baltimore.

Gardner, C.G. (1967). Role of maternal psychopathology in male and female schizophrenics. *Journal of Consulting Psychology*, <u>31</u>, 411-413.

Gottesman, I.I. and Shields, J. (1972). "Schizophrenia and Genetics: A Twin Study Vantage Point". Academic Press, New York.

Gray, J.A. (1971). Sex differences in emotional behaviour in mammals including man: Endocrine bases. *Acta Psychologica*, <u>35</u>, 29-46.

Gray, J.A. and Buffery, A.W.H. (1971). Sex differences in emotional and cognitive behaviour in mammals including man: Adaptive and neural bases. *Acta Psychologica*, <u>35</u>, 89-111.

Greenblatt, R.B. (1955). Metabolic and psychosomatic disorders in menopausal women. *Geriatrics*, 10, 165-169.

Gurin, G., Veroff, J. and Feld, S. (1960). "Americans View their Mental Health". Basic Books, New York.

Hannah, F., Storm, T. and Caird, W.K. (1965). Sex differences and relationships among neuroticism, extraversion, and expressed fears. *Perceptual and Motor Skills*, 20, 1214-1216.

Hare, R.D. (1970). "Psychopathy: Theory and Research". Wiley, New York.

Hinkle, L.E. Jr. and Wolff, H.G. (1957). Health and the social environment: Experimental investigations. *In* "Explorations in Social Psychiatry". (A.H. Leighton, J.A. Clausen and R.N. Wilson, eds.) Basic Books, New York.

Holmes, T.H. and Rahe, R.H. (1967). The social readjustment rating scale. *Journal of Psychosomatic Research*, 11, 213-218.

Ivey, M.E. and Bardwick, J.M. (1968). Patterns of affective fluctuation in the menstrual cycle. *Psychosomatic Medicine*, 30, 336-345.

Jacob, T. (1975). Family interaction in disturbed and normal families: A methodological and substantive review. *Psychological Bulletin*, 82, 33-65.

Johannsen, W.J., Friedmen, S.H., Leitschuh, T.H. and Ammons, H. (1963). A study of certain schizophrenic dimensions and their relationship to double alternation learning. *Journal of Consulting Psychology*, 27, 375-382.

Jourard, S.M. (1964). "The Transparent Self: Self Disclosure and Well-Being". D. Van Nostrand, Princeton.

Kendell, R.E. (1968). "The Classification of Depressive Illnesses". Maudsley monographs, No. 18. Oxford University Press, London.

Kessel, N. (1965). Self-poisoning. *British Medical Journal*, 2, 1265-1270 and 1336-1340.

Kessel, N. and Munro, A. (1964). Epidemiological studies in psychosomatic medicine. *Journal of Psychosomatic Research*, 8, 67-81.

Kimmel, D.C. (1974). "Adulthood and Aging". Wiley, New York.

Leighton, D.C., Harding, J.S., Macklin, D.B., Macmillan, A.M. and Leighton, A.H. (1963). "The Character of Danger: Psychiatric Symptoms in Selected Communities". Basic Books, New York.

Lewinsohn, P.M. (1974). A behavioural approach to depression. *In* "The Psychology of Depression: Contemporary Theory and Research". (R.J. Friedman and M.M. Katz, eds.) Wiley, New York.

Liem, J.H. (1974). Effects of verbal communications of parents and children: A comparison of normal and schizophrenic families. *Journal of Consulting and Clinical Psychology*, 42, 438-450.

Maccoby, E.E. and Jacklin, C.N. (1974). "The Psychology of Sex Differences". Stanford University Press, Stanford.

Manosevitz, M. and Lanyon, R.I. (1965). Fear survey schedule: A normative study. *Psychological Reports*, 17, 699-703.

Maris, R.W. (1969). "Social Forces in Urban Suicide". Dorsey Press, Homewood, Illinois.

Marks, I.M. (1969). "Fears and Phobias". Heinemann, London.

Marks, I.M. (1973). Research in neurosis: A selective review. 1. Causes and courses. *Psychological Medicine*, 3, 436-454.

Mayo, P.R. (1969). Women with neurotic symptoms who do not seek treatment. *British Journal of Medical Psychology*, 42, 165-169.

McClelland, D.C. and Watt, N.F. (1968). Sex-role alienation in schizophrenia. *Journal of Abnormal Psychology*, 73, 226-239.

McCord, W. and McCord, J. (1964). "The Psychopath: An Essay on the Criminal Mind". D. Van Nostrand, Princeton.

Mishler, E.G. and Waxler, N.E. (1968). "Interaction in Families: An Experimental Study of Family Processes and Schizophrenia". Wiley, New York.

Moos, R.H. (1968). The development of a menstrual distress questionnaire. *Psychosomatic Medicine*, 30, 853-867.

Neugarten, B.L., Wood, V., Kraines, R.J. and Loomis, B. (1963). Women's attitudes toward the menopause. *Vita Humana*, 6,

140–151.

Oswald, I. (1970). Sleep, dreams and drugs. *In* "Modern Trends in Psychological Medicine". (J.H. Price, ed.) Vol. 2. Butterworths, London.

Parsons, T. and Bales, R.F. (1955). "Family, Socialization and Interaction Process". Free Press, Glencoe.

Phillips, L. (1968). A social view of psychopathology. *In* "Foundations of Abnormal Psychology". (P. London and D. Rosenhan, eds.) Holt, Rinehart and Winston, New York.

Rahe, R.H. (1968). Life-change measurement as a predictor of illness. *Proceedings of the Royal Society of Medicine*, 61, 44–46.

Rees, W.D. and Lutkins, S.G. (1967). Mortality of bereavement. *British Medical Journal*, 4, 13–16.

Robins, L.N. (1966). "Deviant Children Grow Up". Williams and Wilkins, Baltimore.

Rosenbaum, M. (1967). Peptic ulcer. *In* "Comprehensive Textbook of Psychiatry". (A.M. Freedman and H.I. Kaplan, eds.) Williams and Wilkins, Baltimore.

Rosenthal, D. (1970). "Genetic Theory and Abnormal Behaviour". McGraw Hill, New York.

Rutter, M. (1970). Sex differences in children's responses to family stress. *In* "The Child in his Family". (E.J. Anthony and C. Koupernik, eds.) Wiley, New York.

Rutter, M., Tizard, J. and Whitmore, K. (1970). "Education, Health and Behaviour". Longman, London.

Sainsbury, P. (1955). "Suicide in London". Chapman and Hall, London.

Scherer, M.W. and Nakamura, C.Y. (1968). A fear survey schedule for children (FSS-FC): A factor analytic comparison with manifest anxiety (CMAS). *Behaviour Research and Therapy*, 6, 173–182.

Shaffer, D. (1974). Suicide in childhood and early adolescence *Journal of Child Psychology and Psychiatry*, 15, 275–291.

Shakow, D. (1962). Segmental set. *Archives of General Psychiatry*, 6, 1–17.

Shepherd, M., Cooper, B., Brown, A.C. and Kalton, G.W. (1966). "Psychiatric Illness in General Practice". Oxford University Press, London.

Slater, E. and Cowie, V. (1971). "The Genetics of Mental Disorders". Oxford University Press, London.

Slater, E. and Roth, M. (1969). "Clinical Psychiatry". Bailliere, Tindall and Cassell, London.

Stengel, E. (1964). "Suicide and Attempted Suicide". Penguin Books, London.

Susser, M. (1967). Causes of peptic ulcer: A selective epidemiologic review. *Journal of Chronic Diseases*, 20, 435-456.

Swanson, D.W., Bohnert, P.J. and Smith, J.A. (1970). "The Paranoid". Little Brown, Boston.

Taylor, S.J. and Chave, S. (1964). "Mental Health and Environment". Longman, London.

Trasler, G. (1973). Criminal behaviour. *In* "Handbook of Abnormal Psychology". (H.J. Eysenck, ed.) Pitman, London.

Tyhurst, J.S. (1957). Paranoid patterns. *In* "Explorations in Social Psychiatry". (A.H. Leighton, J.A. Clausen and R.N. Wilson, eds.) Basic Books, New York.

Whitlock, F.A. (1973). Suicide in England and Wales 1959-63 Part 1. The county boroughs. *Psychological Medicine*, 3, 350-365.

Willis, J. (1973). "Addicts: Drugs and Alcohol Re-examined". Pitman, London.

Wilson, G.D. (1967). Social desirability and sex differences in expressed fear. *Behaviour Research and Therapy*, 5, 136-137.

Wolkind, S.N. (1974). Sex differences in the aetiology of antisocial disorders in children in long term residential care. *British Journal of Psychiatry*, 125, 125-130.

Young, M., Benjamin, B. and Wallis, C. (1963). The mortality of widowers. *Lancet*, 2, 454-456.

Zigler, E. and Phillips, L. (1960). Social effectiveness and symptomatic behaviours. *Journal of Abnormal and Social Psychology*, 61, 231-238.

10. BIOLOGICAL EXPLANATIONS OF PSYCHOLOGICAL SEX DIFFERENCES

John Archer

In our culture, men and women differ in a number of general behavioural characteristics. Measures of sensory thresholds, verbal, spatial and musical skills, and aggression show consistent mean differences but overlapping ranges of values.
    Traditionally psychologists have explained these findings in terms of differential learning (see Chapter 2 by Ullian). Kagan and Moss (1962) for example, have suggested that the general classes "male" and "female" are amongst the first types of distinction made by adults in relation to childrens' behaviour. Once the child has been reinforced for sex-appropriate behaviour, it becomes increasingly difficult for him or her to change to the other one without considerable conflict and tension. All the details of the general sex differences in behaviour are thought to arise from these culturally-imposed restraints. A theory of this general type could account for many of the cognitive and motivational differences between the sexes, but it would not cover the following questions. The first is whether the nervous system of the developing child or of the adult, by being male or female, facilitates the learning of certain aspects of the appropriate sex role. The second related question concerns the evolutionary origin of the sex differences, whether they are the indirect consequence of adaptively significant biological sex differences of ancient origin.
    Recently several writers (e.g. Hutt, 1972a, b and c; Dawson, 1972; Brindley et al. 1973; Broverman et al. 1968; Fairweather and Hutt, 1972; Gray, 1971; Gray and Buffery, 1971) have concerned themselves with these issues, and have sought to replace culturally-based theories of sex differences in behaviour with viewpoints which emphasize determinants more firmly rooted in physiology. This change of emphasis

can have implications for social policy, in that culturally-imposed sex differences, unconnected to biology, can be taken as an arbitrary arrangement, which may easily be replaced by any other arbitrary arrangement. On the other hand, the claim that sex roles reflect physiologically and genetically determined sex differences in behaviour that are a consequence of selection pressures which moulded these sex roles, might be taken as providing strong support for the maintenance of "traditional" sex roles, at a time when these are being questioned by the Women's Liberation movement. Hutt (1972a, b and c) and Tiger (1970) view the situation as such, and in a more general context arguments based on biology are being increasingly used in discussions of human social structure, particularly now that our social customs are no longer supported by a strong religious backing.

This chapter describes and examines several biologically-based theories of sex differences in behaviour, and then discusses the implications of these for arguments linking human sex roles and biological determinants of behaviour. Most of the chapter is concerned with theories of the "causation" of sex differences (e.g. their hormonal or developmental bases); the question of evolutionary origin is considered briefly in the last two sections.

SEX DIFFERENCES IN BEHAVIOUR

Garai and Scheinfeld (1968), Oetzel (1967) and Maccoby and Jacklin (1974) have summarized human sex differences recorded from English and American samples during the last 80-100 years, and listed a number of conclusions concerning differences in "identifiable averages" between the sexes. Chapter 6 by McGuinness also considers sex differences in perceptual, motor and cognitive abilities.

The following generalizations are relevant to the biologically-based theories of sex differences discussed in this chapter.

1. Sensory thresholds. Women show lower detection thresholds than men for touch, pain, hearing, taste, smell, and rod (dark) vision, whereas men show lower thresholds for cone (daytime) vision (Garai and Scheinfeld, 1968; Chapter 6 by McGuinness).

2. Males are generally reported to show more "aggression" than females, for measures of aggression taken during school life, and in laboratory measures of aggression taken in adult-

hood (Maccoby and Jacklin, 1974).

3. Motor skills. Men show faster reaction times when a simple task is involved and are faster on rotary-pursuit tasks. These findings are taken to indicate a male superiority in speed and co-ordination of gross bodily movements (Garai and Scheinfeld, 1968, p. 203; see also Chapter 6 by McGuinness).

4. Women perform better on tasks requiring more discrete or finely controlled motor responses, such as typing and other so-called "clerical skills" (Garai and Scheinfeld, 1968, pp. 205-206; Chapter 6 by McGuinness).

5. Women show greater verbal abilities from infancy onwards, and perform better on verbal IQ tests (see Chapter 6 and Maccoby and Jacklin, 1974).

6. Men perform better in tests requiring judgment and manipulation of spatial relationships (Maccoby and Jacklin, 1974). Men and women are also said to show a different perceptual approach to the environment, men tending to concentrate on a particular stimulus, separating it from the background, and women tending to exhibit a more global approach, perceiving both stimulus and setting as inter-related (Witkin et al. 1962). This difference appears to be a consequence of the sex difference in spatial ability (Sherman, 1967; Maccoby and Jacklin, 1974; Chapter 6 by McGuinness) although Witkin and his associates (e.g. Witkin, 1967; Coates, 1974) claim that it reflects a more general sex difference in cognitive style - termed "field independence" and "field dependence" respectively (Witkin et al. 1962). This terminology reflects the implication in most discussions that the (male) characteristic "field independence" is the most desirable of the two styles (see also Chapter 6).

7. Men perform better on tests of mathematical ability (Maccoby and Jacklin, 1974).

BIOLOGICALLY-BASED THEORIES OF THE CAUSATION OF SEX DIFFERENCES

Several biologically-based theories have been proposed to account for different aspects of the sex difference summarized here. These are outlined and discussed below. The first four theories refer to the same sorts of cognitive sex differences, but the explanatory mechanism offered is different in each case.

Dawson (1972). Dawson classed together spatial ability,

numerical ability and verbal fluency as "cognitive style",
and suggested that the typically female cognitive style
(poor spatial ability and better verbal fluency) results
from a female hormone (oestrogen) present during childhood
and from typically female socialization. In formulating
this theory, Dawson must have misunderstood, or been unaware
of, two important aspects of the evidence on early sex differentiation obtained from animal and human studies. First,
in suggesting that sex hormones present after weaning can affect later behaviour, he ignores evidence that it is during
later prenatal and early neonatal life that such long-term
hormonal influences have been found (Money and Ehrhardt,
1972; Chapter 7 by Rogers; also Goy, 1968; Money and Ehrhardt,
1968; Hamburg and Lunde, 1967, for studies on primates). Secondly, in suggesting that oestrogen present early in life
can produce typically female behaviour in the adult, he ignores the abundant evidence that the crucial factor for female differentiation is the absence of sex hormones (both
male and female) early in life; (conversely, the presence of
such a hormone, be it male or female, results in typically
male differentiation). Dawson's theory cannot, therefore,
be taken seriously, and the evidence he has offered from human pathology and animal experimentation is irrelevant in
view of these fundamental objections.

  Buffery and Gray (1972). This theory also concerns verbal and spatial ability, the latter referring to rotary pursuit tasks, tests involving spatial manipulations, and tests
for "field dependence" (see earlier section on "Sex Differences in Behaviour"). Buffery and Gray have suggested that
a linguistic device for speech perception is subserved by an
innate, species-specific, neural mechanism which is lateral-
ized and localized to the dominant hemisphere for language.
They related female superiority in verbal ability to the
more well-developed dominant cerebral hemisphere in young
girls. They then proposed that male superiority in spatial
ability is an indirect consequence of the greater laterali-
zation of language in the female, so that spatial ability is
located more bilaterally for males, giving better three-
dimensional representation. Buffery and Gray have cited a
number of indirect lines of evidence for their theory of
language development which, taken together, appear plausible
at first sight, but their evidence that differences in spatial ability are a consequence of this is tenuous and uncon-
vincing: McGuinness, in Chapter 6, has criticized Buffery

and Gray's theory, on the grounds that many female skills
are located in the right, so-called "male" hemisphere.   The
reader is referred to this chapter for a more detailed discussion.

   Broverman et al. (1968).   This theory involved the following basic premise: that women perform better than men on
simple, overlearned perceptual-motor tasks (e.g. clerical
skills, field dependence tests, verbal fluency), but that
men surpass women on the more complex "perceptual restructuring" tasks which require inhibition of the immediate response to obvious stimulus attributes (e.g. tests of field
independence).   Broverman *et al.* related these differences
to different effects on the brain of the two principal classes of sex hormones, androgens and oestrogens: they suggested that oestrogens facilitate "activation" by stimulating
adrenergic mechanisms, whereas androgens are weaker in this
respect, and facilitate "inhibition".   Thus, in contrast to
Dawson and to Buffery and Gray, Broverman *et al.* stressed
the importance of adult levels of sex hormones rather than
developmental sex differences.

   Broverman *et al.*'s theory has been criticized for its
interpretation of the pharmacological evidence (Singer and
Montgomery, 1969; reply by Broverman *et al.* 1969).   Parlee
(1972) has offered more general criticisms, for example of
Broverman *et al.*'s characterization of tasks in which women
excel: this, she claimed, selectively omitted those tasks
which did not fit the authors' basic premise on the nature
of the sex differences (see above).   Parlee also claimed that
verbal ability should not have been regarded as a simple,
over-learned, perceptual-motor task.   Similarly, she criticized Broverman *et al.*'s use of the term cognitive inhibition
as an explanation of those tasks in which men excelled, because it implied a unitary mechanism where a variety of mechanisms, both physiological and psychological, are known to
be involved.   Parlee also pointed out the ambiguity involved
in terms such as "the most obvious or immediate response"
(which according to Broverman *et al.* is more readily inhibited by men than by women).

   Parlee did not dispute the general premise that women
perform better than men on "simple" and "overlearned"
perceptual-motor tasks.   However, this premise can be dis-
puted, since in their survey of sex differences in mental
abilities, Garai and Scheinfeld (1968) placed these perceptual-
motor tasks into one of two categories.   The first involved

"motor skills", measured, for example, by rotary pursuit tasks and simple reaction times, on which men perform better than women (Garai and Scheinfeld, p. 203; also Botwinick, 1971). The second involved "clerical skills", measured by tasks said to require perceptual speed and frequent shifts of attention, such as typing and checking lists for accuracy, on which women perform better than men. Thus, according to which of these two categories of tests one regards as a rapid, overlearned repetitive task, a different direction of sex difference is obtained. Broverman *et al.* solved this problem by only deriving their evidence from the second category of tests, thus justifying Parlee's criticism that their evidence was selective.

Andrew (1972a). This theory provides an alternative explanation of sex differences in tests involving shifts of attention, in terms of an effect of androgens. It also overcomes the objections which were raised to Broverman *et al.*'s theory. Andrew derived his hypothesis from work on food-searching strategies in young male chicks injected with testosterone (described in Chapter 7 by Rogers in some detail) This work suggested that testosterone increases "persistence", so that the animal attends for longer, either to a spatial locality or to a particular type of stimulus, and is less readily distracted by irrelevant stimuli (Andrew and Rogers, 1972; Andrew, 1972a; Archer, 1974). Andrew (1972a and b) interpreted work on human subjects showing that high-androgen men perform better than low-androgen men in relatively simple tasks involving attention to a restricted set of particular stimuli (Broverman *et al.* 1964; Klaiber *et al.* 1967, 1971a and b) as being essentially similar to the effects of testosterone on visual search in chicks (see Chapter 7 by Rogers for more details). Andrew (1972a and b) has also suggested that a lack of androgen (e.g. in women) is associated with better performance on tests involving frequent switches of attention (e.g. the speed of recognition test described by Klaiber *et al.* 1967, and Garai and Scheinfeld's "clerical abilities").

Although Andrew's hypothesis is not open to the various objections that Broverman *et al.*'s theory raises, for example, that sex differences in "motor skills" and "clerical" tasks cannot share the same causation (see above), it does require further refinement to satisfactorily account for sex differences in "field independence" tests (see Chapters 6 and 7 by McGuinness and Rogers). Men have been consistently

found to attain higher scores in these than women, but other
studies (Broverman *et al.* 1964; Klaiber *et al.* 1967) have
shown that indices of high androgen levels in young males
are correlated with poor performance on one of these tasks,
the embedded figure test. Andrew (1972a and b) has suggested
that this apparent contradiction might be resolved if there
were an optimum degree of persistence which produces high
scores on the test, and that deviations to either side of
this, by females or by high androgen males would both result
in low scores but for different reasons. This hypothesis
has not yet been tested directly, but there is evidence that
performance on the task shows a U-shaped relationship to
"narrow" and "broad" focus of attention (see Chapter 7 by
Rogers).

HORMONE THEORIES: IMPLICATIONS FOR FUTURE RESEARCH

    Thus there have been two main theories proposed to ac-
count for sex differences in cognitive abilities in terms of
adult level of sex hormones. One (Broverman *et al.* 1968)
sought to explain all the differences (and other data) in
terms of "activation" and "inhibition", but is open to a number of objections, e.g. its inability to explain sex differences in simple motor skills. The other theory (Andrew,
1972a and b) sought to explain the differences in terms of
increased persistence induced by male hormones, but at present the precise relationship of this
formance in the embedded figure test requires further clari-
fication before it can adequately account for the sex differences.
    It follows therefore, that two important areas for fur-
ther investigation are the effects of sex hormones on tests
of "field independence" and a fuller investigation of sex
differences in rapid repetitive and clerical tasks. A further crucial research area, relating to these theories, is
ontogeny: theories emphasizing only adult hormonal differences cannot be regarded as entirely adequate if the particular sex differences appear before the pre-pubertal onset
of oestrogen or androgen secretion. The former occurs earlier than the latter, at 10-10.5 years of age according to
studies carried out in the early 1940's reviewed by Tanner,
1962 (these ages would probably be a little lower for a
1970's sample). Recent studies show that the circulating
levels of both sex hormones are low in both sexes until 9

or 10 years of age (Lunde and Hamburg, 1972): however, the
rise in androgen secretion is a gradual one, so that there
is no fixed point when this begins, and it varies widely
from one individual to another. There is at present some
evidence that sex differences in spatial ability do not occur in three to five year olds (Maccoby and Jacklin, 1974;
Dawson *et al.* 1974), but do occur from six to eight years
onwards (Maccoby and Jacklin, 1974; Coates, 1974; Dawson *et*
al. 1974). Immergluck and Mearini (1969) have found a reverse sex difference from that normally reported for adults
in the embedded figure test at 9 years of age (i.e. females
showing higher scores), but no sex differences at 11 or 13
years of age.

If, as some of these studies suggest, the development
of sex differences in spatial ability does approximately coincide with the beginning of hormonal differences, further
credibility is added to the hormonally-based theories discussed above. Nevertheless, the onset of the sex differences
in spatial ability does seem to occur between one to four
years before the levels have risen appreciably (Lunde and
Hamburg, 1972), so that claims that the two coincide (e.g.
Dawson *et al.* 1974) and are causally related, are premature,
and to some extent misleading in the light of the available
hormonal evidence. Similarly, Fairweather and Hutt (1972),
who explain age and sex differences in serial-choice reaction time in terms of possible age and sex differences in
oestrogens and androgens, incorrectly cite Tanner's (1962)
hormonal data, and also the study of Immergluck and Mearini
(see previous paragraph) to support their case. Hormonal explanations provide such easy and simple solutions that we
must always be wary of attempts to misrepresent the evidence.
The lack of clear-cut data, and the anomolous findings of
Immergluck and Mearini make further studies of the subject
desirable.

Gray (1971). This theory concerns differences in "temperament" rather than in cognitive ability. Gray has suggested that hormonal factors can account for animal and human sex differences in aggression and fear. The relationship between androgens and aggression is discussed in Chapter 7 by Lesley Rogers, whose conclusions are much more cautious than the rigid genetic determinism implied by Gray.

Gray's theory also concerned "fearfulness": he argued
that, in rodents, males are more fearful than females, whereas in our own species females are more fearful than males.

I have criticized this suggestion (Archer, 1971) on the grounds that tests of rodent "fearfulness" do not measure a unitary trait (see also Archer, 1973), that different hormonal factors control the different measures, that the nature of rodent sex differences is more variable than Gray suggested, and that his inferences from several specific tests are questionable. I have also outlined in some detail possible alternative explanations which, I suggest, can account for sex differences in a wider variety of tests than those cited by Gray (Archer, 1975).

The evidence from humans used by Gray included reactive depression, neurotic worry, psychosomatic symptoms, crying fits and neuroticism and extraversion. Again, I have pointed out that a unitary description is misleading (Archer, 1971). There may be primary differences in the way the two sexes typically react to threatening situations, but these differences are likely to be only indirectly related to the clinical symptoms listed by Gray. The situation is undoubtedly a complex one, probably involving hormonal, biological, developmental and cultural factors. Mayo has also referred to Gray's theory in an earlier chapter, discussing the possible causal factors of sex differences in psychopathology. The reader is referred to this chapter for a more detailed discussion of this topic.

General Discussion: Inferences from Animals to Humans

One general question raised by all the theories described above is the extent to which they rely on animal studies for their physiological and other evidence. Thus Andrew (1972a) based his theory on work with testosterone-treated chicks, and Dawson, Gray and Broverman *et al.* all laid considerable stress on animal findings. In general, the correspondence between the animal and human tests is not satisfactory, and this criticism can apply even where there seems, at first sight, a close correspondence between animal and human findings as, for example, is apparent in the literature on sex differences in "aggression" (Gray, 1971; Archer, 1976). Even here, the animal findings refer to measures such as the latency of initial attack, threat displays, the duration of fighting and the outcome of fights, whereas many of the human studies refer to rather different measures, e.g. of verbal aggression, teachers' ratings of impulsivity and assertiveness (Garai and Scheinfeld, 1968), laboratory ex-

periments simulating administration of electric shocks, questionnaire and personality studies (see Maccoby and Jacklin,
1974, for a review of these). It seems unlikely, therefore,
that the animal and human data refer to clearly comparable
characteristics.

Other theories involve more obvious attempts to compare
aspects of behaviour unlikely to show common causation.
Broverman *et al.* (1968), for example, included the speed of
colour naming, clerical aptitude tests, manual dexterity,
speech and reading ability, speed of eyeblink conditioning,
and sensory thresholds as their tests measuring "rapid repetitive responding" in human subjects. The same characteristic was measured in the rat by tests of wheel running activity, ambulation in an open field, and speed of avoidance
conditioning.

Similar examples could be cited from the other theories
described in this section, but the two mentioned here should
be sufficient to illustrate the difficulty of comparing sex
differences found in animal and human work. The theories
based on evidence of this type are, therefore, best viewed
as useful in stimulating research on possible biological
factors involved in human sex differences, rather than as
providing any complete or correct answers in the form they
are presented.

In addition to the question of their scientific accuracy, more general issues are raised by the theories, particularly with regard to their emphasis and selectivity. These
general issues, which are discussed in the next two sections,
are important for considering the implications of biological
evidence for the current debate on changing sex roles in contemporary society.

SOME IMPLICATIONS OF BIOLOGICALLY-BASED THEORIES: NATURE AND NURTURE

Two important questions arising from the theories reviewed in the previous sections, and from similar, more general, discussions (e.g. Hutt, 1972a, b and c; Gray and
Buffery, 1971) are, first, whether it is valid to concentrate solely on either the innate or learned aspect of behaviour, and secondly whether mean differences in mental abilities are important and significant as compared to similarities between the sexes. The first of these questions is considered in this section, and the second in the following sec-

tion.

Hutt (1972a, b and c), Gray (1971), Gray and Buffery
(1971) and others (e.g. Freedman, 1964; Scarf, 1972;
Stassinopoulos, 1973; *New Scientist*, 1972; *Daily Telegraph*,
1971) have emphasized "innate" (hormonal) factors as determinants of sex differences. It is clear that behavioural
sex differences are derived in part from genetically influenced processes (as Hutt, for example, has repeatedly emphasized, see 1972b), but what is at issue here is the implication by such writers that there is a major genetic influence important as a determinant of sex roles.

Several aspects of this position can be criticized on
general theoretical grounds. Dividing an individual's behaviour into so-called "innate" and "learnt" components, and
then emphasizing one to the exclusion of the other is an
exercise whose inadequacies have frequently been criticized.
Lehrman (1970) for example, has provided an excellent analysis in which he pointed out that much of the confusion has
arisen from considering behavioural characteristics both at
the level of the species as a whole ("species-typical characteristics") and at the individual level (individual adaptations). At the species level, the term "innate" may be useful to designate that a particular aspect of behaviour is
subject to alteration by genetic selection. The crucial
point for our discussion is that the use of the term "innate"
in this sense does not imply anything about how readily the
underlying developmental processes for such behaviour are
subject to modification by experience at the individual level. Thus the existence of a genetic influence on a sexually-
dimorphic behavioural characteristic implies that such a
characteristic is amenable to alteration by natural selection,
but does not inform us concerning the extent to which the
characteristic can be modified by different environmental
factors. In other words, it can in no sense be used to imply that behavioural sex differences are "determined" by
genetic factors (see also final section).

When we consider the development of sex differences, it
is important to ask how the genetic material or genome
interacts with the environment, rather than seeking to assign
behavioural traits to either nature or nuture. The latter
implies that there are two separate variables bearing an additive relationship to one another, rather than their being
(as they are) abstractions from a process that involves both
components at the onset. Thus to adequately describe develop-

ment, an interactive model involving repeated action and reaction between the organism and its environment has to be
adopted (for a fuller discussion of this point, see Archer
and Lloyd, 1975). By not adopting such an approach but rather treating innate and environmental sources of variation
as if they were additive processes, writers such as Hutt
(1972a, b and c) and the others mentioned earlier in this
section, use a simple, readily understandable, but wholly inappropriate, theoretical model. Since this model inadequate-
ly describes the relation between the variables, certain misleading concepts and conclusions are derived from it, including the notion of "genetic determination" mentioned above,
but also the idea that culture can only accentuate or atten-
tuate sex differences already extant in the genome (Hutt,
1974; 1972c), and that genetic factors can impose readily-
definable limits on behavioural characteristics (implied in
much of Hutt's work).

Adopting an interactive approach, one of the more meaningful questions we can ask is how a genetically-influenced
trait is expressed in the range of environmental conditions
in which it may develop. Even in rodents, which have fea-
tured prominantly in animal-based theories, hormonally-
produced sex differences are environmentally labile. Swanson
(1969) found that testing hamsters in a novel arena in infancy abolished later hormonally-influenced sex differences,
both in activity in a novel arena and in emergence times
from the home cage. Gray *et al.* (1969) found that the extent to which defecation by rats in a novel arena was affected by neonatal injection of testosterone depended upon whether or not the other animals in the litter had received the
hormone.

A similar type of hormonally-based but environmentally-
labile process might underlie some of the findings for human
cognitive abilities discussed above. For example, in relation to "field independence", cross-cultural studies have
shown that the typical sex differences are not detected in
some cultures (e.g. Eskimos and Zambians: Berry, 1966;
MacArthur, 1967; Siann, 1972). It is therefore possible that
if hormonal sex differences influence these attentional processes (see earlier part of this chapter), that these influences interact with the particular individual's educational
and cultural background. Such an interaction could simply
accentuate or minimize the observed sex difference, but it
might just as readily operate in a more complex manner, so

that the same environment would affect the two sexes in opposite directions (cf. the relationship between socialization and IQ discussed by Maccoby, 1967; see also Archer and Lloyd, 1975).

The influence of educational environment has been demonstrated for other sex-typical abilities. In present-day Western society, men typically score higher in tests of creativity (Garai and Scheinfeld, 1968). Torrance (1962) studied scientific creativity and found that with the appropriate form of encouragement and instruction, females were able to utilize their creative potential as well as were males. Similarly, when discussing spatial ability in relation to mathematics, Garai and Scheinfeld (1968) have pointed out that the traditional approach to this subject favours the masculine abilities. Also Carey (unpublished, cited in Maccoby, 1967) attempted to improve problem-solving ability by changing attitudes towards such behaviour in college students, and found that the performance of women but not of men was increased by this procedure.

Theories of sex differences should, therefore, emphasize the interaction between environmental factors (e.g. education, parental attitudes, wider cultural norms) and constitutional ones (e.g. anatomical, developmental and neuroendocrinological differences) rather than being stated in terms of a "learnt" or "innate" dichotomy. McGuinness, in Chapter 6, provides an interactive explanation to account for adult sex differences in cognitive abilities. She argues that perceptual differences observed early in childhood interact with cultural influences to produce adult sex differences in a wide variety of more "cognitive" abilities.

Sherman (1967) has criticized Maccoby for discounting an explanation of a sex difference because it was insufficient in itself. From the viewpoint of an interactive model, this is an important point. Sherman then cited the following example to illustrate the possible development of a particular sex difference. Vocabulary develops earlier in girls whereas boys are more muscular and active: this could lead to girls satisfying their needs more by the use of social communication and boys by physical means. More general differences in "social dependency" could then develop and amplify the original differences in verbal ability: once verbal skills start developing, spatial skills may be neglected in girls, whereas boys would develop these non-verbal skills to a greater extent. Blurton-Jones and Konner (1973) have also

provided an example of how an initial sex difference (in
this case more crying by boys) can interact with maternal
influences to produce later sex differences. An important
point about their example is that they emphasized that later
differences may not be predictable solely on the basis of
either the maternal influence or the initial difference in
crying, but only on the basis of a dynamic interaction between mother and child (see above, and Archer and Lloyd,
1975). Blurton-Jones and Konner remarked that such an interaction would make it pointless to try to apportion responsibility to either innate or cultural factors, and would also
make it unrealistic to refer to culture suppressing or producing sex differences (as stated, e.g. by Hutt, 1972c), conclusions which concur with those presented at the beginning
of this section.

SEX DIFFERENCES AND SIMILARITIES

A second question related to the biologically-based theories concerns the magnitude of the sex differences in behaviour, and thus is related to their general significance.
It was mentioned at the beginning of this chapter that the
sex differences found in cognitive and perceptual tests all
refer to means and that the range of values overlap greatly.
To emphasize these differences is, therefore, a particular
selective viewpoint, which must be considered in any overall
view of sex differences. This illustrates a point made earlier by Strathern, that concern attached to, and social use
made of, a particular sex difference should be the primary
focus of attention, rather than the underlying biological
difference itself. It then becomes pertinent to ask why
physiologically-influenced within-sex variations for these
and other measures have not attracted more research interest,
for it is apparent from several studies that sex hormones
are associated with significant variations within each sex
(Klaiber et al. 1971a and b; studies reviewed by Bardwick,
1971; Lunde and Hamburg, 1972).
Having decided to study *differences* between the sexes
it is easy to overlook that what are studied are only small
differences in mean values: this can lead to some danger-
ous misconceptions. Thus, when discussing "clerical ability",
Garai and Scheinfeld (1968) considered that the superior
verbal fluency and perceptual speed of women enabled them
to be much better equipped than men for almost all secretar-

ial skills: this implied an inherent sex difference which
could be used as a justification for women retaining their
(low status) secretarial employment. Since Garai and
Scheinfeld were, however, referring to mean and not absolute
differences, their argument provided no such justification
for selective employment on the basis of sex: employment
selection should ideally be based on individual differences
in ability rather than differences in the means of groups
to which the individuals belong. The same argument in relation to ethnic groups would be regarded as a "racialist" one,
but where the two sexes are concerned, its implications become obscured. In practical terms, employment differences
between the sexes appear more related to cultural and social
factors rather than to differences in mental and physical
capacity (Davies, 1970; Chapter 4 by Rosenblatt and Cunningham
and Chapter 5 by Kipnis). This again illustrates Strathern's
point about the importance of the cultural elaboration, rather than the biological basis of sex differences.
       Following on from the recognition that there is an em-
phasis on studying sex *differences* rather than similarities,
it is reasonable to suggest that this might be derived from
the general tendency for Western culture to involve a high
degree of division of labour by sex. Thus, it is possible
that because in our culture a large range of activities are
organized more around sex differences than similarities,
small differences in sex-typical mental abilities may become
emphasized in order to justify larger-scale employment and
role differentiation. (Note that the reverse has occurred
for IQ testing, as the tests were constructed so as to minimize sex differences: see Chapter 5 by Kipnis.)

EVOLUTIONARY THEORIES AND THE ORIGIN OF SEX DIFFERENCES

       The theories reviewed in the first part of this chapter
all considered the *causation* of sex differences in behaviour.
A separate but related question concerns their evolutionary
origin. Evolutionary theories generally trace the different
sex roles from the primary division of the sexes for reproduction. Thus Wynne-Edwards (1962) has suggested that the
two sexes have become, throughout evolutionary history, further specialized in more general characteristics, the female
for bearing, brooding, and nurturing the young, and the male
for obtaining food and protection.* Wynne-Edwards' view has
been used by Hutt (1972a and b) to support the hypothesis

that many of the human sex differences discussed in the first
part of this chapter arose, in the evolutionary sense, from
this basic sexual dimorphism. Hutt (1972a) claimed, for example, that "the conformity and consistency" of the female
have evolved as an adaptive consequence of her fulfilling a
predominantly nurturant role, which favoured stability and
reliability in caring for a dependent infant.

Also using Wynne-Edwards' ideas as a starting point,
Gray and Buffery (1971) have discussed, in some detail, the
possible origin in terms of adaptive significance of sex differences in aggression, fearfulness, spatial ability and language ability. The first three were regarded as a result of
the different roles of the sexes in establishing dominance
hierarchies, although as I have pointed out, the concept of
dominance is a limited and inadequate foundation on which to
build a theory claiming to have wide applicability for mammals (Archer, 1971). The greater linguistic ability of women was regarded by Gray and Buffery (1971) as a consequence
of the female playing a major part in teaching the infant to
speak. Gray and Buffery emphasized their viewpoint that
these sex differences are genetic in origin with terms such
as "specified in the gene pool" (p. 107), and they viewed
all the differences as having resulted from the natural selection of traits necessary for the primary division of sex
roles in reproduction.

Tiger (1970) has also argued that the biological basis
of human sex differences extends beyond reproduction, and
suggested that it even covers complex social affairs. In
particular, he views the human female as "biologically un-
programmed to dominate political systems". Tiger suggested
that this had occurred because the male sex possessed a
species-specific pattern facilitating bonding between males,
which arose as a result of selection among primeval hunting
bands against those females willing to hunt and those males
willing to let females hunt. But he offered little evidence
of any substance to support this argument, relying mainly on
a superficial comparison of human society with that of the
baboon which, like the human species, also hunts. Tiger's
argument remained throughout on the level of superficial ana-

* There are certain general difficulties with Wynne-Edwards'
view, principally that it relies on the idea of "group-
selection", which can only occur in a restricted range of
conditions (Maynard Smith, 1964).

logy and nebulous generalization, intended to refer with
equal facility to the mythical primeval hunter and the modern
male chauvinist. Chapter 4 by Rosenblatt and Cunningham discusses some of the evidence against Tiger's viewpoint.

IMPLICATIONS OF THEORIES LINKING SEX ROLES
AND ADAPTIVE SIGNIFICANCE

When discussing the implications of evolutionary explanations of sex differences, we have to distinguish between
explanations which are solely concerned with past selective
advantages for the species as a whole, and those which also
infer from these past advantages that present-day sex roles
are not readily modifiable. The latter are statements about
ontogeny as well as theories of adaptive significance: I
shall refer to this viewpoint as "evolutionary determinism"
(one form of the "biological determinism" discussed by Lloyd
in Chapter 1). Tiger's theory provides a clear example:
he argued that because men evolved characteristics enabling
them to form bonds with other men (originally to facilitate
hunting), they are now "biologically programmed" to dominate
the political and economic life of our communities. In some
of Hutt's writings (e.g. 1972d), she has eschewed such an extreme determinist position, but in other places the tone of
her argument is different. She has claimed (1972a, b and c)
that psychological differences between the sexes have been
clearly selected during the course of human evolution in accordance with particular roles, that these roles are not unique to a particular society, and that cultural influences
can only operate to modify or amplify predispositions already present. The last statement does imply evolutionary
determinism, as does her claim (1972b, p. 133) that it is
doubtful whether new influences could be fashioned with regard to sex roles, or "even whether it is desirable whether
they should".

This position is open to objections of two main types,
the first being conceptual, and the second concerning the
evidence on the plasticity of human sex roles. The conceptual confusion arises when it is assumed that a characteristic with a presumed evolutionary adaptive basis must therefore be fixed in development for every individual of that species. This assumption is implied by Hutt's (1972b) statement that one cannot create new influences with regard to
sex roles, by Tiger's (1970) phrase "biologically programmed",

and by Gray and Buffery's term (1971) "specified in the gene
pool". It is, however, quite unwarranted to argue that because a characteristic can be altered by selection, that it
is not readily amenable to environmental modification (see
Lehrman, 1970, and an earlier discussion in this chapter).
There can be selection for plasticity and flexibility in a
trait, so that the fact that a particular difference is the
product of selection does not mean that it is inflexible.
Kummer (1971, p. 147) and others (e.g. Frisch, 1968) have
argued that primates have evolved flexibility as an adaptive
trait for learning broad sets of tasks.

In addition to their logical faults, arguments that evolutionary adaptations have left a legacy of rigidity in our
psychological make-up also appear unlikely in view of the
known variations in sex roles within the human species.
Mead's (1950) well-known survey of five societies showed
how arbitrarily sex roles and affect differences could be
arranged, with little or no relation to presumed biological
adaptation. For example, in one New Guinea tribe, both sexes
showed traits predominantly considered "feminine" in our culture, sharing the care of the children and other domestic
duties, with less division of labour than that with which
we are accustomed. In a second, both sexes were described
as dominant and aggressive, traits considered to be masculine
in our culture. In a third, the *Tchambuli* the pattern of
sex roles was largely the reverse of that occurring in
present-day Western society, with the women as the dominant
partner and manager of business. The men were described as
more subordinate to, and dependent on, the women, and were
also more responsive to the feelings of the children than
the women were. These sex roles were regarded as "biologically natural" by the members of the *Tchambuli* to the extent
that a man would go into confinement and suffer when his
wife was giving birth. This anthropological evidence contrasts not only with Tiger's views on inherited dominance in
man, but also with Hutt's statement that "cultures and societies cannot create differences – they can only reflect those
which already exist" (Hutt, 1972c, p. 114).

General surveys throughout a large number of different
cultures do show that certain subsistence activities (e.g.
trapping, preservation of meat, grinding grain) commonly
occur in one sex rather than the other (D'Andrade, 1967;
Chapter 4 by Rosenblatt and Cunningham). Anthropological
writers such as D'Andrade (1967) and Murdock (1949) argue

that the consistencies are not evidence for rigidity in the
psychological make-up of the two sexes, but rather a direct
or indirect consequence of physical sex differences (e.g. in
strength). Similarly, Rosenblatt and Cunningham suggest
that mobility restrictions determine what occupations become
regarded as appropriate for women. Certain consistent sex
differences in socialization patterns also occur across different cultures: thus, in their well-known survey of socialization in 110 cultures, Barry *et al.* (1959) found a widespread pattern of greater pressure towards nurturance, obedience and responsibility in girls and self-reliance and
achievement-striving in boys, and more pronounced sex differentiation in societies which hunted large animals. It
was, therefore, possible to relate the extent of sex differences in socialization practices to the economy of the society. This finding, together with the evidence of some instances of reversals of the sex differences in socialization,
and many of no detectable differences, again suggests that
any cultural consistencies are more reasonably viewed in
terms of their being a limited number of ways of coping with
similar external constraints (e.g. in the environment, in
the physical and mobility differences between the sexes),
rather than as evidence for any underlying rigidity of behaviour.

In this section I have argued that "evolutionary determinism" is open to conceptual and practical objections. A
further question involved in its use in justifying a conser-
vative viewpoint of sex roles concerns the argument that because one particular form of sex role differentiation is more
related to biological "function" it is therefore more "desirable" to encourage this form rather than the type of alter-

Case histories taken from our own culture can provide
evidence of a different type for a high degree of plasticity
in human sex role differentiation. Money and Ehrhardt (1972)
describe two examples of physiologically normal males (with
genital abnormalities) who were raised as girls. Both were
able to adopt typically female behaviour patterns and to
learn the appropriate female roles (one exception was their
tendency to show abundant physical energy during childhood).
These case histories also provided an insight into how parents reinforce different criteria in boys and girls with
respect to clothes, adornments, appearance, genital play,
bodily movements and position, play and rehearsal of future
roles.

natives suggested by the Women's Movement (Hutt, 1972a, p. 165; 1972b, p. 133). This argument fails to take into account the difference between environments for which traditional sex roles were originally functionally adapted, and contemporary environmental requirements.

Since most of man's ancestry was probably spent in small groups of hunters and gatherers (Pilbeam, 1972), features which were adapted to these conditions are not necessarily those which are adapted to today's changed conditions. In our society, there is an almost total absence of the types of selective pressures which act on most animal species in their natural habitats (e.g. food shortage, many forms of disease, predation), and these have been replaced by problems of adjustment to the stresses and complexities of modern societies and urban environments. Thus the present changes in the role of women may represent ways of responding to these changed social and physical conditions, and could in this sense be regarded as "functional" or "adaptive" in relation to contemporary requirements, (e.g. in relation to the decrease in the proportion of a woman's lifetime which is required for childbearing in contemporary Western societies). In contrast, sex roles adapted to past environments would only be relevant to present conditions if it could be shown that particular adaptive features involve sufficient rigidity to seriously limit the acquisition of new ways of responding. As indicated above, this rigidity cannot be demonstrated by simply pointing to a likely genetic basis for the adaptive trait, but only by practical evidence that sex roles show little inter-cultural variability, and are resistant to efforts to change them within a culture. The anthropological and clinical studies discussed above have revealed little evidence that this was the case; rather, they suggested that our species possesses a genetic basis for flexibility in its sex role arrangements.

I conclude therefore, that attempts to use biological evolutionary arguments to defend traditional sex roles are not justified. It is interesting to reflect that evolutionary viewpoints were also used over 100 years ago to argue against extending higher education to women (Burstyn, 1971). It is thus ironic that contemporary women who have benefited from this reform (i.e. Hutt, Stassinopoulos) should want to use similar evolutionary arguments against further reforms beneficial to their own sex.

Acknowledgements
I thank Richard Andrew, Tim Clutton-Brock, Barbara Lloyd,
Paul Rosenblatt and Peter Slater for their helpful comments
on earlier versions of this chapter, and the MRC for pro-
viding financial support for my work.

REFERENCES

Andrew, R.J. (1972a). Recognition processes and behavior
with special reference to the effects of testosterone on
persistence. *In* "Advances in the Study of Behaviour".
(D.S. Lehrman, R.A. Hinde and E. Shaw, eds.) Vol. 4.
Academic Press, New York and London.

Andrew, R.J. (1972b). Changes in search behaviour in male
and female chicks, following different doses of testosterone. *Animal Behaviour,* 20, 741-750.

Andrew, R.J. and Rogers, L. (1972). Testosterone, search
behaviour and persistence. *Nature,* 237, 343-346.

Archer, J. (1971). Sex differences in emotional behaviour:
a reply to Gray and Buffery. *Acta Psychologica,* 35, 415-
429.

Archer, J. (1973). Tests for emotionality in rats and mice:
a review. *Animal Behaviour,* 21, 205-235.

Archer, J. (1974). The effects of testosterone on the distractability of chicks by irrelevant and relevant novel
stimuli. *Animal Behaviour,* 22, 379-404.

Archer, J. (1975). Rodent sex differences in emotional and
related behavior. *Behavioral Biology,* 14, 451-479.

Archer, J. (1976). The organization of aggression and fear
in vertebrates. *In* "Perspectives in Ethology". (P.P.G.
Bateson and P. Klopfer, eds.) Vol. 2. Plenum, London and
New York.

Archer, J. and Lloyd, B.B. (1975). Sex differences: Biological and social interactions. *In* "Child Alive". (M.R.
Lewin, ed.) Temple Smith, London.

Bardwick, J.M. (1971). "The Psychology of Women". Harper
and Row, New York.

Barry, H., Bacon, M.K. and Child, I.L. (1959). A cross-
cultural survey of some sex differences in socialization.

Journal of Abnormal and Social Psychology, 55, 327-333.

Berry, J.W. (1966). Temme and Eskimo perceptual skills. *International Journal of Psychology,* 1, 207-229.

Blurton-Jones, N.G. and Konner, M.J. (1973). Sex differences in behaviour of London and Bushmen children. *In* "Comparative Ecology and Behaviour of Primates". (R.P. Michael and J.H. Crook, eds.) Academic Press, London and New York.

Botwinick, J. (1971). Sensory-set factors in age differences in reaction time. *Journal of Genetic Psychology,* 119, 241-249.

Brindley, C., Clarke, P., Hutt, C., Robinson, I. and Wethli, E. (1973). Sex differences in activities and social interactions of nursery school children. *In* "Comparative Ecology and Behaviour of Primates". (R.P. Michael and J.H. Crook, eds.) Academic Press, London and New York.

Broverman, D.M., Broverman, I.K., Vogel, W. and Palmer, R.D. (1964). The automiatization cognitive style and physical development. *Child Development,* 35, 1343-1359.

Broverman, D.M., Klaiber, E.L., Kobayashi, Y. and Vogel, W. (1968). Roles of activation and inhibition in sex differences in cognitive abilities. *Psychological Review,* 75, 23-50.

Broverman, D.M., Klaiber, E.L., Kobayashi, Y. and Vogel, W. (1969). Reply to the "Comment" by Singer and Montgomery on "Roles of activation and inhibition in sex differences in cognitive abilities". *Psychological Review,* 76, 328-331.

Buffery, A.W.H. and Gray, J.A. (1972). Sex differences in the development of spatial and linguistic skills. *In* "Gender Differences: Their Ontogeny and Significance". (C. Ounsted and D.C. Taylor, eds.) Churchill, London.

Burstyn, J.N. (1971). Brain and intellect: Science applied to a social issue. *Actes du XIIe Congres International d'Histoire des Sciences,* Paris, IX, 13-16.

Coates, S. (1974). Sex differences in field dependence among preschool children. *In* "Sex Differences in Behavior". (R.C. Friedman, R.M. Richart and R.L. Vande Wiele, eds.) Wiley, New York.

Daily Telegraph, (1971). Why women become so moody. July 27th.

D'Andrade, R.G. (1967). Sex differences and cultural institutions. *In* "The Development of Sex Differences". (E.E.
Maccoby, ed.) Tavistock, London.

Davies, B.T. (1970). Comparative employability of men and
women in different industries. *Journal of Biosocial Science,* Suppl. 2. 101-106.

Dawson, J.L.M. (1972). Effects of sex hormones on cognitive
style in rats and men. *Behavior Genetics,* 2, 21-42.

Dawson, J.L.M., Young, B.M. and Choi, P.P.C. (1974). Develop-
mental influences in pictorial depth perception among
Hong Kong Chinese children. *Journal of Cross-Cultural
Psychology,* 5, 3-22.

Fairweather, H. and Hutt, S.J. (1972). Sex differences in a
perceptual-motor skill in children. *In* "Gender Differences: Their Ontogeny and Significance". (C. Ounsted and
D.C. Taylor, eds.) Churchill, Edinburgh and London.

Freedman, D.G. (1964). A biological view of Man's social behavior. *In* "Social Behavior from Fish to Man". (W. Etkin,
ed.) University of Chicago Press.

Frisch, J.R. (1968). Individual behavior and intertroop
variability in Japanese macaques. *In* "Primates: Studies
in Adaptation and Variability". (P.C. Jay, ed.) Holt
Rinehart and Winston, New York.

Garai, J.E. and Scheinfeld, A. (1968). Sex differences in
mental and behavioral traits. *Genetic Psychology Monographs,* 77, 169-299.

Goy, R.W. (1968). Organizing effects of androgen on the be-
behaviour of rhesus monkeys. *In* "Endocrinology and Human
Behaviour". (R.P. Michael, ed.) Oxford University Press.

Gray, J.A. (1971). Sex differences in emotional behaviour in
mammals including man: Endocrine bases. *Acta Psychologica,* 35, 29-46.

Gray, J.A. and Buffery, A.W.H. (1971). Sex differences in
emotional and cognitive behaviour in mammals including
man: Adaptive and neural bases. *Acta Psychologica,* 35,
89-111.

Gray, J.A., Lean, J. and Keynes, A. (1969). Infant androgen

treatment and adult open field behavior: Direct effects
and effects of injections to siblings. *Physiology and
Behavior*, 4, 177-181.

Hamburg, D.A. and Lunde, D.T. (1967). Sex hormones in the de-
velopment of sex differences in human behaviour. *In* "The
Development of Sex Differences". (E.E. Maccoby, ed.)
Tavistock, London.

Hutt, C. (1972a). Sex differences in human development.
Human Development, 15, 153-170.

Hutt, C. (1972b). "Males and Females". Penguin Books,
Harmondsworth.

Hutt, C. (1972c). Neuroendocrinological, behavioural and
intellectual aspects of sexual differentiation in human
development. *In* "Gender Differences: Their Ontogeny and
Significance". (C. Ounsted and D.C. Taylor, eds.)
Churchill, Edinburgh and London.

Hutt, C. (1972d). Sexual dimorphism: Its significance in
human development. *In* "Determinants of Behavioral Development". (F.J. Monks, W.W. Hartup and J. de Wit, eds.)
Academic Press, New York and London.

Hutt, C. (1974). Sex: What's the difference? *New Scientist*,
62, 605-607.

Immergluck, L. and Mearini, M.C. (1969). Age and sex differences in responses to embedded figures and reversible
figures. *Journal of Experimental Child Psychology*, 8,
210-221.

Kagan, J. and Moss, H.A. (1962). "Birth to Maturity". Wiley,
New York.

Klaiber, E., Broverman, D.M. and Kobayashi, Y. (1967). The
automatization cognitive style, androgens and monoamine
oxidase. *Psychopharmacology*, 11, 320-336.

Klaiber, E.L., Broverman, D.M., Vogel, W., Abraham, G.E.
and Cone, F.L. (1971a). Effects of infused testosterone
on mental performance and serum LH. *Journal of Clinical
Endocrinology*, 32, 341-349.

Klaiber, E.L., Broverman, D.M., Vogel, W., Abraham, G.E.
and Stenn, P.G. (1971b). Effects of testosterone on mental performance and EEG. *In* "Influence of Hormones on

the Nervous System". (D.H. Ford, ed.) Karger, Basel.

Kummer, H. (1971). "Primate Societies". Aldine, Chicago.

Lehrman, D.S. (1970). Semantic and conceptual issues in the Nature-Nurture problem. *In* "The Development and Evolution of Behavior". (L.R. Aronson, E. Tobach, D.S. Lehrman and J.S. Rosenblatt, eds.) Freeman, San Francisco.

Lunde, D. and Hamburg, D.A. (1972). Techniques for assessing the effects of sex hormones on affect, arousal and aggression in humans. *Recent Progress in Hormone Research,* 28, 627-663.

MacArthur, R. (1967). Sex differences in field dependence for the Eskimo. *International Journal of Psychology,* 2, 139-140.

Maccoby, E.E. (1967). Sex differences in intellectual functioning. *In* "Development of Sex Differences". (E.E. Maccoby, ed.) Tavistock, London.

Maccoby, E.E. and Jacklin, C.N. (1974). "The Psychology of Sex Differences". Stanford University Press.

Maynard Smith, J. (1964). Group selection and kin selection: A rejoinder. *Nature,* 201, 1145-1147.

Mead, M. (1950). "Male and Female". Penguin Books, Harmondsworth.

Money, J. and Ehrhardt, A.A. (1968). Prenatal hormonal exposure: Possible effects on behaviour in man. *In* "Endocrinology and Human Behaviour". (R.P. Michael, ed.) Oxford University Press.

Money, J. and Ehrhardt, A.A. (1972). "Man and Woman, Boy and Girl". Johns Hopkins University Press, Baltimore and London.

Murdock, G.P. (1949). "Social Structure". Macmillan, New York.

New Scientist, (1972). Do their hormones make females more submissive? September 21st, 472.

Oetzel, R.M. (1967). Annotated bibliography. *In* "The Development of Sex Differences". (E.E. Maccoby, ed.) Tavistock, London.

Parlee, M.B. (1972). Comments on "Roles of activation and inhibition in cognitive abilities" by D.M. Broverman, E.L.

Klaiber, Y. Kobayashi and W. Vogel. *Psychological Review*, 79, 180-184.

Pilbeam, D. (1972). "The Ascent of Man". Macmillan, New York.

Scarf, M. (1972). He and She: The sex hormones and behavior. *New York Times Magazine*, May 7th, 30-31 and 101-107.

Sherman, J.A. (1967). Problems of sex differences in space perception and aspects of intellectual functioning. *Psychological Review*, 75, 290-299.

Siann, G. (1972). Measuring field-dependence in Zambia: A cross-cultural study. *International Journal of Psychology*, 7, 87-96.

Singer, G. and Montgomery, R.B. (1969). Comment on roles of activation and inhibition in sex differences in cognitive abilities. *Psychological Review*, 76, 325-327.

Stassinopoulos, A. (1973). "The Female Woman". Davis-Poynter, London.

Swanson, H.H. (1969). Interaction of experience with adrenal and sex hormones on the behaviour of hamsters in the open field. *Animal Behaviour*, 17, 148-154.

Tanner, J.M. (1962). "Growth at Adolescence". 2nd Edition. Blackwell, Oxford.

Tiger, L. (1970). The possible biological origins of sexual discrimination. *Impact of Science on Society*, 20, 29-45.

Torrance, E.P. (1962). "Guiding Creative Talent". Prentice-Hall, Englewood, New Jersey.

Witkin, H.A. (1967). A cognitive-style approach to cross-cultural research. *International Journal of Psychology*, 2, 233-250.

Witkin, H.A., Dyk, R.B., Faterson, H., Goodenough, D.R. and Karp, S.A. (1962). "Psychological Differentiation". Wiley, New York.

Wynne-Edwards, V.C. (1962). "Animal Dispersion in Relation to Social Behaviour". Oliver and Boyd, Edinburgh.

SUBJECT INDEX

A

Accidents, 197

Achievement motivation, 8, 17, 52, 66, 87, 108, 109, 110

Achievement tests, 105

Acoustic sensitivity, 190

Activity, 17

Activity levels, 124

Acts of submission, 84-85

Adrenal cortex, 162

Adrenal glands, 175

Adrenaline, 163

Adrenocorticotrophic hormone, 160

Adrenogenital syndrome, 175, 176

Adventurousness, 5, 52, 67

Affect differences, 258

Affective disorders, 213, 232-233

Agency, 4

Aggression, 3, 5, 6, 10, 13, 17, 26, 29, 49, 63, 66, 67, 79-80, 84, 124, 157, 159, 160, 161, 162, 174, 189, 200, 216, 217, 224, 226, 228, 242, 248, 249, 256, 258

Aging process, 221

Agonistic, 161

Alcoholism, 213, 225, 226, 227, 232

Aldosterone, 198

Ambition, 66

American behaviourists, 15

American sex role values, 5

Anaesthetic effect, 195, 196

Analytic ability, 106, 146

Androgens, 2, 19, 79, 84, 157, 159, 160, 162, 163, 168, 172, 191, 193, 200, 245, 246, 247, 248
ethical problems about possible side effects, 172
organizing effects, 172-177
radioactive, 158

Androgyny, 5, 29, 32, 45

Animal behaviour, 2

Animus and anima, 4

Anthropology, 49-69

Antiandrogens, 166, 167, 171

Anti-social behaviour, 224, 225

Anxiety, 197, 214, 218, 222, 223, 224, 227